The Messianic Kingship of Jesus

WEST Theological Monograph Series

Wales Evangelical School of Theology (WEST) has produced a stream of successful PhD candidates over the years, whose work has consistently challenged the boundaries of traditional understanding in both systematic and biblical theology. Now, for the first time, this series makes significant examples of this ground-breaking research accessible to a wider readership.

The Messianic Kingship of Jesus

A Study of Christology and Redemptive History in Matthew's Gospel with Special Reference to the Royal-Enthronement Psalms

SUNGHO CHOI

WIPF & STOCK · Eugene, Oregon

THE MESSIANIC KINGSHIP OF JESUS
A Study of Christology and Redemptive History in Matthew's Gospel
with Special Reference to the Royal-Enthronement Psalms

Copyright © 2011 Sungho Choi. All rights reserved. Except for brief quotations in critical publications or reviews, no part of this book may be reproduced in any manner without prior written permission from the publisher. Write: Permissions, Wipf and Stock Publishers, 199 W. 8th Ave., Suite 3, Eugene, OR 97401.

Wipf & Stock
An Imprint of Wipf and Stock Publishers
199 W. 8th Ave., Suite 3
Eugene, OR 97401

www.wipfandstock.com

ISBN 13: 978-1-61097-489-9

Contents

Acknowledgements / vii

Abbreviations / ix

1. Introduction / 1
2. Preliminary Survey / 33
3. First-Century Jewish Christians and Their Interpretation of Scripture / 70
4. Psalms in the Context of Israel's Redemptive History / 97
5. Christology in the Gospel of Matthew / 129
6. Analysis of Christological Titles / 180
7. Conclusion / 220

Bibliography / 231

Acknowledgements

THIS BOOK IS A product of research which was originally conducted for my doctoral dissertation. To mention all of the people who have been a source of inspiration and encouragement to me during the years of my research would be impossible here. Indeed, without the prayerful support of many people, the work would have been abandoned long ago. It is with great indebtedness that I would like to sincerely express my gratitude to the following people.

First of all, my special thanks go to my former supervisor (and now a colleague) Dr. Tom Holland whose guidance through the years has been more than just an academic mentoring. His initial comment on the use of the Royal Psalms in Matthew's Gospel in the summer of 2005 was the starting point of this research. His work on Pauline theology has been a major source of influence as I embarked upon the research. Even though the argument of this dissertation has developed independently from Dr. Holland's initial suggestions, his comments have been an invaluable source of intellectual stimulation.

My heartfelt thanks are also extended to my former external supervisor Professor D. P. Davies. Despite his busy schedule he has always greeted me with kindness upon my visits and helpfully offered corrections on the initial draft of my writings. His comments on the final draft of the dissertation were most insightful.

I would also like to express my gratitude to Dr. Wonsuk Ma, the Director of Oxford Centre for Mission Studies (OCMS), for his initial comment on the proposal of my dissertation. His kind invitation for me to give a special lecture at OCMS in December 2008 to the research students was an ideal opportunity for critical feedback and for further research.

My sincere gratitude goes to Mrs. Sung-Joo Kim for her vision and generosity despite her busy business schedule. I should never forget the support of all the people from SaRang Community Church, in Seoul,

South Korea, and especially the senior pastor Rev. Dr. Jung-Hyeon Oh and Rev. Sam Ko for all their commitments for the development of WEST (Wales Evangelical School of Theology). Their support for the publication of this book has been most helpful.

On a personal note, none of this would have been possible without the love and care of my family. The desire to serve the Church and my love for the Bible were planted in my heart in childhood by my parents, whose dedication for the Kingdom of God continues to be the source of inspiration in life. My brother, Jaeho, has been most encouraging in his moral support during the years of my research and work at WEST, which were at times overwhelming.

And finally, there is my wife, Ji Young, whose support and patience have been foundational in all our endeavors. Her fervent prayers are what kept me going through challenges and difficulties. I owe her more than can ever be expressed.

Last but not least by any means, I would like to thank God for leading me to WEST and the work He has graciously allowed me to undertake. It is my profoundest desire that this work would humbly serve His purpose.

April 2011

Abbreviations

AnBib	Analecta Biblica
BAR	Biblical Archaeological Review
BJRL	Bulletin of the John Rylands Library
BS	Bibliotheca Sacra
CBQ	Catholic Biblical Quarterly
EQ	Evangelical Quarterly
EJT	European Journal of Theology
HUCA	Hebrew Union College Annual
HR	Historia Religionum
Int.	Interpretation
JAAR	Journal of the American Academy of Religion
JETS	Journal of the Evangelical Theological Society
JSNT	Journal for the Study of the New Testament
JSOT	Journal for the Study of the Old Testament
JSS	Journal of Semitic Studies
Jub	Jubilees
LXT	Rahlfs' Septuaginta
LXX	Septuagint
NovT	Novum Testamentum
NTK	Neues Testament und Kirche
NTS	New Testament Studies
PTM	Paternoster Theological Monograph
PRR	Presbyterian and Reformed Review
RE	Review & Expositor
RH	Reconciliation and Hope
SBEC	Studies in the Bible and Early Christianity
SBL	Society of Biblical Literature
SBT	Studies in Biblical Theology
SJT	Scottish Journal of Theology
SNT	Studien zum Neuen Testament

SNTSMS	Society for NT Studies, Monograph Series
SSEJC	Studies in Scripture in Early Judaism and Christianity
TyndB.	Tyndale Bulletin
TE	The Expositor
TGM	The Gospel Magazine
TTNTL	The Tyndale New Testament Lecture
WUZNT	Wissenschaftliche Untersuchungen Zum Neuen Testament
WW	Word & World
WTJ	Westminster Theological Journal
ZAW	Zeitschrift für die Alttestamentliche Wissenschaft

1

Introduction

PART ONE: TYPOLOGY AS BIBLICAL HERMENEUTICS

Definition of Typology

AS WE EMBARK UPON the study of Matthew's Christology and Israel's redemptive history with reference to royal-enthronement psalms, we need to first clarify the methodological approach. Before we proceed to defining what typology is and how it can be justified as an appropriate exegetical tool, it is necessary to understand how modern contemporary biblical theologians have approached the Gospel in recent years. This will help us to appreciate the strengths and limitations of the common methodological approach which has dominated the study of Synoptic Gospels in recent years.

First of all, the tradition-historical principle has been the dominant scholarly model in New Testament studies since the post-World War II era in the Western academic setting. The advocates of historical criticism (e.g., form criticism and source criticism) have attempted to unravel the transitional process which the early Church took upon itself in reformulating Jesus' own sayings and self-consciousness into a more refined ideological ingredient that was essential for the newly emerging religious movement. Therefore, they maintain that there is a difference between how Jesus originally understood himself and what the early Church later attributed to him. However, such a view has met serious challenges from those scholars who argue that there was a real continuity and agreement between the self-understanding of Jesus and the early Church's response to it. I. H. Marshall has been vocal concerning this issue; he argues that if it is granted that Jesus expressed his self-understanding explicitly, then the fundamental principle of the tradition-historical method, which is founded upon the conjecture of discrepancy between what the early Church ascribed to Jesus and his self-understanding, cannot be legitimated.[1]

In other words, according to Marshall, the tradition-historical principle relies on an unwarranted conjecture that the early Christians modified the original sayings and put on the lips of Jesus things which he would never have uttered regarding himself. Once it is recognized that there was essentially a congruence between what Jesus actually said and how the early Church at a later stage appropriated the material then the whole concept of historical criticism is found to be on very shaky ground.

More recently, scholars who have acknowledged the weakness of historical criticism have turned to a more synchronic approach to biblical theology. The advocates of literary criticism (e.g., narrative theology) have turned away from preconceived ideas of historical criticism which would fit the descriptions of a diachronic approach to focusing on what the text actually says. According to D. W. K. So, "the literary approach arose out of this context of biblical studies and seeks to study the text as it is, without the reference to hypotheses that cannot be found within the text."[2] This approach is certainly in tune with the fundamental principles of biblical theology. After all, biblical theology is concerned with what the text actually says as opposed to what could have been the underlying principles behind the scene. We therefore need to seek to understand how the first writers and the original recipients understood the text. In this regard, the study of the historical Jesus, that is, how Jesus viewed himself, may not be so vital since it is how the evangelist sees and interprets Jesus that is of prime concern here. This methodological presupposition nevertheless relies on the basic principle that there is a consistency between how Jesus regarded himself and the early Christian understanding which indicates that this congruence needs to be demonstrated in that the study of the historical Jesus is essentially consistent with the study of the early Christian interpretation of Jesus.

---

1. Marshall, *The Origins of New Testament Christology*, 57.
2. So, *Jesus' Revelation of His Father*, 12.

The underlying thesis of this volume relies on the acceptance of the view that there is a big picture that unites all of the writings of the Bible. In other words, the New Testament writers utilized the Old Testament in order to reveal the redemptive function of Jesus in the context of Israel's history. This view is supported by Tom Holland, who argues that Paul draws the reader's attention to the ongoing redemptive act of Yahweh which was decisively manifested in the Exodus. This particular event is historically and theologically significant in defining the people of Israel. The Exodus, according to Holland, is the overarching theme that binds the faith of Israel in Yahweh. The event symbolizes the fulfillment of God's promise to Abraham (Gen 12:2–3; 15:13–14) and signifies the creation of the covenant with Israel under the leadership of Moses. This is demonstrated by the overthrow of the Egyptians in the Passover as the wrath of Yahweh falls upon them. As Israel reaches the promised land, Yahweh establishes the law by entering into a covenantal relationship with Israel and the calling of a priestly people secures the blessing of Israel. On the basis of this prototype redemptive event, the greater deliverance of Israel was anticipated. In other words, the promise of a New Exodus emerged in which David was the central figure. While this is anticipated in the previous events of the Old Testament, the New Exodus will establish a far greater salvation which will entail the overthrow of the Kingdom of Darkness (cf. Isa 11:1–13; 52:7–10; Ezek 44–45; Mic 7:15).[3] Even though there were undoubtedly some promising moments in Old Testament history when Israel seemed to move toward her divine calling, led by Abraham, Moses, and David, her constant rebellion against Yahweh and her sin jeopardized the covenant relationship (Jer 31:31–34). However, Yahweh's faithfulness to the covenant sustained Israel within the divine redemptive purpose as he establishes a new covenant with his servant David (2 Sam 7:12–14; Isa 9:6). Despite the fragile nature of Israel's covenant relationship with Yahweh, she continued to hope that the ultimate salvation would soon be realized. The ultimate salvation and also the ultimate deliverer were yet to be revealed in the Old Testament which indicates that the process of salvation was not completed in the Old Testament period.[4] One of the major characteristics of the Old Testament and its fundamental principles is that it is

---

3. Holland, *Contours of Pauline Theology*. See also Hays, *Echoes of Scripture in the Letters of Paul*.

4. Cf. Pate et al., *The Story of Israel*.

forward-looking in nature. However, the events provide anticipations of later events as the fulfillment of the earlier promises. On the other hand, the New Testament claims that the fulfillment of salvation is made intelligible only within the context of the Old Testament promise of God. F. F. Bruce states that "in the language of typology, the earlier series of events constituted a 'type' of the later; the later series was an 'antitype' of the earlier."[5] For instance, the major Old Testament events of creation, exodus, and restoration from exile are revisited with new meaning attached to them through the works, death, and resurrection of Christ.

It is however imperative that typology be distinguished from allegorical interpretation of the Old Testament. It should not be perceived as a mode of thinking that is figurative by which the original context of the meaning of the Old Testament tradition is somehow distorted by the development of later religious ideas.[6] Rather, the value of the original context and the originally intended meaning of the Old Testament texts are appreciated in their own right. As Israel's redemptive history unfolds, the revelation of Yahweh is progressively disclosed which imparts new understanding on the earlier events in the wider knowledge of Yahweh's redemptive activity.[7] Here, the progressive nature of Israel's faith in Yahweh's redemption is emphasized along with how the emerging historical circumstances affect the covenant relationship with Yahweh.

This is not to say that typology searches for similarities between the details of the old and new events. Such an attempt at analogy is not only artificial but it will also lead to unnatural results. The use of types enforces the underlying theological/historical idea or a principle that God is intimately involved in the life of his people and his redemptive purpose is consistently manifested in history. Even if we discover cases where the details of incidents between the type and antitype are strikingly similar,

---

5. Wood et al., eds., *New Bible Dictionary*, 1214. See also Daube, *The Exodus Pattern in the Bible*; Hanson, *Jesus Christ in the Old Testament*; Davidson, *Typology in Scripture*; Goppelt, *Typos*; Buchanan, *Typology and the Gospel*.

6. Cf. "Allegory" in Kittel, ed., *Theological Dictionary of the New Testament*, vol. 1.

7. Ellison, "Typology," 158–66. The original context of the Old Testament text should properly be acknowledged. For instance, Ellison points out that "to call psalms messianic in the sense that they were written as conscious prophecies of Jesus Christ, and that they refer to him and him exclusively, is to do violence to the Psalter and to misunderstand the New Testament use of the Old Testament." Cf. also Baker, *Two Testaments, One Bible*; Ellis, *The Old Testament in Early Christianity*; Beale, "The New Testament Use of the Old Testament"; Marshall et al., eds., *It Is Written*.

the recognition of a type does not necessarily depend on similarities but on a common spiritual principle operative in history which binds them together. Typology thus points to the fact that God's revelation of his redemptive purpose is consistently manifested in the history of Israel. It is this historical awareness of God's redemptive act that brings the Old Testament types into alignment with those of the New.

Matthew and Typology

The author of Matthew's Gospel exhibits certain characteristics which suggest that he was thoroughly embedded within the Jewish religious mind-set. This will be discussed in greater detail throughout this volume. One of the salient features which demonstrate the Gospel's Jewishness is Matthew's dependence on the Old Testament in various quotations and allusions.[8] C. H. Dodd especially has observed the dominant influence of the Jewish tradition upon the formation of New Testament Christology. He writes, "Others, recognizing that Jewish messianic ideas afford an insufficient basis for the Church's Christology in its early forms, have looked for its origins in Hellenistic conceptions, especially those associated with mystery cults of such writings as 'Hermetica.' That such conception had an influence on the development of Christian theology is probable. But the fundamentals of New Testament Christology can be traced back to a stage when Hellenistic influence was at a minimum."[9]

Although the New Testament was fostered in an environment where Greco-Roman culture was pervasive, the core ethos and principle of Jewish religious identity were never compromised. This was retained in the writings of the New Testament authors who preserved this Jewish heritage. When we accept that Matthew was keen to demonstrate that the Old Testament redemptive history of Israel reached its culmination in the ministry of Jesus, typology becomes an exegetical tool through which the reader can decipher the intention of Matthew's message.

---

8. Dodd, *According to the Scripture*. He also points out that "the Psalms as a whole was clearly regarded as a source of testimonies to the passion of Christ and his ultimate triumph (e.g., Ps. 31:13 has helped to construct Matthew's account of the plotting of the Sanhedrin against Jesus, cf. Matt. 26: 3–4)." Cf. Hays, *Echoes of Scripture*. See also his chapter titled "Echoes and Inter-textuality: On the Role of Scripture in Paul's Theology," in Evans and Sanders, eds., *Paul and the Scriptures of Israel*; Marshall et al., eds., *It Is Written*.

9. Dodd, *According to the Scripture*, 115. Cf. also Hays, *Echoes of Scripture*.

One may also argue that typology is in fact inherent within the Gospel of Matthew, as any claim regarding Jesus as the Messiah is meaningless without the Old Testament as its supporting background. As a Jew, Matthew was familiar with the Jewish Scripture and its original meaning. When the evangelist draws the readers to Old Testament prophecy, he is intending something much more than just drawing fanciful parallels without regard for the original meaning of the text. He is in fact drawing the readers to the ongoing pattern of God's redemptive activity in Israel's history which reaches its ultimate fulfillment in Christ Jesus. We would argue that such typological reference is common among all New Testament writers. For instance, Richard B. Hays would be inclined favorably to this notion. In his study of Pauline epistles, Hays raises an important question: "In what sense are the Israelites of the exodus the fathers of the Gentile Corinthians?"[10] In other words, would the Apostle Paul justify typological understanding of the Scripture? He argues that "it is no accident that Paul never uses expressions such as 'new Israel' or 'spiritual Israel.'"[11] As far as Paul was concerned, there was no distinction between the two periods of the Old Testament and the era of Christ Jesus. It is still a single corporate entity of Israel into which Gentile Christians are now incorporated. For this reason, Hays affirms that Paul could freely deploy the words of the Old Testament for the community of Christians (cf. 1 Cor 5:13). He notes, "The scriptural command is treated as a self-evidently valid word addressed immediately to these Gentiles, who are thereby encouraged to assume an extraordinarily daring hermeneutical posture: they are to stand with Israel and join in the covenant confession (Deut. 5:2–3)."[12]

It seems plausible to suggest then that the typological correspondence is inherent in the mind-set of Paul as he addresses the Gentile Christians as children of the covenant (cf. 1 Cor 5:13; 10:1–22). The redemptive purpose of God is thus consistently revealed throughout Israel's history which reaches its decisive climax in Christ Jesus. This is certainly a salient feature within Matthew's Gospel, as the evangelist is particularly keen to draw attention to typological connections.[13]

---

10. Hays, *Echoes of Scripture*, 95.
11. Ibid., 96.
12. Ibid., 97.
13. France, *Matthew*, 185–86.

On the basis of our definition, Matthew's reliance on typology indicates that the evangelist is acutely aware of Israel's redemptive history. Hermeneutically, if allegory is characterized by a much more rigid attachment to the text and the very letter of it, typology, on the contrary, is relatively free from attachment to the word or the letter.[14] Instead, it is bound to a much greater degree by historical awareness. This prevents biblical thought from being diluted into an abstract spiritual notion. In other words, the redemptive act of God is demonstrated in concrete historical reality. The concept of the redemptive history of Israel will be discussed in more detail in chapter 4.[15]

Gerhard von Rad aptly describes the nature of typological interpretation in relation to the redemptive history of Israel when he writes, "It is not at all as if such promises only, so to speak, moved on before Israel, and remained till the end something to be hoped for. On the contrary, Israel told of manifold instances of divinely given fulfillment that had already been brought to pass in history . . . Yet this historical fulfillment notably did not diminish the actuality of the promise that had once been given; it did not fall before the law of history. Rather, the promise of land, in spite of its initial fulfillment, remained in force for Israel."[16]

This historicizing tendency of typology is in fact shared by scholars who argue that typological interpretation is reinforced by the historico-critical exegetical process.[17] Although it is impossible to describe the relationship between the Old Testament and New Testament in only one way, one of the major characteristics of typology commonly understood by biblical exegetes is the historical correspondence between the two traditions. While we would agree that the Old Testament type should be appreciated in its own terms within the framework of typology, one is likely to miss the fundamental meaning if God's redemptive action in history is neglected. Typology keeps the reader's attention to the overarching framework of God's redemptive purpose in the history of Israel, and without this sense of continuity the Old Testament on its own is

---

14. Von Rad, "Typological Interpretation," 21.

15. Ibid., 27. Von Rad states that "the concept of *Heilsgeschichte* is here sketched as a course of history which is kept in motion and guided to its God-ordained goal, by the constantly intruding divine Word."

16. Ibid., 33.

17. Cf. Cullmann, *Christ and Time*.

believed to be incomplete.[18] Peter Legarth concurs that "the designations type and antitype do not belong to two-world thinking, but to a line of thought dominated by salvation history."[19] Since the early Christians believed that the same God is operating in the old and new covenants, the concept of redemptive history is an essential foundation for understanding the nature of typology found in the New Testament. In this mode of thinking a theological and historical coherence between the old and the new covenants is implied. Although the Old Testament on its own is considered to be incomplete, it provides the primary background to the message and theology of the New Testament authors. The exclusive authority of the Old Testament for the message of the New is easily recognizable in the Bible. In conjunction with this, Legarth notes that "Paul and the others at times refer to Hellenistic poets and to the world of ideas of Ancient Judaism. However, phenomena in Rome and Athens, and in contemporary Jerusalem, are not portrayed as 'type.' They can merely be parallels, capable of confirming, but not normative. The authors of the New Testament find 'type' exclusively in the Old Testament."[20]

Walter Eichrodt points out that even in the Old Testament prophecy typology is inherently playing a part which indicates that it is not an ordinary exegetical tool formulated and utilized by modern biblical scholarship in an attempt to decipher the meaning of the text. It is something that is inherent within the religious text of Israel itself. For instance, as Eichrodt writes, "It is Hosea who speaks of a new wilderness period on the model of the first one (2:14ff.) and this is taken up again by Jeremiah (23:7). But it is Deutero-Isaiah who first gives full force to this theme, setting the deliverance from Exile in parallel with the fundamental act of deliverance by Yahweh in the escape from Egypt, and using the colors of the Exodus story to paint this new picture (Isa. 40:3; 41:17ff.; 42:16; 43:17; 48:21; 49:10f.; 52:12; Jer. 31:2f.)."[21] It is foretold that

---

18. Legarth, "Typology and its Theological Basis," 143–54. Legarth states that "undoubtedly the authors of the New Testament regarded the types as 'historical realities.' Consequently, the point is that the theological substance of the type is contained not behind or under the historical incident, but in it."

19. Ibid., 146.

20. Ibid., 148. It is further noted that typology is not an exegetical method, and the interpreter can utilize it only in cases where it is evident that New Testament authors do so. Under other circumstances this option in the hermeneutical process is closed. Cf. also Eichrodt, "Is Typological Exegesis an Appropriate Method?"

21. Eichrodt, "Is Typological Exegesis an Appropriate Method?" 234.

the later redemptive act of Yahweh would be far greater than what Israel had previously experienced (cf. Isa 43:17; 52:12).[22]

The importance of the Old Testament for typological interpretation is axiomatic. However, Eichrodt notes that the difference between typology and the interpretation of the Old Testament as prophecy of the fulfillment which is found in the New Testament is the objective historical outlook of the former. They are interdependent to a certain degree as each of them sees in the Old Testament the announcement of the completion of salvation by God. The difference is that while "in prophecy the messenger of God proclaims the future which has been seen by him, a type possesses its significance, pointing to the future independently of any human medium and purely through its objective factual reality."[23] What is also stressed is the attachment of typology to the historical reality of God's redemptive act for his people. Eichrodt advances this view, arguing that "typology is not exhausted by the correspondence of external facts but relates itself to the intercourse between God and man made real through them . . . But the fact that the salvation was prepared upon a historical path removes this salvation from any attempt to spiritualize it, and places it within historical concreteness."[24]

All these elements of typology and historicizing tendencies are characteristic of Matthew's Gospel. The evangelist is clearly interested in the redemptive history of Israel, as he begins his Gospel with exclusive reference to Jesus' genealogy by tracing his ancestry. Moreover, the fulfillment quotations are embedded in the entire literary structure of the Gospel. It covers the events of Jesus' birth (Matt 1:23; 2:6, 15, 18, 23), the beginning of his ministry in Galilee (4:15–16), his healings (8:17), his compassion and gentleness (12:18–21), his teaching in parables (13:35), his entry into Jerusalem (21:5), and his passion and death (26:56; 27:9–10).[25] Even though most of the fulfillment quotations are found in the first thirteen chapters and especially in the passages that are most uniquely Matthean, such as the infancy narratives (chs. 1 and 2), it shows Matthew's reliance on the Old Testament and his aware-

---

22. Ibid., 235. "It can hardly be doubted, however, in face of passages like Isa. 11:1; Jer. 23:5; Ezek. 34:23; 37:24; Isa. 55:3, 5, that David was considered a type for the coming deliverer-king."

23. Eichrodt, "Is Typological Exegesis an Appropriate Method?"

24. Ibid., 240.

25. Senior, *What Are They Saying about Matthew?* 51.

ness of the redemptive act of God manifested in the history of Israel.[26] These "historicizing tendencies" in Matthew are not only present in the genealogy and infancy narratives, but apparently in other chronological references that reveal the evangelist's historical interest. At three crucial moments of Jesus earthly ministry (Matt 4:17; 16:21; 26:16), Matthew inserts the phrase "from that time." This supports the thesis that typology in relation with Israel's redemptive history is inherently characteristic of Matthew.[27]

This further suggests that Matthew retained his Jewish mind-set and that the primary audience was his Jewish counterparts. It is in the context of Israel's historical and theological background that he wished to convey the message of Israel's Messiah. His typological use of the Old Testament quotations indicates that Matthew's Gospel is designed to reach out to his Jewish brothers and sisters (cf. Matt 10:5). However, Israel's rejection of her own Messiah will give way to the Gentiles who will constitute the new Israel (cf. Matt 12:18, 21). As Hays remarks, "The relation between Israel and Church is one of positive correspondence, not antithesis."[28] This suggests that the fundamental characteristics of the Jewish mind-set were not compromised even in the context of the Gentile Christians (cf. 1 Cor 5:13; 10:1–22). As noted earlier, it is often assumed in New Testament scholarship that the early Christian authors were Hellenistic in their thinking. This has led scholars to draw evidence from Hellenistic sources in order to explicate the New Testament text and its mind-set.[29] For instance, R. H. Fuller argues for the "two stage

---

26. Cf. Stendahl, *The School of St. Matthew*. He is known for his argument that Matthew was a creative writer who was at liberty in his use of the Jewish Scripture. In the fulfillment quotations, the text form, although composed in Greek, is closer to the Masoretic text while displaying "deviations from all Greek, Hebrew and Aramaic types of texts known to us." He arrives at his conclusion by comparing Qumran texts with Matthew's in which the former practiced similar techniques in shaping the text in the light of their convictions about its fulfillment. Cf. also Gundry, "The Use of the Old Testament in St. Matthew's Gospel," 18, who also argues that the practice of making one's own translation of Old Testament texts rather than relying on the Septuagint or Masoretic text was widely prevalent in the early Christian setting. This is analogous to that of the rabbinic practice of "targumizing," which is a "free interpretive rendering of biblical quotations and stories."

27. Cf. Strecker, "The Concept of History in Matthew," 219–30; see also Meier, "Salvation History in Matthew," 203–15; Levine, *The Social and Ethnic Dimensions of Matthean Salvation History*, 14.

28. Hays, *Echoes of Scripture*, 97.

29. Cf. Gilfillan-Upton; also Fuller, *The Foundations of New Testament Christology*, 62–63, who argues that the ethical teachings attributed to Jesus were derived from

Christology." He notes that a Hellenistic Jewish Christianity first emerged in Palestine which was an originally Aramaic speaking community. It is presumed that it was here that the Aramaic Christological terms were first translated into the Greek language. As the early Christian message was circulated it had to undergo certain changes for the purpose of mission. Fuller points out that "it was impossible for the Greek speaking Jewish Christians simply to repeat the tradition or even merely to develop it along the lines laid down by the earliest Aramaic speaking Christians." According to Fuller, the process of Hellenization took full effect as the use of the Septuagint led to important and far-reaching developments for Christological titles such as *Kyrios, Christos, Son of God*, and *Son of David*.[30] However, caution is in order when one argues that the fundamental ethos of a religion is compromised as it took on a missionary outlook. What Fuller is implying is that the context in which the message is proclaimed affects the perception or even determines the essence of the message being delivered. This is in fact undermining the tenacity of the Diaspora Jewish community and their adherence to their religious tradition and custom. This is what most New Testament scholars who argue that the New Testament writings are Hellenistic in nature often overlook. Being in a foreign environment does not necessarily dilute the communal identity. Indeed, Matthew and the rest of the New Testament writers display their dependence on the parent body of religion by making references to the Old Testament. Even if there are certain similarities between the vocabularies of the New Testament and the Hellenistic world, the core of the religious meaning is different. This view is shared by Holland, who points out that the *Jewishness* of the Bible is often undermined by modern contemporary scholarship in biblical theology at large. He writes, "The Hebrew meaning had been poured into the text of the Greek translation to produce a language that had its own particular lexicon. It was Greek in its alphabet and vocabulary, but Hebrew in its mindset and essential meaning. It was this very language

---

Hellenism, since the tradition would have influenced not so much the prophetic eschatology but ethical and cosmological categories.

30. Fuller, 182–86, advances this view in relation to fundamental Christological implications which are generated as a result of Hellenistic influence. It is noted that "in the earliest Palestinian community no attempt was made to evaluate the present status, dignity and function of Jesus in heaven. *Kyrios* Jesus becomes the proclamation of the Hellenistic Jewish missionaries." It is claimed that Hellenistic influences allow LXX passages to be applied to Jesus which were originally reserved for Yahweh-Kyrios.

that Judaism bequeathed to the infant Church as she interpreted and proclaimed the message of the prophets."[31]

The Jewish heritage of the Christian message remained intact and formed the structural core of the message concerning Christ. Therefore, the understanding of the Old Testament texts becomes the crucial text for interpreting the New Testament.

This renders the use of the extrabiblical sources somewhat unreliable for the study of Matthew's Gospel, which displays clear attachment to the Old Testament prophecies. In principle, this would cohere with the rest of the New Testament writers. Recently, however, there has been an ever-increasing tendency to use intertestamental literature in New Testament studies as a result of the discoveries at Qumran. Undoubtedly, these writings provide insights into this particular period of Judaism, but to what extent these prove to be of value for the New Testament message needs to be critically reexamined.[32] Even if common terminology was utilized in the New Testament and in the intertestamental literature, its original context of meaning may not be consistent for any sound theological comparison to be conducted. Holland points out that "the common terminology is not evidence of a common theology and its literature is of limited value for New Testament research."[33] What these do provide, Holland argues, "is evidence as to how widely different themes were discussed but this evidence does not give us the details that we need to map the theology of these documents accurately."[34]

In fact the sheer diversity of messianic concepts found in intertestamental literature is so overwhelming that any analogy with the Matthean Christology becomes somewhat tentative. For instance, in the Qumran community, it may be that they also possessed the belief that the exile continued and the promises of salvation still remained unfulfilled. In this regard, there exists a common belief system with Matthew's community who also held that the exile was an ongoing reality for Israel and the significance of Jesus' ministry was a divine manifestation of messianic

---

31. Holland, *Contours of Pauline Theology*, 52.

32. Jacob Neusner claims that Judaism must not be reduced in simplistic terms. It is not a homogeneous system but rather a complex entity. He also shows that Judaism did not have a unified expectation of Israel's Messiah, but rather various and often conflicting theories; Neusner et al., eds., *Judaism and Their Messiahs*.

33. Holland, *Contours of Pauline Theology*, 68.

34. Ibid.

restoration from the exilic plight.[35] However, Matthew never refers to these post-Old Testament Jewish literatures in the way he quotes and alludes to the Old Testament. This is also pointed out by Nolland, who writes that "it is hard to tell to what degree the books of the Apocrypha are part of his repertoire."[36]

G. R. Beasley-Murray examined the messianic concept in apocalyptic literature and came to the conclusion that the various teachings of messiah often contradict one another and cannot be traced uniformly. He notes that in the Psalms of Solomon (chapters 17–18), "an anticipation of a purely earthly kingdom of Israelite domination over the nations invites the idea of a purely earthly Messiah-king of the order of David."[37] On the contrary, however, the concept of a kingdom of God envisaged in the Similitudes of Enoch especially concerning the Son of Man indicates that the Messiah is attributed qualities that are beyond ordinary human beings. Moreover, the messianic expectation in apocalyptic writings such as Jubilees, 1 Enoch 1–36 and 91–104, Assumption of Moses, 1 Baruch, 2 Enoch, and various books of the Apocrypha (1–2 Macc, Tob, Wis, Jdt, and Sir) is not so apparent in their anticipation of the kingdom of God.[38]

Perhaps relevant to the subject under consideration is the Testaments of the Twelve Patriarchs, where two different types of Messiah are expected. Beasley-Murray notes that in this literature there are various passages which deal with a Messiah who will come from Levi (cf. esp. Test. Reuben 6:5–12 and Test. Levi 18:2–14), while other passages speak of a Messiah who will emerge from Judah (e.g., Judah 17:5–6, 22:2–3, 24:1ff.). He notes that some passages bring the two together as follows: "And now, my children, obey Levi and Judah, and be not lifted up against these two tribes, for from them shall arise unto you

---

35. Nolland, *The Gospel of Matthew*, 37.

36. Ibid., 38. Nolland nevertheless comes to the conclusion that Matthew does relate appreciatively to Sirach (e.g., Matt 11:28 echoes Sir 51:27).

37. Beasley-Murray, *Jesus and the Kingdom of God*, 52.

38. Ibid. It is noted that "the Psalms of Solomon are exceptional but explicable in that they represent the Pharisaic reaction to the Hasmonean kingship. In their rejection of the Hasmonean usurpation of kingship, the Pharisees looked to God to raise up a king of David's line but the apocalyptic movement itself rejected the messianic expectation." Cf. also Müller, *Messias und Menschensohn in Jüdischen Apokalypsen und in der Offenbarung des Johannes*.

the salvation of God. For the Lord shall raise up from Levi as it were a High-Priest, and from Judah as it were a King."[39]

Furthermore, ever since the discoveries at Qumran, a major shift of perspective in biblical scholarship has taken place. The scholars who advocate the view that these texts shed light on the New Testament texts draw references from them to understand Jesus and Christian origins.[40] However, the question of whether the Qumran documents can be a reliable source of reference to Jesus needs to be critically evaluated. F. F. Bruce suggests that caution is in order when a biblical exegete relies on these texts for New Testament interpretation.

First of all, he argues that "the Qumran community withdrew as far as possible from public life and lived in its wilderness retreat; Jesus carried on his ministry in places where people lived and worked, mixing with all sorts and conditions and by preference with men and women whose society pious men like those of Qumran would rather avoid."[41] In other words, the nature of the environment and perhaps the cultural context from which the New Testament message concerning Christ and the Dead Sea Scrolls emerged is quite different for a convincing analogy to be drawn.

Secondly, the messianic connotation in the New Testament and the Dead Sea Scrolls is not homogeneous although there are ancillary similarities. The Dead Sea Scrolls are in general forward-looking in nature, as the Messiah is still eagerly awaited by the community, whereas in the New Testament the message is dominated by the proclamation that the Messiah has finally come. In the New Testament the Messiah is not only identified with the royal figure from the house of David but also with the Servant of the Lord in the book of Isaiah and the Son of Man in the book of Daniel. However, these figures, according to Bruce, have not influenced the messianic doctrine of the Qumran community. The language that is ascribed to the Messiah in the New Testament such as "Servant of the Lord" and "Son of Man" does not appear in the Dead Sea Scrolls.[42] Rather, it seems that there is emphasis upon the priestly function of the Messiah in the order of the Levitical priesthood. This is entirely devi-

---

39. Beasley-Murray, 54, 61. It is also noted that Levi was superior to Judah (cf. the Testament of Judah 21:1ff.).

40. Cf. Brooke, *The Dead Sea Scrolls and the New Testament*.

41. Bruce, *Jesus and Christian Origins outside the New Testament*, 66.

42. Ibid., 73, 74.

ant from the portrayal of the Messiah in the New Testament where the writers, especially Matthew, seek authority from the Old Testament for Jesus' identity and his redemptive ministry. It will become clearer as we progress that the Messiah in the New Testament is identified as the anointed king of David's line as described in the Psalter (cf. Ps 110:4).[43]

These widely diverse ramifications regarding the messianic understanding in the Jewish apocalyptic literature suggest that these books are perhaps too easily assimilated into the New Testament scholarship as if they are a reliable source for sound exegesis. However, we need to critically evaluate the use of such texts since there is so little evidence, at least that which is convincing, which could be of significance for biblical studies. We know very little about the original context from which these texts emerged and the mind-set of the authors in relation to the New Testament authors. Even if it is granted that these New Testament writers were somehow familiar with intertestamental literature, there is no proof that the evangelists depended on or drew from them. Matthew's Christology, as we shall see in more detail in subsequent chapters, exhibits characteristics that are derived exclusively from the Old Testament tradition. We are not denying that even within the Old Testament it is unrealistic to hope for a uniformly traceable expectation of Messiah. Sometimes it seems that Israel is longing for the Messiah but, on the other hand, any messianic hope seems to be dominated by Yahweh as Israel's sole redeemer. We shall discuss these in more detail in chapter 2. All in all, Matthew displays his allegiance to Jewish religious tradition which is inherent in the Old Testament.

For Matthew, there is no doubt that the Old Testament is the foundational source of influence. The fulfillment motif is prevalent within the Gospel, as there are approximately sixty quotes from twenty-five books and seventy-six allusions to the Old Testament which indicates that Matthew is distinctly attached to the Old Testament. It is of paramount importance for Matthew to demonstrate that Jesus and the events of his life are "fully shadowed" in the Old Testament. Throughout the Gospel there are ample incidents where the authority of the Old Testament is properly acknowledged. For instance, Jesus declares that he has not come to abolish the law or the prophets but to fulfill them,

---

43. Ibid., 78. Incidentally, the anointed king of David's line is declared as "a priest forever after the order of Melchizedek," which is regarded as more prestigious than Levi's in ancient Israel.

which underlines the divine quality of Torah (Matt 5:17–20). The reason for Jesus' critical attitude against the Jewish authorities is precisely due to the fact that the Pharisees and the scribes were not practicing what they were preaching, and not because what they were teaching was obsolete. The demand of a righteousness exceeding that of the scribes and Pharisees suggests that Jesus is calling Israel back to the fundamentals of Torah and awakening her leadership to its true values rather than invalidating it. It is significant that only Matthew records this word of Jesus (5:20) within the synoptic tradition.[44]

Along this line of thought, D. J. Moo argues that "Jesus' criticism of the scribes and Pharisees is not that their attention to the details of the law is in itself wrong, but that, as a result of such attention, more fundamental demands of God are often neglected." In other words, Jesus did not bring about a radically new principle for the interpretation of the law but he sought to revive the original value and intention of Torah which is entirely in keeping with the prophetic tradition.[45]

It is nevertheless important to appreciate that while the teaching of Jesus maintains clear links with the Old Testament and Matthew's claim regarding Jesus would be meaningless without the foundation of the Old Testament, he does not confine Jesus within the boundary of Judaism in the strictest sense. Jesus has not come to abolish any Old Testament commandment, but neither can it be conceived that he fully advocates the law. With regard to Jesus' teaching, D. J. Moo notes that, "Some of them might be best described by the terms 'deepening' or 'radicalization' but some of Jesus' teaching cannot be understood in this way. What is the dominant note, hinted at in the emphatic 'I say to you', testified to by the crowds at the conclusion of the sermon and observed in all the antitheses, is the *independent, authoritative teaching of Jesus*, which is neither derived from nor explicitly related to the Old Testament."[46]

---

44. It is also noteworthy that only Matthew records the incident regarding the temple tax in which Jesus paid the tax and abided by the Jewish law (Matt 17:24–25).

45. Moo, "Jesus and the Authority of the Mosaic Law," 3–49, utilizes Robert Bank's model which distinguishes between the written law, the oral law, and customs in assessing Jesus' relationship to the Judaism of his day. It is noted that "as the Sabbath became increasingly important in post-exilic Judaism, the need was felt to define more clearly the kinds of activity prohibited, and this led to the development of the oral Sabbath law. It appears that it was only this scribal tradition, not the written law, which Jesus and the disciples violated."

46. Ibid., 22; emphasis added.

This statement is supported by Luke 16:16 where a clear distinction is drawn between the era of the prophets and that which is inaugurated by Jesus. "The law and the prophets were until John; since then the good news of the Kingdom of God is preached, and everyone enters it violently." A fundamental shift in the redemptive history of Israel has taken place with the coming of Christ. John the Baptist marks the end of the Old Testament era by preparing the path for Jesus' ministry to take effect in order to inaugurate the coming of the New Era. However, in the light of the immediately succeeding verse, Jesus clearly does not regard the Old Testament tradition as obsolete, but he is rather saying that "the period during which men were related to God under its Old Covenant has ceased with John."[47] It seems, therefore, that there is an element of both *continuity* and *discontinuity* in the way the New Testament uses the Old. The authority of the Old Testament not only remains authoritative and valid but it is also expanded with the fulfillment of Jesus, who brings it to a decisive culmination. In other words, the authority of the Old Testament is determined by its fulfillment.[48] It is this seemingly paradoxical balance which is inherent in the teachings of Jesus as he fully preserves the authority of the law in general (cf. Matt 5:17, 18; 7:12; also 23:23), but, in the Kingdom of God which Jesus establishes, little use of the law is made in the formulation of its ethics. This view is shared by Moo when he states that "on the basis of Jesus' teaching, it does not seem that any Mosaic commandment can be assumed to be directly applicable to the believer. Jesus' authority as the law's fulfiller stands even over the Decalogue."[49]

PART TWO: CONSISTENCY OF THE CONCEPT OF SALVATION

Continuity and Discontinuity

This brings us to a more specific question: To what extent does the conception of salvation in the Old Testament remain consistent with that of the New Testament? After all, without the sense of continuity from the Old Testament Matthew's Gospel quite simply has no foundation. The

---

47. Ibid., 23.
48. Ibid., 28, 29.
49. Ibid., 29. Cf. also Banks, *Jesus and the Law in the Synoptic Tradition*; Bacon, "Jesus and the Law," 203–31; Branscomb, *Jesus and the Law of Moses*; Kaiser, *The Uses of the Old Testament in the New*.

issue must have been poignant for the early Christians, since without the consistency of the concept of "promise and salvation" from the Old Testament the messianic era brought about by Jesus might be seen as an illegitimate claim. This was clarified in the previous section, as we have seen how Jesus displayed his adherence to the law. However, there is also a sense of radical disjuncture, at least implicitly, in that the New Era brought about by Jesus does mean that a fresh insight to the Jewish Scripture is now in effect (cf. Matt 11:13).

This also affects the Christological discussion, as the promise of the Messiah foretold in the Old Testament is consistently fulfilled in the New but in a way that exceeds the common understanding of the Messiah in Judaism. In other words, the concept of salvation remains consistent in that Jesus is the Messiah in the line of David, as Israel was promised, but his identity and redemptive function differ greatly, as Jesus is far more authoritative in terms of his messianic status than David could ever have been (cf. Matt 22:43–45).

It might be suggested that the nature of salvation somehow changes in the New Testament which places more emphasis on the matter of sin in a spiritual sense, as is evident in some of the claims of Jesus which deal predominantly with the doctrine of sin and salvation (cf. Matt 12:31; 13:41; John 1:29; 5:14; 8:34; 9:41; 15:22; 16:8, 9). The prophetic tradition of the Old Testament does have a more nationalistic connotation which deals with the actual liberation of Israel from the oppression of foreign tyrants. G. B. Caird describes one of the chief characteristics of the New Testament message thus: "The New Testament was written by those who had entered on a new life of freedom and dignity, opened to them by the *forgiveness of sins*, and who believed that their experience was offered to all human beings as God's universal answer to the world's universal need (cf. Rom. 3:23; 1 John 5:19; Heb. 10:3)."[50]

The issue of sin and the need for forgiveness are what characterize the fundamental creed of the Christian movement. This is certainly the major aspect of John the Baptist's ministry, as he calls Israel to repentance so that she may be spared the impending judgment and wrath of God (Matt 3:1–12; Mark 1:4; Luke 3:3). The blood of Jesus Christ will be shed for the forgiveness of sins (Matt 26:28). Whereas the New Testament writers explicitly stated the universality of sin and the death of Christ as the means of saving humanity from the consequences of

---

50. Caird, *New Testament Theology*, 74; emphasis added.

sins, the Old Testament on the contrary seems less clear in this respect. G. B. Caird also makes the observation that "even in some of the great penitential Psalms, it is not clear whether the Psalmist's confession is the genuine recognition of a specific fault or simply an assumption that, since God is just, the disaster must have been deserved."[51] In other words, it is not always clear whether the sense of guilt is caused by the profound acknowledgement of sin or by the national atrocities which arouse a sense of guilt and regret.

It may well seem that there is a discontinuity in terms of the nature and concept of salvation. Whereas the Old Testament was concerned more or less exclusively with the state of Israel and her position in world politics, the New Testament rarely relates salvation with the actual state of Israel. This issue is also recognized by John Goldingay, who notes that "in the New Testament God's activity centers on the life of his people and the individuals, and his chief blessing is forgiveness and spiritual renewal. The Old Testament God is involved in this world, in politics and war, and his blessings are this-worldly."[52] However, as F. F. Bruce notes, it is important to remember that "Israel's political and historical atrocities were caused by the sin of the people of Israel."[53] In effect, this is fundamentally consistent with the salvation that the New Testament proclaims which promises triumph over death and sin (cf. Matt 13:41; John 1:29; Rom 5:12; 6:13; 7:13; 8:2). Ultimately, the entire prophetic tradition of the Old Testament is essentially proclaiming that judgment is impending from Yahweh which is indeed manifested through neighboring foreign nations for her transgressions and sin. On the same principle, F. F. Bruce notes that "Jesus deals with redemption at a more fundamental level and his messiahship is not merely confined to national redemption but deals with the greater cosmic level of redemption."[54] David's messianic role is inherently embedded in the identity and the redemptive ministry of Christ, and it would seem that Matthew is particularly keen on this theme (as we shall see in more detail in the subsequent chapters). It seems, then, that political stability and national welfare were directly dependent upon Israel's spiritual relationship with Yahweh. This is perhaps what is unique about Israel's religion—both religion and politics

---

51. Ibid., 75.
52. Goldingay, *Approaches to Old Testament Interpretation*, 29.
53. Bruce, "The Sure Mercies of David."
54. Ibid., 20.

were inextricably intertwined. After all, David is not just a king in a political-military sense but also assumes priestly status (cf. Ps 110:4). In this sense, Jesus' role as the Messiah in principle is not inconsistent with the messianic understanding of redemption in the Old Testament. It is ultimately sin before Yahweh which incites judgment upon Israel. David is remembered as such an authoritative royal figure precisely because he was able to deliver Israel from its enemies and elevate the status of Israel among foreign nations. However, this is only the superficial aspect of salvation; he could not deal with the more fundamental issues of redemption. This would be achieved by the greater Son of David who establishes salvation from all causes of sin (cf. Matt 13:41).[55]

For Israel, the religious dimension of faith played a vital role in her understanding of historical reality in which Yahweh is in control. This will be discussed in more detail in the next chapter, which deals with the "Redemptive History of Israel." This is perhaps an unacceptable position for a postmodern Western way of thinking where a clear distinction is drawn between the religious and political realms. However, the two were closely bound with each other for ancient Israel, as sin was the cause of political atrocities. The people of Israel saw the exile as God's punishment for their sins. Viewed in this way, the major events of Yahweh's redemption of Israel dealt fundamentally with the matters of sin. Undoubtedly, the Exodus is one of the key events in the history of Israel, if not the dominant representative redemptive event. While it is commonly regarded as Israel's liberation from a foreign oppressor and the bondage of slavery, it has a deeper significance. Holland argues that the Exodus motif is prevalent in the mind-set of the New Testament writers and is indeed what forms the bedrock of the message concerning Christ's redemptive work. He advances the discussion by pointing out that it is the Passover which is the driving force within the Exodus motif. For most biblical interpreters, Passover has no propitiatory value.

---

55. Matthew 13:41 reads that it is the "Son of Man" who will effect judgment. We shall see in more detail in the subsequent chapter how different Christological titles do not conflict with each other but interact to form a dynamic portrait of Jesus. Cf. also Rev 5:5ff. In the apocalyptic vision John sees the celebration of the triumph of Jesus, in which the conqueror's arrival is heralded as the "Lion of the tribe of Judah" and the "Root of David." For a contrary view, see Bentzen, *King and Messiah*, 39, who underlines the inconsistency of the concept of messiah in the Old and New Testaments. He argues that "he [the Messiah of the Old Testament] comes *in* history, called by the God of history, *not* at the end of history and of time, between the aeons. The Messiah of pre-exilic days is not an eschatological figure."

However, Holland argues that there is biblical evidence within the Old Testament prophetic tradition which suggests otherwise.[56] During the exilic period, the prophets predict that the New Exodus will soon be established by the Davidic Messiah, and the prototype Exodus provided the basis for the assurance and the future messianic hope. Holland writes that "a crucial contributor to this expectation was Ezekiel, who, like Isaiah, saw the importance of the raising up of a Davidic prince (Ezek 24:23–24; 37:24–25; cf. also 45:25). Ezekiel saw the prince's main function was to build the eschatological temple and to provide sacrifices for the sins of the covenant community."[57] Since Ezekiel records that the sacrifices offered by the prince come during the Passover, Holland suggests that "Ezekiel is emphasizing the importance of the Passover for dealing with the sins of the people." During the Passover, the Davidic prince will offer a sin offering for the atonement of his people (Ezek 45:21ff). Any redemptive event depicted in the Old Testament, therefore, is fundamentally related with Israel's sin. This imagery is essentially congruent with what the Gospels present, that is, the sacrificial death of Jesus the Son of David, which is reminiscent of the Passover sacrifice, brings about the New Exodus, thereby redeeming Israel from the judgment of death and sin.

One of the chief characteristics of the prophetic tradition is that it pointed forward to the greater salvation which is yet to be established. The exile was a temporary measure, as the punishment of Israel's sin and even the return from the exile was not the final salvation. The ultimate redemption, which the prophets anticipated, was to deal with sin in a completely different way. Holland writes that "The nature of the exile caused by Adam is of a different dimension and order, and requires an act of cosmic redemption. The redemption achieved by Christ is totally unique. It could not take place without the death of the Son of God. Here the emphasis is on removing man from the condemnation that sin has brought about."[58]

---

56. An understanding accepted by Marshall, *Aspects of the Atonement*. Cf. also Thiselton, "Influences on Paul," 425–26, a review of Holland's *Contours of Pauline Theology*. Both scholars express support for this claim.

57. Holland, *Contours of Pauline Theology*, 161.

58. Ibid., 170. Cf. Rom 8 where Paul explains the cosmic dimension of Christ's redemption.

It seems fair to suggest that the fundamental principle of salvation remains consistent although what the New Testament proclaims regarding Jesus expands the Old Testament concept of redemption. This is not a deviant perspective that is newly generated by the New Testament writers. As mentioned earlier, even though the majority of biblical commentators do not associate Passover with atonement, there is evidence that suggests that "the early Church through the influence of Ezek. 45:25 saw the anticipated eschatological Passover to be a sacrifice of propitiation."[59] This is also supported by S. J. L. Croft's observation of Psalm 51 in particular; Croft writes, "as there is clearly a strong association between the sin of the community, or of the individuals within the community, and the disaster which has befallen the nation, the psalm is grouped here with others which reflect a background of war." In other words, sin was the direct cause of political and national atrocities. He argues that "the psalm should be seen as forming part of a liturgy for a day of penitence either amongst the exiles or, more probably, in Jerusalem."[60] It is noted that the concepts of sin, repentance, God's forgiveness, and the like, are all inextricably connected to the outcome of political reality, as these concepts assumed a prominent position within the theology of Israel's prophetic tradition.[61] J. H. Eaton has also argued that the kings of ancient Israel had a priestly role, as they sought to make atonement for Israel's sin (cf. Ezek 45:17).[62] When we look at the Son of David's role as a mediator and the salvation from sin which the New Testament claims has been manifested in Jesus, the king's role as the representative of the

---

59. Ibid., 171, 174. Holland notes that "further support is found for the link between atonement and Passover in Gal. 1:3, overtly New Exodus material. The cultic event, which describes the means of deliverance from God's wrath, is clearly presented in terms of a sin offering, which again is fused with the imagery of redemption and is in a New Exodus context." This position is further advanced with the reading from Colossians 1:12–14, which "speaks in New Exodus language for it is saturated with redemptive/Paschal imagery, while 1:20 describes the effect of the redemption (1:14) as the reconciliation of all things, which is again atoning imagery."

60. Croft et al., eds., *The Identity of the Individual in the Psalms*.

61. Cf. Engnell, *Studies in Divine Kingship in the Ancient Near East*; Hooke *Myth, Ritual, and Kingship*; Johnson, "The Role of the King in the Jerusalem Cultus"; Mettinger, *King and Messiah*; Mowinckel, *The Psalms in Israel's Worship*; also Ollenburger, *Zion, the City of the Great King*.

62. Eaton, *Kingship and the Psalms*, 177. It is further noted that "Solomon's great prayer at the autumn festival and consecration of the temple (1 Kings 8) founds a way of reconciliation."

nation is in principle what Jesus fulfilled as Israel's Messiah.[63] Both concepts of redemption found in the Old and the New Testaments offer messianic deliverance from the wrath of God and the impending judgment. This indicates that the New Testament is essentially congruent with the Old Testament, and the New is indeed the continuation of the Old.[64] Goldingay succinctly summarizes this point: "If the two testaments have a different range of concerns and insights, this does not mean that one testament ought to be the basis for narrowing our interests in relation to those of the other; and if they have different emphases in relation to themes they have in common, these may be seen as complementary rather than as alternatives to each other."[65]

What Goldingay suggests is that although there are clear differences between the two testaments in that the Old Testament's witness to Christ is often implicit (as it is essentially a witness to Yahweh), for the early Christians, Yahweh's redemptive activity is made intelligible only in the light of Christology.[66]

This has wider implications, since the question of at what point Christianity becomes a distinct entity from Judaism comes to the fore. This is of particular interest for Matthew's Gospel, since he displays his adherence to the Jewish tradition but at the same time detaches himself

---

63. Ibid., 178. Eaton notes that "it is possible that in Psalm 56 we have a prayer of the king recited at a ceremony of expiation quite similar to that of the scapegoat." Furthermore, "Psalm 102 may disclose to us, the custom of the king, afflicted in penitential rites of fasting and weeping in sackcloth and ashes, pleading for the good of Zion." Cf. also Bentzen, *King and Messiah*; Bleeker, "The Religion of Ancient Egypt," 40–114; Cooke, "The Israelite King as Son of God," 202–25; Frankfort, *Kingship and the Gods*; Gadd, *Ideas of Divine Rule in the Ancient East*. See also Wright, *Jesus and the Victory of God*.

64. Cf. van Groningen, *Messianic Revelation in the Old Testament*, 32, 37. The question of whether the messianic concept remains consistent in the Old Testament and the New Testament is a subject that deserves an in-depth discussion in its own right. This will be dealt with in chapter 2. Regarding the office of the anointed, there is clearly a composite picture which needs to be taken into account. According to van Groningen these are the office of priest (Exod 29:41), the office of prophet (Deut 18:15), and the office of king. A close relationship existed between kings, prophets, and priests, as all three groups were considered to be the "anointed" and were respected as God-honoring covenant servants. Since the specific functions performed by the anointed ones are by nature mediatorial, it seems fair to assume that the Messiah would exhibit all these characteristics.

65. Goldingay, *Approaches to Old Testament Interpretation*, 34.

66. Ibid., 37.

from it to such an extent that he is known to be the most "anti-Jewish" author in the New Testament (cf. chapter 2). In other words, as A. G. Fruchtenbaum pointed out, "the terms Jewishness and Judaism need to be clearly defined and delineated."[67] For Matthew, who most distinctly displays adherence to the Jewish tradition, the question arises, To what extent can the "Jewishness" of his Gospel be embraced without violating the fundamental ethos of the New Testament?[68] This is where the discussion may seem somewhat paradoxical, but the fine balance of continuity and discontinuity must be grasped in order to appreciate the relationship between the Old and New Testaments. It would be nothing short of a complete disregard of the uniqueness of both Judaism and Christianity to suggest that they share the same concept of God. They may share a common scriptural heritage, but the God of the Old Testament, Yahweh, is not the same divine being which forms the Trinity of Christian understanding. The latter is precisely the type of deity which Judaism repudiates. Even though certain commentators are beginning to appreciate the approach and understanding of the New Testament writers' mind-set from a Jewish perspective, which has yielded useful interpretive insights, it should be stressed that the "Jewishness" cannot be the dominating factor in the biblical studies of the New Testament (cf. Phil 3:3, 11).[69] The danger is that when one overemphasizes the importance of the Jewish aspect of the New Testament, one may give the impression that it is simply an extension of Jewish Scripture. The uniqueness of the message concerning Christ lies precisely in the fact that there is "newness" in terms of the redemptive history of Israel and in terms of the fulfillment of the prophecies concerning the Messiah.[70] In conjunction with this, Walther Zimmerli makes a critical observation which should be taken into account in our discussion of typology and in particular Matthew's use of the Old Testament: "Less and less will the Church be able to avoid

---

67. Fruchtenbaum, "The Quest for a Messianic Theology," 13.

68. Ibid.

69. Cf. Fruchtenbaum, "The Quest," 16. See also Holland, *Contours of Pauline Theology*, and D. H. Stern's response to Fruchtenbaum. Stern argues that "by understanding Paul from a Jewish perspective, the whole Church will understand him better and will see that he is the most articulate promoter of Torah in the New Testament."

70. Cf. Gray, *Sacrifice in the Old Testament*; see also Ringgren, *The Messiah in the Old Testament*.

the question as to what is involved in this claim to be Israel, the question as to where its rights, its limits, its temptations lie."[71]

Therefore, the Church's claim to be Israel needs to be understood in a context which generates a unique experience of the salvation established by Christ Jesus by incorporating the past legacy of Jewish religion. It is the construction of something new built upon its historical heritage which offers a new interpretation of the entire religious stratum.[72]

PART THREE: TRINITARIANISM IN A JEWISH-CHRISTIAN CONTEXT

Christological Implications

We have discussed thus far how typology can be justified as a biblical hermeneutic and how it generates ramifications regarding the relationship of the Old and New Testaments. If our thesis that typology in our interpretation of Matthew's Gospel is a plausible methodological approach, then the fundamental question of to what extent does the concept of redemption remain consistent and yet take on a different meaning becomes an important aspect of our study. If indeed the New Testament message concerning Christ is based on the Old Testament, then the understanding of the relationship between the two testaments becomes a crucial methodological starting point. This also affects the study of Christology to a large extent, since the writers of the New Testament firmly believed that Jesus was the fulfillment of the messianic expectation of the Old Testament. When we think about the tone of the New Testament understanding of Jesus as "the second person of the Trinity," which is certainly implied in John's Gospel, we need to decipher to what extent the Jewish religion justifies Jesus' claim to be divine, and whether this understanding is present elsewhere. This is certainly an appropriate enquiry for the study of Matthew's Gospel. Although Matthew's Jesus does not explicitly claim the status of deity for himself, the Great Commission portrays the risen Messiah as one of the "constituents" of what later developed into the doctrine of the Trinity. Since we have established that Matthew regarded himself to be Jewish, we need to ask whether this particular aspect of his Christology can be justified by the Old Testament belief in Israel's Messiah.

71. Zimmerli, "Promise and Fulfillment," 122.
72. Dewey, "The Locus for Death," 124.

It seems that the Old Testament regards the Davidic kingship to be the manifestation of Yahweh's reign, which means that the Messiah is the representative of Yahweh's authority in Israel. B. C. Ollenburger makes an observation regarding the Jerusalem cult, affirming that there was a close connection between the portrayals of the Messiah's authority and that of Yahweh in the Psalter. He writes, "The royal associations of Yahweh's subjection of the waters in Pss. 24:1–2 and 89:10–11 are clearly evident here and are made explicit in 89:26. Here, in a derivative sense, the representative of Yahweh, David his anointed (v. 21), is secured on his throne through his delegated power to subjugate the waters . . . Thus the creation wrought by the cosmic king is administered in the mundane realm through his regent, whose earthly throne is founded in righteousness and justice according to the pattern of Yahweh's heavenly throne (vv. 15, 30–34)."[73]

Of course, the degree to which the king's power actually corresponds to that of Yahweh within the Psalter is another matter for discussion. However, the overarching concept that Yahweh's throne (Pss 97:2; 89:15) forms the foundation of the royal throne (Ps 89:30–34) seems undisputed.[74] Nevertheless, this does not necessarily warrant the claim that the Old Testament regarded Israel's Messiah as a deity.[75]

Recently, R. M. Bowman Jr. and J. Ed Komoszewski have put forward the case for the deity of Christ.[76] They argue that when the New Testament refers to Jesus it does so by quoting from, or alluding to, Old Testament texts about God. For instance, the New Testament calls Jesus "Lord" and "Savior" (e.g., John 20:28; Titus 2:13; 2 Pet 1:1; 1:11), which

---

73. Ollenburger, *Zion*, 54, 57. "The defense of Israel is narrated in terms of Yahweh's conquest of chaos, i.e., in his creative activity (Ps 93), while this mythological pattern is itself given a particular historical valence with the incorporation of references to the defense of Israel (Ps. 99)."

74. Ibid., 59. Psalm 97 is commonly designated as one of the enthronement psalms, which were written to celebrate the Kingship of Yahweh, whereas Psalm 89 would most likely fall into the category of royal psalms, which celebrate the kingship of Davidic monarchy. It is reasonable to suggest that there is theological or even perhaps an ideological connection between the two types of psalms.

75. Cf. Hahn, *The Titles of Jesus in Christology*. It is argued that "the constitutive element of the 'divine-man' conception, the divinity of man or the possibility of his participating in what is divine, indeed of his deification, is unthinkable in the Old Testament." However, this does not negate the possibility that the Messiah could have divine attributes which are characteristic of Yahweh.

76. Bowman and Komoszewski, *Putting Jesus in His Place*.

are not applied to anyone else except Jesus. Peter quotes from Joel 2:32 in Acts 2:21 and 4:12 where "he appears to be equating the name that Jesus has with the 'name of the Lord.'"[77] It is noted that Isaiah is one of the major contributors in designating divine attributes to the future Messiah (in Isa. 9:6, the future Messiah is called "Wonderful Counselor, Mighty God, Everlasting Father, Prince of Peace"; see also Isa 10:21; 40:9–11; 43:10–13; 59:15–20).

John's Gospel stands out from the synoptic tradition in its affirmation of Jesus' divinity and in the claim that salvation can only be attained through faith in him. Bowman and Komoszewski state that "for the early Christians the belief in Jesus' deity was not just a doctrinal affirmation but was the crux of their entire value system."[78] Although the general consensus in the New Testament is that the resurrection of Jesus is an act of God, there are nevertheless implications that Jesus plays a part in his resurrection on the basis of the evidence that the temple is referring to his body. In other words, even though God takes the initiative (cf. Gal 1:1), Jesus' role in resurrection is not merely passive. This is evident in John 2:19–22: "Jesus answered them, 'Destroy this temple and I will raise it again in three days.' The Jews replied, 'It has taken forty-six years to build this temple, and you are going to raise it in three days?' But the temple he had spoken of was his body. After he was raised from the dead, his disciples recalled what he had said. Then they believed the Scripture and the words that Jesus had spoken."

The hearers initially misunderstand Jesus to be referring to the temple in Jerusalem, but John explains that Jesus was referring to his own body in the event of resurrection (cf. John 10:27–28; also Deut. 32:39).

It would be fair to suggest that Paul also shares the same conviction regarding Jesus and his divine-messianic identity. On numerous occasions in his epistles he refers to the eschatological Day of Judgment as the Day of the Lord Jesus Christ (1 Cor 1:8; 5:5; 2 Cor 1:14; Phil 1:6, 10; 2:16; 1Thess 5:2; 2 Thess 2:1–2; 2 Tim 1:18; cf. 2 Pet 3:8–10, 12). Indeed, on the basis of such evidence, one is inclined to agree with the statement that "the use of such a familiar Old Testament idiom in reference to the

---

77. Ibid., 133.
78. Ibid., 134.

Lord Jesus' exercising the same function of judgment strongly identifies the Lord Jesus with the Lord Yahweh."[79]

However, the writers of the Synoptic Gospels are not as explicit about the nature of Jesus as a deity. This is not to repudiate certain evidence which very likely points to Jesus' divine nature. For instance, one aspect of Jesus' ministry was that he forgave the sins of those whom he healed (cf. Matt 9:3; Mark 2:7; Luke 5:21; also chapter six), and the scribes accused him of blasphemy since it was a prerogative which was exclusively reserved for Yahweh alone. The conflict with the Jewish authorities reaches its climax when Jesus is brought before the Sanhedrin, where Jesus he is asked whether he is the Messiah. Mark is more emphatic in affirming the identity and also stresses Jesus' authority to be something far beyond a mere human savior, whereas Matthew dilutes the directness of Jesus' answer to Caiaphas' interrogation (Mark 14:62; cf. also Matt 26:64).[80] Mark's more emphatic affirmation—"I am, and you will see the Son of Man sitting at the right hand of the Mighty One and coming on the clouds of heaven"—may suggest that he is less conservative than Matthew in ascribing to Jesus the divine traits which are associated with the Son of Man. In comparison, Matthew's Jesus answers the High Priest's question with less clarity which may provide possible ground for an argument that Jesus here is referring to a figure other than himself. However, we shall see that the textual evidence does not permit the distinction between the Son of Man and Jesus as separate entities.

Compared with John's Gospel and the Pauline epistles, Matthew is more cautious in disclosing Jesus' identity as God. In this regard Matthew's Christology is relatively conservative and might be considered to be early.[81] However, as Bowman and Komoszewski point out, if "a figure is the recipient of honors reserved exclusively for God, or a wide

---

79. Ibid., 230.

80. The Old Testament texts used in Jesus' answer to Caiaphas' question are Psalm 110:1 and Daniel 7:13.

81. Dodd, *The Authority of the Bible*, 228–29, notes that the Synoptic Gospels were constructed early, whereas John's Gospel is late and thus presents a more developed form of Christology. Dodd notes that "we may now say with confidence that for strictly historical material, with the minimum of subjective interpretation, we must not go to the fourth Gospel. The religious value stands beyond challenge, and it is the most fully appreciated when its contribution to our knowledge of the bare facts of the life of Jesus becomes a secondary interest." He goes on to say, "This is not to say that it makes no such contribution. But it is the Synoptic Gospels that we must go to if we wish to recover the oldest and purest tradition of the facts."

range of honors normally associated with God, and if believers express such honors in contexts of religious activity or spiritual devotion, such honors do indicate that those according him such honors regard him as God."[82] If Matthew's Jesus was attributed traits that were characteristically applied to God in the Old Testament, then we need to at least allow the possibility that Matthew's community regarded Jesus as far more than a human Messiah.[83] If Mark was written prior to Matthew and the former was more emphatic in Jesus' affirmation of his identity in response to the High Priest's interrogation, it may be that Matthew wanted to take on a different approach or wanted to reinforce the understanding by highlighting a different aspect of Jesus. However, it is difficult to imagine that Matthew disagreed with Mark in the fundamental principles of his theology. It is unlikely that the two evangelists would have diverged in opinions on the fundamental issues of Jesus' self-consciousness. We suggest that these textual variants should be seen within the overall context of the audience which the evangelists are addressing rather than the contradictory statements of the texts.

This may well lead to the view that the authors of the New Testament on the whole share the same mind-set with one another and present Jesus in divine terms which are reserved exclusively for Israel's God. In

---

82. Ibid., 270.

83. Cf. Lee, *From Messiah to Preexistent Son*, 115, who emphasizes the importance of the early Church's role in the formation of Christological development to which Matthew's community belongs. He notes that "it is therefore most likely that there was not a coherent concept of a pre-existent messiah before Christianity for the early church to readily apply it to Jesus. This assessment, however, does not completely rule out the possibility that some of the LXX texts (especially Ps 110:3) might have been interpreted as entailing the pre-existence of the messiah at a later stage by early Christians. The evidence thus strongly suggests that it would be more profitable for us to focus our attention to how the early Church made use of these Old Testament messianic texts in such a way that led to an understanding of Jesus' pre-existence than finding a ready-made category of pre-existence in pre-Christian Judaism into which Jesus could be placed." Cf. also Fuller, *The Foundations of New Testament Christology*, 197, 248, 249, who argues that the Gentile mission necessarily required ontological input in the statements about Christ if the church was to be successful in reaching out to the Greco-Roman world. Fuller notes that "while Hellenistic Jewish milieu (and its missionaries) could apply to Jesus in a functional sense Old Testament texts originally referring to Kyrios-YHWH, it had not yet raised the ontic question of the divinity of the exalted Lord. But it had laid the necessary foundations for these developments in the Gentile mission." The ontological language of the doctrine of the Trinity therefore is deemed to be a missiological tool with which Christians appealed to the Greco-Roman audience.

the context of the fundamental principles of typology, can the doctrine of Trinity be upheld? Can the New Testament claim regarding Jesus' divinity be justified on the basis of the Old Testament tradition? This is a crucial question which we must bear in mind throughout our discussion. If the Christology of the New Testament is viewed as in essence deviant or detached from the guiding principles of the Old Testament expectation of the Messiah, then typology could not be justified as a key biblical hermeneutic, since the relevance of the Old Testament would be very limited. There are, however, evidences in the Old Testament that support the view that the messianic being possessed divine attributes and indeed shared the authority of Yahweh. On the basis of Ezekiel 1 and Daniel 7, N. T. Wright points out that the imagery of the exaltation and heavenly enthronement of a figure who is possibly identified as the Son of Man support the thesis that the messianic being is not only believed to represent Yahweh's throne but also shares the divine authority of the "Ancient of Days."[84] C. C. Rowland concurs with this observation: "The Son of Man is in fact the embodiment of the person of the Ancient of Days. In other words the original scene in Daniel 7, where two figures exist alongside each other in heaven, is changed so that the vice-regent, the Son of Man, takes upon himself the form and character of God himself."[85]

It is reasonable to suggest that the notion of the Messiah with divine elements attributed to him is not necessarily regarded as a threat to Jewish monotheism. In this light, Jesus' self-understanding in Matt 11:25–27 and Luke 10:21–22, which describe his unique relationship with God the Father, is not deviant from how the Old Testament portrays the Messiah. In these verses of the Scripture, the evangelist is clearly conscious of Jesus' status and authority to the extent that Jesus speaks as if he were in some sense the one who had power over Torah itself. This is clearly evidence with which one can argue for the starting point of the later development of the doctrine of incarnation and the Trinitarian concept within Christianity. However, as Wright points out, "awareness of vocation is by no means the same thing as Jesus having the

---

84. Wright, *Jesus and the Victory of God*, 2:624.

85. Rowland, *The Open Heaven*, 98. Cf. also Wright, *Jesus and the Victory of God*, 626: "Other Jewish teachers of the period (late first and early second century AD) seem to have speculated similarly on the possibility of a plurality of powers within heaven."

sort of supernatural awareness of himself."[86] This is a critical point which we need to take into account since the Old Testament concept of the Messiah, who is attributed with divine qualities, would never make the statement that the Messiah would be God Himself. Indeed, even though there are clues which indicate Jesus' divinity, Christology according to the Synoptic Gospels never goes as far as explicitly affirming the case. The discussion of "high Christology," especially in Matthew's Gospel, which primarily targets a Jewish audience, will therefore need to be conducted in a critical manner and with objectivity.[87]

Summary

In this chapter we have attempted to justify typology as an appropriate exegetical tool for Matthew's Gospel in the context of a brief survey of other methodological approaches. We have established the importance of acknowledging the essential character of the New Testament as dependent upon the Old Testament which suggested that the fundamental mind-set of Matthew is rooted in Jewish religious tradition. This naturally diverts our attention from the pursuit of interpretative insights gained from the realm of Hellenistic thinking and directs our attention to the Jewish Scriptures. In so doing, we need to bear in mind that the use of Old Testament in the New Testament is based on historical awareness of Yahweh's redemptive activity. In other words, typology points to the ongoing redemptive work of God in the history of Israel. In summary of this, C. H. Dodd's statement is worthy of mention: "It is characteristic of Christianity to find its Christ in history as well as above history. Those who would neglect the Gospels as mythical or obsolete and point us to the eternal 'Christ within' as the only object of faith, no less than those

---

86. Wright, *Jesus and the Victory of God*, 652–53.

87. Cf. So, *Jesus' Revelation of His Father*, 5–6, who highlights the importance of Trinitarianism in biblical theology. The basis of his argument is: "1. Doctrinal criticism is inclined to understand doctrines as the products of historical circumstances rather than 'the inner logic of faith.' 2. The influence of natural religion in modern theology had meant that God was conceived of in generic terms. Natural religion cannot in itself conceive specifically of the triune God who is made known only in revelation. 3. God is not conceived of as the Trinity from the beginning but only in the later discussion of a systematic theology." He argues for the divinity of Christ within Matthew's Gospel in particular. Jesus' personal divine authority in offering forgiveness of sins and in modifying the Law in the Sermon on the Mount (e.g., abrogating provisions for oath and divorce) indicate that Jesus is portrayed as a deity, i.e., Yahweh Himself.

who will allow us nothing but a 'Jesus of history,' are proposing an unreal simplification contrary to the genius of our religion—the unity of the eternal with the historical."[88]

The Christology of Matthew which is the fulfillment of the messianic expectation of the Old Testament brings into focus the redemptive activity of Yahweh, which reaches its culmination in the New Testament and is now manifested in Christ's death and resurrection.

---

88. Dodd, *The Authority of the Bible*, 232.

2

Preliminary Survey

PART ONE: CONTEMPORARY SCHOLARSHIP ON THE THEOLOGICAL PURPOSE OF THE GOSPEL ACCORDING TO MATTHEW

Comments on Methodology

THERE IS NO SCHOLARLY consensus with regard to the purpose and function of Matthew's Gospel, and the debate still continues as to how the Gospel was interpreted and understood in the early Church. Indeed, it would be extremely artificial and unrealistic to restrict the author's aim and to classify the various functions which Matthew's Gospel served within the life of the early Christians into one unifying category. Scholars from various fields of Matthean studies argue that the Gospel is to be read as a catechism, or a lectionary, an apologetic or even a polemical treatise. With the rise of redactional criticism, G. D. Kilpatrick in 1946 and Krister Stendahl in 1954, following the discovery of the Dead Sea Scrolls, put forward the thesis that Matthew revised the existing Marcan text and Q source (common to both Luke and Matthew but absent in Mark) and expounded them for liturgical use.[1] Stendahl goes further to suggest that the Matthean School, analogous to that of the interpretational institution found at Qumran, originally designed it

---

1. Kilpatrick, *The Origins of the Gospel according to St. Matthew*, argues that the Gospel is primarily designed for liturgical purposes. However, he also points out that the function of the Gospel is much more than merely the instruction of the proselytes.

as a manual of instruction and administration.[2] He proposed that the Matthean School provided a milieu in which students of Matthew were engaged in interpretational activities with Old Testament quotations which closely resemble commentaries found in Qumran.

In modern contemporary New Testament scholarship, it has become quite prevalent to draw analogies from such extracanonical texts, and so it is necessary to make a few comments for the sake of methodological clarity before we embark upon the survey of Matthew's Gospel. Although such comparative studies have provided intriguing insights which stimulated the debate concerning the contemporary understanding of the New Testament texts, it should be stressed that such analogy between two religious texts with an undoubtedly different theological ethos is to be conducted with a caution that many do not exercise.[3] There are several reasons that scholars have turned to extracanonical texts such as the Dead Sea Scrolls. Perhaps the major reason for such comparison is that the writings discovered at Qumran show a keen expectation of the Messiah who will inaugurate the Kingdom of Heaven on earth and the unusual events that are related with it, such as the resurrection of the dead during the time of the Messiah (Matt 27:51-53).[4] This is described in a language that is reminiscent of the words of the Gospel tradition, and this is what has attracted New Testament scholars to the study of these texts. However, one soon discovers that there are many more differences than commonalities between the Dead Sea Scrolls and the Gospel tradition such as Matthew, which puts the use of such texts for New Testament studies in serious doubt. For instance, M. O. Wise and J. D. Tabor note that "scholarship on the Dead Sea Scrolls by now

---

2. Kilpatrick, *The Origin of the Gospel according to St. Matthew*, and Stendahl, *The School of St. Matthew*, both cited in Hill, *The Gospel of Matthew*, 34, 35.

3. See Horbury, "Messianism in the Old Testament Apocrypha and Pseudepigrapha." Horbury provides the following definitions of the Apocrypha and the Pseudepigrapha: "Apocrypha: Writings associated with the Old Testament but outside the Hebrew Canon. A Western view advocated by Augustine and approved by two councils of Carthage (397, 419) and Pope Innocent I held them to be in principle fully as authoritative for Christians as the books of the Hebrew Canon. However, the designation of the relevant Old Testament books as apocryphal which had hitherto been widely current was now soon to be discouraged by the Council of Trent. Pseudepigrapha: Writings outside the Hebrew Canon but dubiously ascribed with biblical authors, which early Christians generally disapproved."

4. Wise and Tabor, "The Messiah at Qumran," 60-65, examine messianic apocalypse in 4Q521 (document 521 from Qumran cave 4).

almost takes it for granted that the Qumran community expected not one but two messiahs. It is this that is supposed to provide one of the major differences between the messianic expectation at Qumran, on the one hand and Christianity, on the other."[5]

Further to this fundamental difference, it is noted that the more prominent of the two messiahs is the priestly figure from the line of Aaron. The second messianic figure, who is portrayed to be lower in rank than the priestly being, is the messiah from the line of Davidic monarchy.[6] In the scrolls, it is the priestly messiah who will accompany the Davidic Prince, and the former wields greater authority than the latter. Likewise, William Horbury notes that "1 Esdras honors Ezra 'the high priest' (9:40) as well as the Davidic Josiah and Zerubbabel (1:32; 4:13; 5:5–6); in Judith the high priest Joakim has a central place (4:6–15, 15:8), and in 2 Maccabees Onias the high priest has the attributes of a saint (3:1–36; 15:12–15)."[7] All these texts which were composed during the Second Temple period seem to envisage the glory and, moreover, the messianic status of the high priest.[8] Nowhere in the Gospel of Matthew is Jesus designated as the priest, even though there may be implications in the passages dealing with the purity and the destruction of the temple (cf. Matt 21:12–17; 24:1–2), where Jesus could be seen as pronouncing judgment upon the temple leadership as the true High Priest. Consequently, the designation of Priest lacks christological capacity and plays a minor role in formulating the identity of Jesus in Matthew. The evangelist makes it clear from the beginning of his Gospel that Jesus is primarily identified as the Son of David, and although a royal psalm associates Yahweh's king with priestly status in the order of Melchizedek (Ps 110:4), Matthew does not make this connection. The image of the

5. Ibid., p.60

6. Ibid. "This Qumranic concept of two messiahs was supposedly derived from post-exilic biblical literature, which portrays both Zerubbabel (a Davidic descendent) and Joshua, the High Priest, as 'anointed ones.'" Cf. Talmon, "Waiting for the Messiah at Qumran," in Neusner, Green, and Frerichs, eds., *Judaism and Their Messiahs at the Turn of the Christian Era*. See also Allison, "The Baptism of Jesus and a New Dead Sea Scrolls." Brooke, "Kingship and Messianism in the Dead Sea Scrolls," 443, also comments that "the term 'Messiah' is used in the plural of a priestly and of a kingly figure, 'the Messiahs of Aaron and Israel' (1QS 9, 11)."

7. Horbury, "Messianism in the Old Testament Apocrypha and Pseudepigrapha," 414.

8. Ibid. Horbury nevertheless notes that in Ecclesiasticus and 1 Esdras the Davidic monarchy is also mentioned.

priestly messiah who has higher authority as depicted in the scrolls is simply absent in Matthew's Gospel.[9] It seems evident that there is such a gulf between the communities of Matthew and Qumran in terms of religious and cultural dimensions that any hope of comparative study is extremely tentative. Even if it is conceded that there are some verbal parallels between the Gospel and the Dead Sea Scrolls, the fundamental ethos concerning the messianic expectation is different. G. J. Brooke notes that the Dead Sea Scrolls speak of the royal Messiah, but the paucity of those texts leaves the impression that the ideology of kingship was based fundamentally upon theocracy rather than the messianic agent.[10] On the contrary, however, Matthew's single most pressing concern was to present Jesus as the messianic king in the line of David who brings the history of Israel to a decisive culmination.[11] Matthew as a Jewish writer remains faithful to the ongoing Old Testament expectation of the Messiah and now believes that the prophecy has come to a fulfillment in Jesus Christ. Scholars who employ the kind of methodological approach in which the use of extrabiblical sources is justified often miss the

---

9. Horbury, "Messianism in the Old Testament Apocrypha and Pseudepigrapha," 406, offers an insight to the apocrypha and the question of a messianological vacuum. He notes that one might expect to see a mention of the Messiah in Baruch, Tobit, Judith, 1 and 2 Maccabees, and the Wisdom of Solomon—but this is in fact absent. He writes, "The Apocrypha and Pseudepigraph which enjoyed more authority among early Christians and probably also among Jews, seems almost to suggest the unimportance rather than the importance of messianism." Not overlooking the fact that the messianic expectation within these texts is diverse and complex, it does nevertheless put the use of these texts in serious doubt when we study Matthew's Gospel in particular, which is predominantly concerned with the issues of messianic promise and its fulfillment.

10. Brooke, "Kingship and Messianism in the Dead Sea Scrolls," 436, 439, notes that "as for God himself, several non-sectarian compositions refer to his kingship; for example, God is described as 'King of all the ages' (1QapGen 2:4, 7) and 'King of heaven' (1QapGen 2:14), 'King on Mt. Zion' (4Q216; Jub. 1:28)."

11. Tasker, *Matthew: An Introduction*, 17, 19, 21 regards Matthew's Gospel as "ecclesiastical" in its function since it provided the church with three major tools: defending its beliefs against attacks from Jewish opponents, instructing converts from paganism, and helping its own members live a disciplined life. In essence, he argues that the Gospel functioned as an apology. Moreover, he also conceives that the major characteristic of Matthew is to present Jesus as the royal Messiah. He contends that the textual evidences are in support of this claim. In the Gospel of Mark, for instance, the title "Son of David" is only once given to Jesus (by blind Bartimaeus), whereas in Matthew not only blind men on two occasions (9:27; 20:30) but also the woman of Canaan (15:22), the crowds as Jesus entered Jerusalem (21:9), and the children in the temple (21:15) address him this way (cf. also 12:23).

obvious Old Testament background which forms the crux of the evangelist's mind-set and that of his audience. They tend to overlook the unique aspects of Matthew's theology and the primary concern of the evangelist, namely, Old Testament themes relating to the story about Jesus in the overall scheme of the redemptive history of Israel.[12] The uniqueness of the New Testament message concerning Christ in the early Christian community must be borne in mind by scholars who rely on the extracanonical texts to understand the Gospel. This is also pointed out by C. C. Rowland, who states that "there is little in the extant literature that resembles the peculiar features that characterize the emergence and development of Christianity."[13] This shifts our attention away from the extracanonical texts to something more obvious and textually evident in the Gospel of Matthew, that is, the Old Testament, which the evangelist entirely depends upon for his Christological message.[14]

Jesus and the Kingship Theme

In Matthew's Gospel, the evangelist systematically presents Jesus primarily as the long-awaited messianic King from the house of David.[15] It is clear from the genealogical introduction of the Gospel (Matt 1:1) that the evangelist intends "Son of David" to be perceived as one of the most important Christological titles, which is emphasized throughout the Gospel narratives. In fact, the importance of this title has been pointed out and examined in detail by Otto Michel, who, in discussing the final scene of the Gospel (28:16), has pointed out that there is strong formal similarity between the structure of the passage dealing with the Great Commission and the ancient Near Eastern liturgy for the enthronement of the king in the "three consecutive acts of elevation, presentation, and formal investment with power."[16] The analogy of Jesus' resurrection and his appearance before the disciples and investiture with heavenly power before the ascension suggest that the evangelist was elucidating the fact

---

12. Bauer and Powell, *Treasures New and Old*, 6.
13. Rowland, "Christ in the New Testament," 493–94.
14. See Ridderbos, *Redemptive History and the New Testament Scriptures*, 26.
15. Rowland, "Christ in the New Testament," 476, notes that "Christ as king is particularly prominent in Rev. 1:5 and 19:16 and the messianic reign on earth has a central place in the vision of the eschatological future in that book, something which may be hinted at elsewhere in 1 Cor. 15:24."
16. Cited in Rengstorf, "Old and New Testament Traces," 229–44.

that Jesus is here presented as King according to the enthronement liturgy of an ancient Near Eastern context.

A parallel example is drawn from Psalm 2 (known to be one of the psalms belonging to the enthronement ritual of the king) and the final passage of the Gospel of Matthew.

| "Ask of me, and I will make the nations your heritage, and the ends of the earth your possession." (Ps 2:8) | "All authority in heaven and on earth has been given to me. Go therefore and make disciples of all nations, baptizing them in the name of the Father and of the Son and of the Holy Spirit . . ." (Matt 28:18–19) |

Here, the observation is made that a part of the Jerusalem-Judean royal ritual has become christologically significant in that it describes the sovereignty of Jesus after the resurrection and his dominion at the moment of his heavenly ascension.[17]

This leads Rengstorf to contend that the common designation of the last passage of Matthew's Gospel should no longer be called the "Great Commission." Rather, it should be acknowledged that this passage deals with the disciples' universal proclamation of the heavenly enthronement of Jesus and of his assumption of power.[18]

Rengstorf thus postulates that various features of the Jerusalem-Judean royal ritual and its fundamental ideas remained alive for centuries, and this became a dominant source of influence for primitive Christianity and its conception of Christ.

Jesus' royal ancestry is introduced in the prologue of the Gospel as a prelude to his birth, and in the infancy narrative Jesus is presented as the true king of the Jews in contrast to Herod (Matt 2:2). Later in the narrative, the entry of Jesus into Jerusalem (Matt 21:4–5) is said to be the fulfillment of the prophecy of Zechariah, and the title "King of the Jews" appears again in the trial narrative (Matt 27:11, 29, 37, 42) where Jesus is charged by the Jewish authorities.

A pertinent question emerges here as to the nature of Jesus' kingship depicted in the Gospel Tradition. Matthew 25:31ff shows that the

---

17. Rengstorf, "Old and New Testament Traces," 238, 239.
18. Ibid., 240.

heavenly descriptions and splendor attached to the Son of Man are reminiscent of the royal traits attributed to Yahweh in the Old Testament. Jesus' ministry was to establish God's Kingship and his Kingdom on earth, and, assuming that Son of Man here refers to Jesus, the passage under discussion seems to imply that the Son of Man's royal dominion and his function as the judge of men (Matt 13: 41; 16: 27; 19: 28; 25: 31ff.) is on a par with God's royal authority. This is further reinforced when one observes that the criterion in the judgment is how men respond to him (7: 21–23; 25:34ff.). R. T. France also notes that such language takes us well beyond any normal idea of messiahship that the title "King of the Jews" might have suggested.[19]

Such a lofty description of Jesus takes us far beyond any Israelite monarch in the antecedent historical account, and the uniqueness of his Kingship is emphasized in the Gospel narrative, as Warren Carter observes, in the genealogical prologue, the tragic history of the kings' "misrule" from David to the deportation to Babylon (1:6–11). Fifteen kings are named in the genealogical account and only two appear in 1 and 2 Kings and 1 and 2 Chronicles as good kings. Carter posits that the kings constitute a long tradition of unfaithfulness and disappointment which resulted in disastrous punishment from imperial Babylon (1:11–12).[20]

G. M. Styler makes a similar point about the narrative of the Triumphal Entry. Here Matthew elicits what is implicitly hinted at in the Markan passage—that Jesus is the Davidic King, which Matthew makes more explicit and central. C. C. Rowland is in agreement with this view, as he also states that the situation is slightly different in Mark's Gospel. He notes that the title Cristo,j is used only seven times and "Son of David" significantly fewer times than in Matthew.[21] Again, in

---

19. France, *Matthew*, 46, 47.

20. Carter, "Resisting and Imitating the Empire," 264.

21. Rowland, "Christ in the New Testament," 479, 480–81, points out that the reason for such difference in Christological emphasis is possibly due to Mark's narrative-theological design, which is commonly designated as "Messianic Secrecy" in modern New Testament scholarship and which basically indicates that Jesus was reticent in revealing his identity as the Messiah during his earthly ministry. He also notes that "the subordination of David to the Messiah in Mark 12:35 suggests a separation of messianism from the Davidic tradition." In general, the language of king, Davidic dynasty, and the centrality of Jerusalem are contrasted with the new way, the suffering and humble obedience of the Servant. In Luke, the importance of the Davidic legacy to Jesus' messianic identity is highlighted in 1:32 and 2:11, where it is specifically connected with the history of salvation.

the controversy about plucking corn on the Sabbath, Mark's Christology has an element of ambiguity, but Styler points out that Matthew gives more prominence to the argument that Jesus has authority over religious regulations with his affirmation that "something greater than the temple is here." Moreover, it is also pointed out by G. Bornkamm, G. Barth, and H. J. Held that "Lord" (κύριε) in Matthew's Gospel is not simply an expression of human respect, but is intended as a term of majesty. "It is the form of address to Jesus as the miracle-working savior (8:2, 6, 8; 9:28; 15:22, 25; 17:15; 20:30, 33)."[22] This clearly suggests that the royal attributes Matthew places on the Christological portrait are superior to any qualities attributed to the kings of Israel.[23]

However, it must be noted that such qualities of Jesus' royal personage must not be viewed in isolation from what the evangelist paradoxically presents in his gospel, namely, that Jesus' kingship and his greatness cannot be fully grasped unless one understands that this is displayed precisely in terms of obedience, lowliness, and self- sacrifice. Such a paradoxical presentation of Jesus' kingship has led Dorothy Jean Weaver to examine Matthew's use of irony in portraying the political leaders in contrast to Jesus' true kingship. She employs the literary technique of narrative criticism to unveil the use of irony, which is most evidently seen in the characterization of the three political leaders:

1. Herod the King (2:1–23)

2. Herod the Tetrarch (14:1–12)

3. Pilate the Governor (27:1–2, 11–38, 54, 62–66; 28:1–15)[24]

Matthew presents Jesus in kingly terms: "the One who has been born King of the Jews" (2:2); "the leader who will shepherd God's people Israel" (2:6); and "God's Son" (2:15). However, Weaver points out that with lofty descriptions of Jesus' kingship comes the single most prominent term used to designate Jesus throughout this narrative, namely, "child" (2:8, 9, 11, 13, 14, 20, 21), a term which has connotations of "weakness" and "dependence" in contrast to "political power."[25] Such a

---

22. Bornkamm, Barth, and Held, *Tradition and Interpretation in Matthew*, 42.

23. Styler, cited in Hill, *The Gospel of Matthew*, 64.

24. Weaver, "Power and Powerlessness: Matthew's Use of Irony in the Portrayal of Political Leaders," 179.

25. Ibid., 184.

paradoxical representation of Jesus' kingship can also be detected in the Transfiguration scene (17:1–9), where the disciples, after witnessing an epiphany, are instructed to maintain silence until the Son of Man has been raised from the dead (17:9). This implies that Jesus' glorious kingly power cannot be understood in isolation from suffering, obedience, and humility in accordance with the will of God.[26] It is in the light of the resurrection that the enigmatic nature of Jesus' kingly authority finally discloses itself. Weaver thus affirms that "in the light of Jesus' resurrection human power is robbed of its potency and human powerlessness transformed by the power of God. This is the ultimate irony of power."[27]

It is clear, then, that Matthew's primary concern is to present Jesus as the long-awaited messianic King in the line of David. However, the adequacy of the Christological title from a Christian point of view has been recently reexamined by Israel Selvanayagam in his article "Jesus' Subversion of the Davidic Legacy,"[28] where he argues that the title Son of David has been uncritically accepted and glorified by Christians, whereas it is clear from the gospel that Jesus was cautious about revealing his identity as the Davidic Messiah for fear of being understood in military and/or political terms when he clearly understood his own ministry in a quite contrary way. Selvanayagam points out that the reason for the preservation of the Davidic legacy in Christian tradition is due to the poetic achievement and a charismatic charm attributed to him, attested to especially in royal psalms. It is evident that certain royal psalms such as Psalms 2 and 110 portray the kingly authority as being derived directly from YHWH himself, and the demand for submission to the king is clearly intimated. Selvanayagam's main argument is that, rather than Jesus viewing himself to be the culmination of Davidic legacy, he was, in fact, achieving a silent revolution in subverting this legacy of David. He draws an example from the incident in the Gospel where, after the cleansing of the temple, Matthew notes, "in the temple the blind and the crippled came to Jesus and he healed them" (21:14). In order to appreciate the significance of this event, Selvanayagam mentions the great massacre of the handicapped when David captured the city of the Jebusites

---

26. Rowland, "Christ in the New Testament," 477, also notes that "Jesus' kingship is most evident at the time of greatest humiliation and dissonance with a conventional understanding of kingship (Matt. 27: 29)."

27. Ibid., 195.

28. Selvanayagam, "Interpreting a Riddle."

(an ethnic name for a Canaanite people) in 2 Samuel 5, where one reads that "no one who is blind or lame is to come into the Lord's House" (v. 8). In light of this, a close reading of the Gospel soon shows that the two kinds of people who referred to Jesus as the Son of David were the handicapped and the Gentiles, both enemies of David (Matt 9:27–30; 20:30–34; Mark 10:47–52; Luke 18:35–43).[29]

Although Son of David is clearly the most prominent Christological title in Matthew, such an argument has merit when we read the passage in 22:41–45 where Jesus explicitly regards his authority as far above that of David, in answer to the Pharisees' statement concerning the notion of the anointed messianic Deliverer. Jesus' messianic authority differs fundamentally from the concept of the Davidic reign, which was primarily a form of human/political leadership, and differs also in its nature in the sense that Jesus was victorious over death and is attributed divine character, whereas to regard David as a deity would be blasphemous in Judaism. However, we read in Psalm 2:7 that David is attributed the status of son in direct relation to YHWH, which has led some to the conclusion that the neighboring nations in the ancient Near East have influenced the Israelite religion in which kings were deified. However, a close examination of the words of this verse and its nuance reveals a rather strong ritualistic tone:

διαγγέλλων τὸ πρόστιγμα κυρίου κύριος εἶπεν πρός με υἱός μου εἶ σύ ἐγὼ σήμερον γεγέννηκά σε

The noun πρόστιγμα, meaning "ordinance" or "command," indicates a highly formal setting possibly for public display and chronological distinction indicated by σήμερον points towards the idea of a special occasion of royal coronation ceremony when kings were formally empowered before the nation. This suggests that a king's authority is derived from God and, indeed, divinely blessed but is far from suggesting that the essence of the king is divine.

This leaves us with a crucial question as to why Matthew is so keen to present Jesus as the Davidic Messiah which seems neither to capture his divinity nor adequately to portray his relationship to Joseph who is, in fact, a Davidic descendant but is not responsible for Jesus' birth.

---

29. Ibid.

It must be acknowledged that the mention of the name David and its related themes are not designed to liken Jesus to the person of David himself, but are only mentioned because of the conviction that Jesus fulfills the messianic expectation of the Old Testament, which has David as the central figure of Yahweh's salvation of Israel. It is often assumed by scholars that the reason for Jesus' apparent reluctance to accept the title Son of David or to use the title Messiah to refer to himself may be that the terms had military/political connotations.[30] Jesus' messianic identity and ministry obviously do not conform to such nationalistic expectations which could well be one of the major reasons why Jesus never explicitly uses the titles for himself. Or, it could be that Jesus considered himself higher than the Davidic Messiah, and therefore the titles could not fully portray his heavenly authority. Having said this, Jesus is nevertheless proclaimed as the Son of David who fulfills the ancient Jewish messianic prophecy in the decisive moments of his earthly life.

What is intended is not a comparison between David and Jesus, *per se*, but the redemptive function of Jesus in the scheme of Israel's redemptive history, which now endorses a seemingly different concept of redemption. It was from endless foreign political oppression and military tyranny that Yahweh promised to liberate his people through the agent of the Davidic king, but it is stressed that in the New Era of Jesus, it is liberation from the bondage of sin. Although the concept of salvation seems to have undergone transformation from a politico-historical realm into the spiritual dimension of sin and atonement, the entire Old Testament attests to incidents of Israel's sinfulness and disobedience which result in direct consequences in her political and historical circumstances. The two are inextricably intertwined, which is a unique character of Israel's history, as the political and religious worlds are inseparable.

It is the pattern of God's ongoing redemptive act that is displayed through the Davidic royal motif, and this history reaches its pinnacle in the person and the ministry of Jesus.[31] This does not necessarily mean

---

30. Rowland, "Christ in the New Testament," 485.

31. Ibid., 487. This common understanding of the Davidic legacy can be found in the Pauline Epistles. Bearing in mind that "Messiah" originally means the "anointed," the equivalent term in Greek, *christos*, is frequently found in the Pauline corpus. In these epistles the title seems little more than a way of referring to Jesus in which specifically messianic connotations are not emphasized. Rowland notes that "its ubiquitous presence reminds us of how deeply rooted it has become in early Christian discourse, that, at least as far as Paul is concerned, it needed no explanation (cf. Rom. 5:6; 8; 6:3–4; 8:9–10; 10:4; 14:9, 15; 15:3; Cor. 8:11; 15:3, 12; Gal. 3:13)."

that the "Christology" of Matthew is subordinate to his "Theology." We shall discover throughout this volume that messianic kingship and God's Kingship do not stand in tension against one another; rather, they are mutually complementary and, indeed, each reinforces the understanding of the other.

Fulfillment Theme

Matthew's dependence on the Old Testament, compared to the other Synoptic Gospels, is displayed by the frequent explicit citations, forty in all, with twenty-one implicit quotations, and numerous allusions to the Old Testament motifs.[32] These are accentuated throughout the Gospel, and the distinctive feature of the "formula quotations" is convincing evidence that the idea of the fulfillment of prophecies through the person of Jesus Christ was of paramount importance to the evangelist.

The unique literary feature of Matthew's formula quotations "this was to fulfill what was spoken by the prophets" (1:22–23; 2:15; 2:17–18; 2:23; 4:14–16; 8:17; 12:17–21; 13:35; 21:4–5; 27:9–10) has been explored by scholars. R. T. France notes that among the formula quotations, the only one to offer a text identical to the LXX is 1:23, while others differ significantly from the LXX. In fact, Matthew's version offers a more direct translation of the Hebrew (2:15/8:17).[33] However, their general nonconformity to either the Masoretic text, or the LXX, or indeed any known Targum indicates that Matthew was a creative writer and editor of concomitant textual materials, as he collected and discarded certain texts for the overall scheme of his theological design. This has led Krister Stendahl, known for his theory of the Matthean school of interpretation, which is closely analogous to the interpretative institution found at the Qumran community, to suggest that "formula quotations" are so unique and integrated into the text that they cannot be classified as entities which have roots in special sources outside the known tradition. He contends that such formal similarities between the two enterprises of interpretation stand strongly in favor of the notion of a school of interpretation comparable to that reflected in the *lemmata* in the Qumran Habakkuk commentary, which contain similar textual abnormalities due not to dependence on any familiarity with texts outside the tradition, but to

---

32. Beaton, *Isaiah's Christ in Matthew's Gospel*, 18.
33. France, *Matthew*, 173.

the creative interaction of the writer as he sought to analyze details of fulfillment in accordance with its antecedent prophecy of Scripture.[34]

An attempt at deciphering the function of these "formula quotations" in their contemporary social setting has been carried out by Bertil Gärtner,[35] who argues that in origin, the formula quotations have been designed as a "missionary preaching tradition," which through the use of scriptural citations and proofs sought to combat Jewish opponents based on the conviction that Jesus' messiahship was the fulfillment of Old Testament prophecies. For Matthew and his community, the kingly authority of Jesus can only be divulged through the knowledge of the Old Testament. The interpolation of Old Testament passages and the theme of fulfillment work to procure the notion of God's continuing act of redemption in the history of Israel which reaches its culmination in Christ Jesus.

Moreover, the deployment of the fulfillment theme in the Gospel is not necessarily confined to the formula quotations. The theme is distributed throughout the entire Gospel; formula quotations are simply one way of achieving the effect. R. T. France shows that we should not imagine that formula quotations exhaust the entire theme of fulfillment, as Matthew did not single out this particular group for this specific purpose. It simply represents one expression of the fulfillment theology which rests upon the entire structural scheme of his presentation of Jesus. This is sometimes conveyed in formal quotations, sometimes in allusions, sometimes in the manner in which a plot progresses in disclosing Jesus' messianic identity so that a reader acquainted with the Old Testament will perceive the ongoing patterns of God's redemptive act in the history of Israel.[36]

However, there is a certain level of reluctance to finding Christological themes in the preceding Jewish tradition.[37] The advocates of this view contend that the Old Testament is a product of a particular history and religion which are exclusively Jewish in their content and style. The identity generated from these texts is most certainly not

---

34. Stendahl, *The School of St. Matthew*, cited in Hill, *The Gospel of Matthew*, 36.

35. Gärtner, cited in Hill, *The Gospel of Matthew*, 37.

36. France, *Matthew*, 184. This also explains why a reference to particular psalms in this volume must not only include direct literal quotations by the evangelist but also allusions and echoes which would have been picked up by the implied readers.

37. Reimer, "Old Testament Christology," 382–84.

Christian.[38] These scholars argue against the "Christianization" of the Old Testament and propose that the original context of textual meaning should be appreciated in its own right. Along similar lines, D. J. Reimer notes that the concept of the "messianic deliverer" is at best muted in the Old Testament, even in its later stages. The general concern for the advocates of this view is to preserve the Jewish tradition liberated from Christian dialectics, which read into the Jewish texts preconceived notions and ideological interests that are simply absent. Such an argument, stemming from a growing appreciation of the comparative study of religions, deserves credit for the attempt to study the religious traditions exclusively in their own right. However, the complex process of the separation of "Christianity" from its parent Jewish body adds to the difficulty of ascertaining when Christians actually started to address themselves as "Christians" or when the designation became known to others as distinct from Judaism. More simply put, we, as modern contemporary readers, have access to the entire canon of the Scripture, and we can neatly divide between Old and New Testaments. However, we must remember that the early Christians did not have this privilege that we take for granted. For them the distinction between the Jewish identity and Christian mind-set is not so obvious, since the Jesus movement was a newly emerging religious campaign that professed its faith in the God of Israel. This problem becomes more acutely poignant in relation to Matthew's Gospel, where it seems that the community and the evangelist still regard themselves to be within the boundaries of Judaism. Their corporate identity distinct from the parent body of Judaism seems at best rudimentary in the contemporary setting, and the polemic against the Jews seems more of an internecine strife between members of the same group. This indicates that an attempt to find "New Testament innovation" in the Old is a misguided approach to the matter under discussion. It is more plausible that the community of Matthew regarded themselves as the true remnants of Israel in thorough accordance with Jewish faith, and Jesus' teaching was a reinterpretation of the Jewish Scripture and its ethos, rather than a radical rupture from its parent tradition.

---

38. Ibid. The scholars mentioned above are cited by D. J. Reimer as an example of the scholarly trend to reject the simplistic view of Jesus as the answer to the Old Testament promises.

Structure of Matthew's Gospel

The ongoing discussions with regard to the ramifications of the structure of the Gospel have by no means reached a conclusive end, as various proposals continue to be examined based on the understanding that structure is the means used to convey a particular message.[39] Numerous scholars have come up with suggestions as to the possible epideictic structural form intended by the evangelist, and to varying degrees they all have plausibility, even though they may not necessarily concur with one another.

One of the pioneering works on the Synoptic Gospels by means of literary criticism has been initiated by Jack Dean Kingsbury, whose scholarly work has provided a context for further investigation of the Christology and the related titles and their interaction in the narrative dimension. He put forward a possible structural outline for the Gospel of Matthew based on three major divisions:

1. The Person of Jesus the Messiah (1:1—4:16)

2. The Proclamation of Jesus the Messiah (4:17—16:20)

3. The Suffering, Death, and Resurrection of Jesus the Messiah (16:21—28:20)[40]

He is certainly correct in arguing that the theme of salvation history is ubiquitous in the Gospel, as the overall function of the structure is to set forth the claim that through the person of Jesus Christ, his ministry and death—and the subsequent triumph over death in his resurrection—are of ultimate significance for the salvation of both Israel and the Gentiles. The major turning points, in Kingsbury's view, are the vague chronological indications ("From that time on") which occur in 4:17 and 16:21 as pointers to a new phase of Jesus' ministry. It is noticeable from these two turning points that the geographical locations of Jesus' ministry also changed, as the public ministry in Galilee moves to the Passion context when the story reaches its climax in Jerusalem. However, the idea of regarding geographical locations as an indication of crucial points in the development of the story is somewhat tenuous, as it is highly doubtful that the evangelist would have considered

---

39. See Combrink, "The Structure of the Gospel of Matthew as Narrative," 61–90.
40. Kingsbury, *Matthew: Structure, Christology, Kingdom*, 9.

the changes of location as the crux in his presentation of the story.[41] An ambiguous reference to time indicated in 4:17 and 16:21 shows that Matthew is not interested in chronological or geographical details, but rather it is much more likely that the Gospel is structured according to the development of Christology, the progressive disclosure of the messianic identity of Jesus which is the prime concern of Matthew. This is inextricably intertwined with Matthew's conception of Israel's redemptive history. According to Kingsbury, Matthew has a tendency to use temporal expressions to designate some point in time, such as "at that time," "at that hour," and "on that day," which seem rather indistinct and vague but nevertheless play a significant role in the chronological movement to the text.[42] However, the ambiguity of the expression points not to Matthew's interest in chronological details in his story of Jesus but his historical awareness in the context of eschatology. In the same manner, the geographical locations during the earthly ministry of Jesus are quite insignificant details in comparison with his overarching concern for Israel's history and God's fulfillment of redemptive purpose for her. Analysis of the structure of Matthew's Gospel based on the geographical movement or chronological expression as indicators of the development of the story should not undermine the evangelist's redemptive historical perspective, which is closely connected with his Christology. When Matthew uses expressions such as "day" or "hour," their meaning stretches beyond the ordinary perception of time.[43] They point to a more urgent reality of eschatological judgment which also presupposes salvation manifested through Christ Jesus. In a similar manner, a phrase such as "on that day" has no distinct chronological value in the ordinary sense of the word but is intelligible only in the context of Israel's redemptive history. The term denotes the eschatological "day of the Lord" which points to the impending divine judgment (Matt 7:21; see also 25:13; 24:37).[44] Kingsbury adds that Matthew's strong eschatological outlook

41. France, *Matthew*, 152. France here presents his own critique of Kingsbury's structural thesis. Cf. also Taylor, *The Names of Jesus*, who advocates the view that geographical movements indicate crucial stages of development in the story.

42. Kingsbury, "The Structure of Matthew's Gospel," 467.

43. Combrink, "The Structure of the Gospel of Matthew as Narrative," 66, also notes that "Matthew's Gospel is a narrative with plot, which is less often chronological and more often arranged according to a preconceived artistic principle determined by the nature of the plot."

44. Kingsbury, "The Structure of Matthew's Gospel," 468.

and redemptive historical perspective can be seen in the way he employs the term *end*—which is used four times in the Gospel, whereas Mark uses it only twice (13:7, 13) and Luke only once (21:9)—in its absolute sense. Moreover, he notes that "it is only Matthew who brings the expressions 'on the day of judgment' and the 'consummation of the age.'"[45] The pressing question is, How are Matthew's redemptive historical perspective and his eschatological awareness reflected in the overall structure of the Gospel?[46] Does he indicate when this eschatological time began? In the Gospel, the disciples address this very question in 24:3. Kingsbury contends that the answer to this question is answered prior to Jesus' public appearance in the introductory scene of John the Baptist (3:1). It is indicated here that the eschatological period is imminent, which is the motif behind the urgency of his message of repentance.

However, the problem with Kingsbury's structural analysis is the grouping of Matthew 3 with chapters 1 and 2 in the prologue of his structure, which is plausible as far as it is restricted to the general introduction of Jesus' person. However, I find problematic Kingsbury's specification that it is the recurrent theme of the "Son of God" climactically sounded at the end of the baptismal scene 3:17 that compels us to regard chapter 3 as internally related to the antecedent chapters.[47] If Kingsbury's conviction that the preeminence of "Son of God" dominates the entire structure of Matthew's narrative, it would be difficult to explain why the evangelist bothered to employ other Christological titles throughout the Gospel. The distribution of different Christological titles throughout the Gospel structure compels us to adopt a different approach; for example, the primary concern for Matthew in chapters 1 and 2 is not essentially Jesus as the Son of God but the explicit presentation of Jesus as the Son of David and Son of Abraham (1:1), which indicates that Christological titles and themes interact with each other to convey a dynamic portrait of Jesus rather than Kingsbury's simplistic notion of

---

45. Cf. Feuillet, *The Background of the New Testament and Its Eschatology*.

46. If it is accepted that the structure of Matthew's Gospel is connected with the perspective of Israel's redemptive history, it also becomes necessary to acknowledge the importance of the Old Testament narrative. Cf. Patte and Patte, *Structural Exegesis*. See also Combrink, "The Macrostructure of the Gospel of Matthew," 1–20; Malina, "The Literary Structure and Form of Matt. 28"; Brooks, "Matthew 28:16–20 and the Design of the First Gospel," 2–28.

47. Kingsbury, "The Structure of Matthew's Gospel and His Concept of Salvation History," 451–74.

Son of God exhausting the full identity of Jesus. Besides, based on the assumption that structure is the means by which the plot (i.e., message) is conveyed, it is difficult to see how his broad classification of structural outline necessarily supports the claim that Son of God is the most preeminent Christological trait dictating its entire literary structure.

With regard to the subsequent chapters of the Gospel (4:17 to 16:21), which deal largely with the public ministry of Jesus before the Passion Narrative, Donald Senior aptly points out that Matthew 4:17 represents the commencement of Jesus' public ministry. But his ministry does not conclude with 16:20, since the proclamation of the imminent Kingdom of God which continues to the very end of the Gospel takes on a new form in the context of suffering, death, and ultimately resurrection.[48]

The second example is that proposed by B.W. Bacon, who argues that the Gospel is divided into five discourses and is deliberately designed after the Five Books of Moses in order to present a polemic against the Jews.[49] He noted the presence of the recurrent statement that appears five times in the Gospel of Matthew (7:28; 11:1; 13:53; 19:1; 26:1) which begins in a similar manner ("And when Jesus finished these sayings . . ."). The reason for such intended resemblance to the Pentateuch is to emphasize its continuity with the precedent Jewish Scripture. The Gospel is designed in such a way as to imply that it is the new followers of Christ who are truly the legitimate descendents of Israel and heirs of the Torah. On the other hand, through its polemical nature, it criticizes the Jewish community for having thrown away its privileged status as the People of God by their consistent failure to recognize their Messiah.

The total structure of the book, using Bacon's headings, is as follows:

The preamble: chapters 1–2
Book 1—concerning discipleship: chapters 3–7
Book 2—concerning apostleship: chapters 8–10
Book 3—concerning the hiding of revelation: chapters 11–13
Book 4—concerning church administration: chapters 14–18
Book 5—concerning the judgment: chapters 19–25
The epilogue: chapters 26–28[50]

---

48. Senior, *What Are They Saying about Matthew?* 31.

49. Bacon, "Studies in Matthew" and "The Five Books of Matthew against the Jews," 55–66.

50. Adapted from Bacon's structural proposal as illustrated in France, *Matthew*, 144.

The fundamental flaw of this five-book scheme is that the author places the opening chapters (1–2) and the concluding chapters (26–28) in peripheral sections which nevertheless have a huge impact upon the entire structural scheme of the Gospel. The structural outline proposed by Bacon undermines the prime theological concern of the evangelist, which is Christological, and the single most decisive factor in the Christological portrait of Matthew is not so much the ethical teaching or healings Jesus performed, although they do have an important place in the overall picture, but it is predominantly the "messianic identity" of Jesus revealed by the narratives. Matthew's first and foremost concern is to proclaim Jesus as the long-awaited messianic deliverer. The genealogy makes an explicit statement concerning Jesus' messianic identity, and the infancy narratives that immediately follow portray Jesus' birth as divinely conceived by the Holy Spirit. The beginning of the Gospel, therefore, exerts a decisive impact upon the rest of the story. In fact, the charge made against Jesus at the trial scene (Matt 26:63–68) is not based on his ministerial activity, but essentially on his identity as the Christ, the Son of God. In the same respect, the concluding chapters (26–28) have their crucial function in the Gospel, since in the light of the Passion, crucifixion, and resurrection the story reaches its denouement (see Matt 27:54) and the enigmatic identity of the suffering Messiah finally becomes clear.

Moreover, the notion that the Gospel is modeled after the Five Books of Moses implies that the author had in mind Jesus as the "New Moses" to whom the Torah is attributed.[51] However, this title exerts relatively little influence in the entire structure of the Gospel compared to the preponderance of other major Christological titles such as Son of David.[52] Nowhere in the Gospel of Matthew do we find Jesus designated as the New Moses. Therefore, Bacon's structural analysis based on this Mosaic theme (which is not even a widely accepted Christological title in New Testament scholarship) in fact has no textual support from the Gospel itself. Rather, it is evident that the Christology of Matthew is most concerned about presenting Jesus as the Davidic Messiah who draws the redemptive history of Israel to a decisive fulfillment. In which case, if

---

51. Cf. Allison, *The New Moses*.

52. It will be argued that while the figure of Moses plays a vital role in the Exodus, the prototype redemptive event in the history of Israel, it is later merged with the messianic figure of Davidic monarchy, which dominates the redemptive history of Israel.

the analogy between Moses and Jesus is not intended but Davidic kingship is the model for Jesus' messiahship, it is reasonable to presuppose that the language attributed to David in the Old Testament is retained in Matthew's Christological statements. This naturally draws our attention to an enquiry about Matthew's use of the Psalms in his Gospel. This will be examined in more detail later on in this volume.

The sheer diversity of structural outlines and alternatives proposed by scholars with different theological perspectives may possibly suggest that the evangelist perhaps did not seek to establish a set pattern of literary structure.[53] This view is shared by R. T. France, who points out that rather than seeking indications of the structure in an aesthetically satisfying manner, one should pay closer attention to the overall thrust of the movement of the story, which is essentially about progressive disclosure of the person of Jesus the Messiah and his unique ministry. Perhaps the author of the Gospel did not originally envisage a neatly constructed pattern of literary elements but rather a compelling story which reaches its climax in Jerusalem as Jesus triumphs over death. Assuming that the Gospel was originally composed to be delivered orally,[54] it is unlikely that people who would hear the Gospel being read aloud in public would assimilate and remember the literary structural pattern of the text; it is more likely that the audience would pick up the actual content of the dialectical message.

---

53. Senior, *What Are They Saying about Matthew?* 36, proposes the following structural outline of the Gospel:

1:1—4:11

4:12—10:42 (The entire scene of 4:12–17, not just a single verse, is a key transition moment.)

Galilean ministry: (*a*) chs. 5–7, teaching; (*b*) chs. 8–9, healing; (*c*) ch. 10, model for the apostles' own mission. (In this section Matthew introduces significant material not found in Mark's Gospel and imposes his own order.)

11:1—16:12 (varying responses to Jesus)

16:13—20:34 (The entire Petrine story in 16:13–23 is a "bridge," with the blessing on Peter serving as a culmination of some of the discipleship themes apparent in the previous section and the orientation to the Passion.)

21:1—28:15

28:16-20 (found only in Matthew)

Cf. also Krentz, "The Extent of Matthew's Prologue," 409–14.

54. Stanton, *A Gospel for a New People*, 75. Cf. also Gilfillan-Upton, *Hearing Mark's Endings*.

Structure of Matthew's Gospel Proposed in This Volume

There is no doubt that the evangelist's concerns for the early Church are varied. Matthew clearly has a range of concerns and is anxious to maintain the social, ideological, and theological solidarity of the community. For instance, the theme of discipleship and community intertwined with other theological concerns such as apocalyptic beliefs resulted in a Gospel which has a versatile theological purpose and function within its community. However, behind the multifaceted character of the Gospel lies the prime concern of the evangelist: Namely, the conviction of Jesus Christ as Israel's Messiah. The accentuation of Jesus as the long-awaited messianic deliverer who is the fulfillment of the Old Testament prophecies is propagated throughout the entire Gospel structure. The unique kingship of Jesus becomes progressively disclosed as the story reaches its denouement. The primary concern of the evangelist is therefore Christology. Although the Gospel needs to be understood in its overall context, it must be pointed out here that the major objective of this volume is to focus on the significance of Matthew's message about Christ not so much in his ethical teaching, his healing of the sick, and his performing wondrous miracles (although they contribute to a crucial part of Jesus' earthly ministry), but it is the esoteric nature of Jesus' person and messianic identity that distinguishes him from the mundane and attributes him divine character.

This view is generally accepted by New Testament scholars. R. V. G. Tasker contends that "the teaching of Jesus cannot be classified and evaluated separately from a consideration of His person and claim, because His greatest lesson was Himself."[55] G. Bornkamm concurs: "it is not the teaching of Jesus, as contained in the Sermon on the Mount, which is the motive for the disciples following him. Even at the point where they are actually charged with the teaching, 'to obey everything I have commanded you' (28:20), it is preceded by the call 'all authority in heaven and on earth has been given to me' (v.18),[56] based on the resurrection of Jesus and his power over heaven and earth."[57] On this fundamental principle—that Jesus' authority was the very essence of himself rather than what he demonstrated in his speeches and actions—we shall

---

55. Tasker, *Matthew: An Introduction*, 20.
56. I have changed the biblical quotation to the NIV.
57. Bornkamm, Barth, and Held, *Traditions and Interpretation in Matthew*, 40.

examine how Matthew defines Jesus' person. Of course his authority is manifested through the wondrous deeds and teachings during his earthly ministry but these are merely signs of his divine power rather than what define his identity. This volume seeks therefore to focus on the messianic identity, i.e., the "person" of Jesus presented in Matthew's Gospel, and the key Christological passages dealing with the matter are selected to explore this theme. They will be examined and close attention will be paid as to how these passages interact with one another in presenting a complex and dynamic portrait of Jesus:

1. The Genealogy of Jesus and the Infancy Narrative (1:1—2:12)

2. The Baptism of Jesus (3:1–16)

3. The Transfiguration of Jesus (17:1–13)

4. The Climax of Jesus' Ministry

    The Last Supper (26:17–30)

    b. The Trial of Jesus (26: 57–67)

    c. The Crucifixion and Resurrection (27:32—28:10)

5. The Great Commission (28:16–20)[58]

PART TWO: CONTEMPORARY SCHOLARSHIP ON THE MESSIANIC EXPECTATIONS OF THE OLD TESTAMENT

Jewish History of Exile

Since Matthew saw himself and the community within the broad spectrum of Judaism and sought to define Jesus' messianic identity in terms of the Davidic legacy, it is appropriate to examine the historicity of the Christological title "Son of David," which necessarily entails a discussion of the messianic expectations of the Old Testament. The coming of the Messiah who will restore the covenantal relationship between Yahweh and Israel is the central message that the prophets preached in response to the threat of the exile. The national theology of Israel and the

---

58. A detailed Christological exegesis will be conducted later on in this volume according to the structure proposed.

messianic expectation are products of Israel's political crisis, as she was repeatedly attacked and invaded by foreign tyrants. During the Assyrian invasion prior to the Babylonian captivity, the national theology of Israel—anchored in the affirmation of Yahweh's choice of Zion and his promise to the Davidic dynasty of an everlasting reign—was thrown into crisis. Although Josiah's reform seemed to reestablish the nation's spiritual welfare by reviving the Jewish cult which commemorates Yahweh's redemptive act (2 Kings 23:23, 24), this came to a disappointing end with the tragic death of Josiah (2 Kings 23:29). This no doubt must have been a huge disillusionment for the people of Israel, who saw glimpses of an ideal ruler in Josiah.[59] The prophetic response to the national crisis seems somewhat varied. J. Bright notes that "Jeremiah rejected the national confidence in the Davidic promises utterly. He did not deny its theoretical validity nor did he reject the institution of the monarchy as such. But he was convinced that, since the existing state had failed in its obligations, neither it nor its kings would know anything of promises."[60] Ezekiel on the other hand spoke of the greater New Exodus (20:33–38) as he eagerly anticipated the restored nation under Davidic kingship (34:23f.; 37:15–28). However, it seems that Yahweh will be the one who will accomplish this, as the prophet encourages Israel to put her hope and faith not in human kings but in Yahweh alone as her King (ch. 34).

The time of the exilic plight for Israel was a time of testing not just for the political tenacity of the state but also for her faith in Yahweh's redemptive plan. On the one hand, the period could be seen as a judgment upon unfaithful Israel, who was guilty of breaching the covenantal relationship with Yahweh, and therefore it was a well-deserved punishment for her stubborn and unrepentant heart. On the other hand, it could be argued that the period had a didactic purpose for Israel, as the crisis of the exile forced her to reassess her faith in Yahweh and her wrongdoings. It provided an opportunity to purge Israel of sin and look to a new future of national restoration.[61] It was undoubtedly the most challenging time for Israel but it was also the time when she grew in

---

59. Bright, *A History of Israel*, 331.

60. Ibid., 334.

61. Bright, *A History of Israel*, 350, argues that "the cultic laws which comprise the bulk of the so-called priestly code, and which reflect the practice of the Jerusalem Temple were likewise collected and codified in definitive form at about this time." Also, "the priestly narrative of the Pentateuch (P) was composed, probably during the 6th century BCE and probably in the exile."

spiritual maturity. In Deutero-Isaiah the entire prophecy is dominated by the consolation and conviction that Yahweh as Israel's true King will come and redeem his people from the tyranny of foreign oppressors. In Isaiah 40:1-11 the prophet comforts Israel, assures that her penalty has been paid, and offers the profound explanations of her suffering. The God of Israel Himself will be the good shepherd and will lead His flock through the wilderness to Zion. In that dwelling place of Yahweh He will establish His kingly rule (Isa 51:17—52:12).[62] Those who returned from the Babylonian exile under the leadership of Zerubbabel, were obviously eager to reinstitute the cult of Israel and reconstruct the temple, but the early years of the restoration community (538-522 BCE) again proved bitterly disappointing (see Hag 1:3-11; 2:15-17). Bright notes that "eighteen years after work on the Temple had begun by Shesh-bazzar it had not progressed beyond the foundations—indeed, had stopped altogether. The community was too poor, too harassed, and too dispirited to keep it going."[63] In this dire predicament, the prophets Haggai and Zechariah give a message of comfort and encouragement that Yahweh will not abandon Zion and affirmed the fulfillment of Yahweh's promise in the national theology of Israel and the Davidic dynasty. The prophet Haggai charged people with the conviction that Yahweh will defeat the enemy nations and will shortly restore Israel (Hag 2:20-23). With this encouragement, the temple was completed and dedicated in 515 BCE (Ezra 1-6), which marked the beginning of the Second Temple period in Judaism.[64]

However, the prophetic tradition reveals that the ideal Davidic Messiah had not appeared as Israel had so desperately hoped. What happened to Josiah and Zerubbabel only yielded confusion. Although these figures displayed traits which led the prophets to believe that each was perhaps the Messiah, they only added to the disillusionment and frustration. In general, the kings of Judah and Israel constantly failed to

62. Ibid., 357.

63. Ibid., 367, 368. Bright also notes that "the community was divided into two ill-reconciled segments: those—mostly of the returning exile—who were moved by lofty prophetic ideals and traditions of the fathers; and those—including probably the bulk of the native population—who had absorbed so much from the pagan environment that their religion was no longer Yahwism in pure form."

64. Ferguson, *Backgrounds of Early Christianity*, 377, notes that "the great work of Ezra was the restoration of the law (cf. Neh. 8-10). The post-exilic community was dedicated to the study of the law."

live up to the standard prescribed in the Davidic covenant throughout its history; the prophets as a whole had a critical perspective and distrust of the monarchy.[65] The tenacity of Israel's faith in Yahweh's redemption did not die easily. The prophets in the exilic context did not give up their hope but continued to assert that Yahweh would establish the greater New Exodus event, through which He would redeem the true remnants of Israel. What is significant here is that despite countless disappointments and failures, Jewish eschatology never detached itself from the messianic hope of Israel and still managed to maintain its faith in the Davidic dynasty and, in the end, that Yahweh would fulfill His promise by sending the Messiah to establish salvation for the elect and judgment upon Israel's foes.[66] Bearing in mind the turbulent relationship of Israel with Yahweh and the resulting political atrocities due to the failures of the kings, it would be absurd to think that the prophets were naïve enough to put their hope in another Davidic king. If anything, our brief outline of Israel's exilic history serves as a painful reminder that putting trust in human leadership is futile. Therefore, we may presuppose that when the prophets speak of yet another Davidic king as Israel's Messiah, they are not merely pointing to another human kingly figure that is susceptible to temptations and failures. It is thus reasonable to suppose that the kind of messiah which the prophets have in mind after a series of tragic events of exile will surely not succumb to human limitations and will indeed surpass all political leadership. He will be an ideal Davidic Messiah who possesses heavenly qualities, and when he appears in the last days, he will surely not disappoint as his predecessors have done.[67]

---

65. Blair, "Kingship in Israel and its Implications for the Lordship of Christ Today," 74, 75, argues from a Christian perspective as he states that "Isaiah looked forward unwaveringly to the coming of a king with the spiritual gifts—this hope is abundantly realized in Jesus Christ."

66. Bright, *A History of Israel*, 456, notes that "Obadiah looked (vs. 15–21) for a restoration of the Davidic boundaries at the Day of Yahweh, and even the Chronicler desired a rehabilitation of the national-cultic institutions after the order of David (Ezra 3:10; Neh. 12:45)." On the contrary, passages such as Zechariah 9:9f. and 12:1—13:6 lack messianic hope in the line of David.

67. Ibid., 459, 460, refers to the later portions of 1 Enoch (chs. 37–71) where the Son of Man, who is possibly an individual redeemer, clearly appears as a preexistent heavenly deliverer. The notion of the messianic king associated with Yahweh in his authority is in conjunction with the observation that the origins of this cosmic redeemer may well reach back to very ancient figures of Oriental myth, as these had been fused in popular thinking with the concept of the Davidic Messiah. Cf. also Ferguson, *Backgrounds of*

What Was the Nature of the Messianic Promise?

According to John Barton, the definition of the Messiah in the Old Testament is related to the Israelite king, and the expected deliverer would be regarded as the Messiah only if he was a new David (Jer 23:5–6; 33:14–18),[68] which explains Matthew's emphasis on Jesus' messiahship as the Son of David (Matt 1:1). This naturally leads to an enquiry with regard to the content of the Davidic promise. In other words, what was the nature or the essence of the Davidic covenant?[69] Usually, one may presume that the Davidic promise is mainly concerned with the succession to the throne and Yahweh's anointing of the descendents of David so that the monarchy would rule forever (Ps 89).[70] The everlasting nature of the Davidic reign throughout the ages is what characterizes the covenant. A. R. Johnson notes that "David has an 'everlasting' covenant with Yahweh, so that failure at any point to fulfill the conditions, while it must meet with suitable punishment, will not be allowed to annul the promise which was originally made to the founder of the royal house."[71] Even though it may seem that the Davidic covenant is essentially a political tool which is designed to secure the royal authority of the monarchy, G. N. Knoppers argues that a "close study of the principal passages dealing with the Davidic promises reveals that there is a concern with much more than royal rotation and the ancient Israelite authors draw links between the fate of the Davidic dynasty and the fate of other institutions,

---

Early Christianity, 381, 383, 388, 398. Of course, the Jewish history of exile does not end here. "In the Roman Period (from 63 BCE) Psalms of Solomon is the first Jewish writing to express complete hostility toward Rome. The author expresses the ardent expectation of a Righteous Davidic King-Messiah who would deliver the holy land from unholy enemies." Even when Matthew's Gospel was composed, which is believed to be around 70 AD, it was the time of the First Jewish Revolt (66–70 AD).

68. Barton, "The Messiah in Old Testament Theology," 373.

69. Knoppers, "David's Relation to Moses," 92, distinguishes two different views concerning the Davidic promise: "1) Integrationists have proposed analogies of ancient Near Eastern vassal treaties with both the covenants between Yahweh and Israel at Mt. Sinai (Exod. 19–24) and the covenant between Yahweh and David (Pss. 89 and 132). 2) Segregationists are hesitant to employ Hittite or Assyrian treaties as any sort of parallel to the Davidic promises. They view the Davidic promises as distinctly different from any ancient Near Eastern treaties."

70. Ibid., 95. The Mosaic covenant established at Sinai deals with the divine administration of the Israelite people as a nation, and the law forms the basis of the morality of the society. The Davidic covenant has a more political connotation in which David is the central figure and the succession to the throne is promised to his descendents.

71. Johnson, *Sacral Kingship in Ancient Israel*, 25.

which demonstrates the relevance of the Davidic promises for national life."[72] The unique character of Israelite faith was that Israel's political welfare was directly linked with the righteousness of the people. All the political atrocities and oppression from foreign nations are in fact portrayed as punishments of Israel's sin. Although it seems that the covenant deals exclusively with the succession of David's kingly power, we need to bear in mind that the king had a representative function in both the political and the religious life of Israel. In other words, the king's righteousness and his relationship with Yahweh define the quality of his political leadership. Therefore, Israel was directly affected by the king's representative function. So, we would agree with Knoppers' statement that what seems like an exclusive preservation of the Davidic kingship is in fact dealing with the nation as a whole, since the two entities are interchangeable; that is, the king represents the nation, and his righteousness determines the welfare of the nation. A. R. Johnson highlights the importance of the religious role of the king as the representative of Israel: "The king is not only found leading his people in worship with the offering of sacrifice and prayer on important occasions in the national life, but throughout the four hundreds years of the Davidic Dynasty, from the time of David's active concern for the Ark to that of Josiah's thoroughgoing reform, himself superintends the organization of the cultus in all its aspects."[73]

It seems evident that the king was deeply involved in the sacral dimension of Israel's religious life. In fact, in the act of anointing in 1 Samuel 14:13, the Spirit of Yahweh came upon David, which in itself has a profound religious connotation.[74] In this vein, D. W. Rooke notes that "the most explicit reference to the monarch's priestly prerogatives is that of Psalm 110:4." Here, the importance of the king's role is vividly described in the religious dimension of the Israelite cult. At a glance, it may seem from the statement that the assurance of Yahweh is given to the priestly figure who is endowed with the kingly authority, but D. W. Rooke points out that it is in fact the other way around. It is noted that the "psalm clearly addresses a royal figure to whom priestly prerogatives are subsequently granted by divine oath, and not a priestly

---

72. Knoppers, "David's Relation to Moses," 95.

73. Johnson, *Sacral Kingship in Ancient Israel*, 13–14.

74. Ibid., 15. The act of anointing in the Old Testament is reminiscent of the descent of the Spirit from the heavens in the baptismal narrative of the New Testament.

figure who is being granted some kind of kingly rule."[75] It seems that the sacral nature of Israelite kingship arises not out of the king's pursuit of priestly prerogatives within the Jewish cult but from his unique, intimate relationship with Yahweh.[76] On the basis of the king's position before Yahweh, even though the king may not be expected to carry out the actual functions of priesthood within the temple, his role as a mediator between the people of Israel and Yahweh is in principle the same as the priestly function.[77] This shows how prominent a position the king assumed in the religious and political life of Israel.[78]

Moreover, the content of the Davidic promise is most vividly portrayed in the Psalms which support the thesis that the Davidic promise extends beyond the immediate Davidic lineage.[79] For instance, in Psalm 89:27, Yahweh anoints David and confers upon him the status of the firstborn whose authority extends beyond Israel to the whole earth. This is a widely ambitious statement for a nation that was relatively insignificant compared with the surrounding powerful nations. The psalmist could not have been unaware of the political situation of his time, especially in the exilic context, as Israel could not have been serious about the statement unless it is granted that the promise of a messiah

---

75. Rooke, "Kingship as Priesthood," 187, 188.

76. Ibid., 196. E.g., "When the King Ahaz has consecrated a new altar of Damascene design for the house of the Lord by making offerings upon it himself, he tells Uriah, the chief priest, to offer upon it among other things the king's burnt offering and his grain offerings (2 Kings 16:12–15). That Ahaz is perfectly entitled to make his own offerings is evidenced by the fact that he does so for the first use of the altar; but then delegates the responsibility to the chief priest, who thereby acts in his place (2 Kings 16:16)."

77. Ibid., 199. In the postexilic period, "both monarch and high priest appear as representatives of the whole community before Yahweh." Moreover, "the high priest became the equivalent of the monarch in the post-exilic society after the demise of the Davidic line." Durham, "The King as 'Messiah' in the Psalms," 425–35, also points out that "Israel's own relationship to Yahweh was itself a pattern for understanding the relationship of the Messiah to Yahweh."

78. Ibid., 207, 208. On the basis of the analysis of Psalms of Solomon 17:5–8, it is noted that "the perceived usurpation of the monarch was a far more serious crime than the illegitimate assumption of the high priesthood. To claim to be monarch when the evidence of such an adoption or election is absent is equivalent to blasphemy of the worst kind."

79. Ibid., 106. "The author of Psalm 132 commemorates the connections between the ascent of the Ark, the participation of the priests and Yahweh's selection of Zion. Unlike the Chronicler, who ties the dynastic promises to the accession and activities of Solomon, the Psalmist ties the dynastic promises to the ritual procession of the Ark (vv. 6–8) and Yahweh's election of Zion (vv. 13–16)."

may extend beyond the immediate Israel and Davidic monarchy.[80] In short, the context of the Davidic promise is the king's religious role as Israel's representative, since the spiritual relationship between Yahweh and the king determined the welfare of the nation as a whole. Secondly, the Davidic promise should primarily be understood in the context of the contemporary reigning king of Judah, but the nature and the content of the promise also extends beyond the monarchy.[81] The kings failed to live up to the claims they were called to fulfill. This is one reason why the sacral kingship of Israel never fully recovered after the exile.[82] This has led some to argue for a more developed messianic presence in the Old Testament. For instance, J. I. Durham notes that the Old Testament writers shifted their emphasis from a human king to a "more-than-human king who is at once an eschatological figure, a deliverer without parallel, who is yet to come, and an anointed one who will be Yahweh's servant with a loyalty and status no human king could ever exemplify."[83] This is not to say that David as a royal figure was considered to be deified. However, the messianic expectation came to entail within its concept much more than a mere Davidic king but a "divine-royal" figure who exceeds what Israel has previously known.

Conflicting Evidence of Davidic Messianic Expectation

Having said this, not all theologians are convinced that Israel expected a Davidic Messiah to bring her liberation from exile. When Israel first asked for a monarchy they were in fact admitting that an invisible divine King was not enough for them. Therefore, the institution of monarchy tacitly represents Israel's lack of faith in Yahweh.[84] Even though Israel's desire for a monarchy expresses Israel's weakness and disbelief, Yahweh

---

80. Ibid., 115. It is concluded that "in dealing with the Davidic covenant one is confronted with different passages and many ancillary differences." He argues that it is more appropriate to speak of Davidic covenant(s) than to speak of a single pact.

81. Johnson, *Sacral Kingship in Ancient Israel*, 27–28. "The coronation Psalms do not refer merely to the individual whom we know as David; they must be read in the light of what we know about Israelite ideas of 'corporate personality.'"

82. Durham, "The King as 'Messiah' in the Psalms," 430, points out that this is why the priesthood moved with so little resistance into royal functions after the exile.

83. Ibid., 430.

84. Motyer, *Look to the Rock*, 26, notes that "from that moment, Samuel's task was to make sure that monarchy in Israel was founded and was known by all to be a theocratic institution."

was still her King, and the monarchy was ultimately dependent on Him. From the beginning, the monarchy was supposed to be a visible form of theocracy in action, and the king was a gift from Yahweh for His people. However, the heightened expectation of the true royal king who would manifest Yahweh's divine reign often ended in disappointment and disillusionment. The search for the ideal king who would match the Judges' ideal continued. It seems that in the south, the royal succession was based on the covenantal stipulation as originally prescribed to David, as the rightful heir sat on the throne of the Lord (1 Chr 29:23) and the legitimate royal succession continued for five centuries in accordance with the covenant. However, the situation seems to have been very different in the north. There was complete disregard for the Davidic covenant, as men without legitimate royal rights rose to power by their own political ambitions. J. A. Motyer notes that "there were in total nineteen different kings of whom only a minority succeeded in passing the throne to their sons, and the kingdom ended in a climax of unrestrained individual ambition with six kings reigning briefly in quick succession until the kingdom ended in Assyrian exile (2 Kings 17)."[85] Even though the south was more faithful in maintaining their Davidic legacy, the kingdom also ended in failure, which seems to have been initiated by Rehoboam (1 Kings 12) and ultimately brought to an end by Zedekiah (2 Kings 24–25). From this failure of monarchy two diverging perspectives emerge. The disappointment at monarchy may have resulted in complete distrust and rejection of the kingship in general and forced the nation to regret their desire for a king. Or, the disappointment could have been the motif to hope for a more ideal king in the future. In fact it seems that the Old Testament's perspective towards the ideal king, that is, the Messiah, retains both hopeful and skeptical views. However, it needs to be pointed out that the skepticism towards the kings and their failure led to the hopefulness of the future king who would fulfill the criteria of the true ideal leader. Indeed, the Psalms were used with this in mind, as Motyer also notes that "many of the royal psalms are best explained if we assume that they were composed deliberately in order to hold up before a new David at his coronation a mirror of a true leader."[86] Despite the fact

---

85. Ibid., 29.

86. Ibid., 31, 32. It is also pointed out that "alongside this persistent notion of the ideal ruler there was a backward look of longing to the 'golden days' of David himself, for, without a doubt, he was beyond compare." Motyer summarizes the material offered

that the Old Testament texts in general seem forward-looking in nature, the scholarly debates concerning the messianic expectation of the Old Testament can be broadly divided into two different perspectives:

1. Those who accept the view that the prophetic message of the Old Testament has found its fulfillment in Israel's Messiah, which is realized in the death and resurrection of Jesus Christ. The advocates of this view express positive attitudes concerning the presence of the Davidic promise in the Old Testament texts, which is central to the Redemptive History of Israel.

2. On the contrary, there are scholars who express skepticism towards the "Christianized" interpretation of the Old Testament texts in which any trace of messianic hope is simply absent or scanty at best. They argue that Christians have read into the Old Testament without appreciating the original context of the texts that they quote.

It is interesting to note that there should be such diverging opinions on the same texts. A brief examination of the general division of scholarly opinions outlined above is in order. T. D. Alexander is strongly in favor of the former view, namely that the presence of the messianic promise in the Old Testament is clearly central from the very beginning. He argues that the starting point for the discussion of the Messiah ranges from Genesis to Kings and that the content of these books is central to the understanding of the Old Testament witness to the Messiah realized in the New Testament.[87]

Alexander notes that the Abraham narrative in Genesis 22, which deals with the divine oath given after the testing of Abraham's faith, is the crucial point of the Messianic promise in the Old Testament. Here, in Genesis 22:16-18, Yahweh makes an oath to Abraham which recalls

---

in Psalms as follows: "the expected king would meet world-opposition (2:1-3; 110:1ff.) but, as a victor (45:3-5; 89:22-23) and by the activity of the Lord (2:6, 8; 21:1-13; 110:1-2) he would establish world-rule (2:8-12; 45:17; 72:8-11; 89:25; 110:5-6), based on Zion (2:6)." "He would rule forever (21:4; 45:6; 72:5), in peace (72:7), prosperity (72:16) and undeviating reverence for the Lord (72:5). Pre-eminent among men (45:2, 7), he would be the friend of the poor and the enemy of the oppressor (72:2-4, 12-14). He is the recipient of the Lord's everlasting blessing, the heir of David's covenant (89:28-37; 132:11-12) and of Melchizedek's priesthood (110:4)."

87. Alexander, "Royal Expectation in Genesis to Kings," 191-212.

the initial divine speech in Genesis 12:1–3, where Yahweh reaffirms His initial promise. The divine promise can be classified in two distinctive parts: First, Abraham's seed will become numerous, and second, Abraham's "seed" will defeat Yahweh's enemies and become the source of blessing for the nations. Here, Alexander contends that in contrast to the first, the second expression of "seed" refers to a single descendant of Abraham.[88] The identity of this figure is thought to be messianic in character, as the Abraham narrative indicates that the line of seed will give rise to royal descendents (Gen 17:6; cf. 17:18). Although Abraham is nowhere designated as king, he is nevertheless addressed in royal terms, as Yahweh's promise that Abraham's name will "become great" and other various episodes where his status is analogous to that of a king are supported by this messianic reading (Gen 14:1–24; 21:22–34; 23:6).[89] Alexander thus contends that the Abraham narrative focuses on this future individual through whom the nations will be blessed (Gen 22:18; cf. 12:3) and by whom the serpent will be defeated (Gen 3:15).[90] If Alexander's reading is correct, then one may presume that there is a link between Abraham and David in the messianic expectation of the Old Testament. Indeed, Yahweh's promise that he will make David's name great in 2 Samuel 7:9 finds its echo in the promise made to Abraham in Genesis 12:2. This reading finds its support in Matthew's Gospel, as Jesus is first and foremost designated as the Son of Abraham along with the title Son of David in the opening sentence of the prologue (Matt 1:1).

By contrast, Joachim Becker argues that there was no widespread messianic movement in the Old Testament and that the texts with messianic attributes were not originally intended to be messianic in nature. Israel did not particularly look for the coming of an idealized deliverer.[91] Becker's presupposition is strongly in favor of the idea that any trace of faith in a Davidic deliverer is either absent or is reduced in such a way that a more prominent theological concept of theocracy prevails. In other words, Israel longed for Yahweh to deliver her from the exilic plight rather than depending on a messianic agent. Becker does have a valid point in arguing that the central tenet of Israelite religion was the

---

88. Ibid., 194–203.
89. Ibid., 205.
90. Ibid., 208, 210.
91. Becker, *Messianic Expectation in the Old Testament*, 38.

focus upon God rather than a kingly figure. However, his argument has room for a more balanced perspective to the subject under discussion.

To understand such contrasting views concerning the messianic hope in the Old Testament, one needs first to examine one of the most significant events in the history of Israel which functions as the decisive landmark for the precipitation of messianic thought: namely, the period of Exile and the destruction of the first temple by the Babylonians (586–538 BCE), otherwise known as the period of the prophecy of the New Exodus.

The situation of the exilic period was that of historical crisis, as the temple lay in ruins following its destruction by the Babylonians (Isa 44:26–28; 51:3; 52:9); the elite members of society were forced out of the country (42:22); and the failure of the Davidic monarchy led to utter hopelessness of the nation ever recovering from such a downfall.[92] T. N. D. Mettinger notes that this historical crisis affected more than just the external and tangible aspects of Israel's communal life, as the period represented an intense test of faith.[93] It was more than national disaster, for it represented the termination of Israel's covenant with Yahweh. Her relationship with God had been utterly severed. It was a period of sheer disappointment and hopelessness, which has led various scholars who have examined the Jewish messianic faith to come up with two contrasting observations:

1. Disappointment at the failure of the Davidic monarchy and the termination of the Davidic covenant by Yahweh redirected the people's hope to a theocratic sovereignty, as YHWH alone is the King of Israel. Becker's argument fits this category of observation.

2. However, on the contrary, the historical crisis of exile kindled a hope of a future messianic deliverer whose redemptive authority would far exceed the previous monarchs and who would succeed in delivering Israel, in contrast to the failure of the Davidic precedents.

This period surrounding the fall of Jerusalem is certainly the most decisive event in the formation of apocalyptic thought.[94] The compo-

---

92. Mettinger, *In Search of God*, 158.
93. Ibid., 159.
94. Cf. Heim, "The (God-)forsaken King of Psalm 89," 304.

sition of the royal psalms which are clearly messianic in content took place about this time. This inclines favorably towards the idea that exilic/postexilic times[95] were the crucial period in which the messianic hope was more pervasive than is usually allowed.[96] This need not mean that Jewish religion prior to this historical event was averse to the idea of a messianic deliverer. Rather, the exilic/postexilic period was a time when Israel looked for the "New Exodus," and this emphasized messianic hope by drawing references from the past events in their history. T. N. D. Mettinger aptly points out that the "historical context under discussion provided double exposure for the people of Israel; the oppression imposed by Babylon and the deportation from their homeland and the subsequent liberation of Israel recalled the redemptive event of Exodus."[97] In Jewish tradition, Moses is regarded practically as the messianic deliverer and very much the central figure in the narratives of the Exodus, as he took the role of leadership in liberating Israel from the bondage of slavery.[98] The memory of the redemptive act of God in the past, which is effected by the servant Moses, helped to consolidate Israel's faith in the midst of historical crisis that God will once again faithfully deliver His people through the chosen servant and reestablish the covenant with Israel. In this vein, Motyer writes, "The Old Testament uses its own times and characteristic norms and forms as building blocks of the future reality which it foresees, much as Jesus used the ordinances of his own time in his parables of the kingdom. Within the Old Testament the 'Exodus' events provided funds of imagery and motifs regarding the future acts of God for his people."[99]

We may observe that from very early on in the history of Israel the Exodus event always included the messianic agent as the crucial element

---

95. Exilic/postexilic times need to be seen as one entity since the period in its entirety was a test for the faith of Israel in Yahweh.

96. De Vaux, *Ancient Israel*, 110. The period of the destruction of the First Temple (586 BC) is also relevant in our discussion of Matthew's Gospel, which is dated immediately after the destruction of the Second Temple by the Romans in 70 AD. The resemblance between the two historical realities is possibly the reason for the rekindling of the messianic hope among Matthew's community as it did in the exilic/postexilic times. However, during exilic/postexilic times, the messianic hope was directed towards the future, but for Matthew the messianic hope is finalized in Jesus.

97. Mettinger, *In Search of God*, 181.

98. Ibid., 161. Cf. also Holland, *Contours of Pauline Theology*.

99. Motyer, *Look to the Rock*, 37.

in the redemptive act of God. The significance of the exilic/postexilic period lies precisely in the way the messianic thought is emphasized in texts such as the royal psalms. These are picked up by the evangelist and applied to Jesus as he brings Israel's redemptive history to its decisive climax. This demonstrates Becker's argument that there was practically no trace of messianic hope in the Old Testament tradition to be a misguided perception of the history of Israel. The nation of Israel did long for divine intervention, and, as Becker argues, her faith in Yahweh's kingship probably grew more strongly than ever. However, the divine deliverance will be wrought by His chosen servant, who will assume the role of the Messiah and inaugurate the new covenant. The disappointment in the Davidic monarchy is best explained as the indignation and frustration expressed at individual kings who failed to live up to the idealized standard prescribed in the Scripture. Discarding the whole concept of the messianic deliverer and its monarchic institution would be to forfeit the core identity of Israel's historical and spiritual heritage.

The primary reason for Becker's rejection of the concept of the Messiah is due to the observation that the prominence of Yahweh's kingship leaves little or no room for the idea of messianic kingship and that the two notions are intrinsically antagonistic to each other. However, Davidic kingship and Yahweh do not stand in tension but reinforce each other in that Davidic reign is a manifestation of theocracy in action.[100] The notion of coexistence between theocracy and Davidic monarchy is well attested in Psalm 2:8. K. H. Rengstorf notes that the divine invitation "Ask of me," which is followed by the divine promise "I shall give thee," shows that the Davidic king and Yahweh's reign are seen as mutual collaboration, and it is clear that the authority of the Davidic king is derived from his privileged relationship with Yahweh.[101] This idea is not confined within the Hebrew canon, but is also expressed in the apocrypha. William Horbury notes that the messianic overtone in the texts depicts not only Israel's divine ruler, but also the earthly ruler which is a crucial element in the redemptive history of Israel. He cites Exodus as an example which is referred to in the apocryphal texts as the most significant redemptive event in Israel's history and argues that, although

---

100. Blair, "Kingship in Israel and its Implications for the Lordship of Christ Today," 70–77.

101. Rengstorf, "Old and New Testament Traces of the Formula of the Judean Royal Ritual," 229–44.

the redemptive act is wholly attributed to Yahweh, it is nevertheless affirmed that Moses as an agent of salvation assumed a crucial role in the redemptive act of Yahweh. From the very beginning of Israelite history in its archetypal form, the divine redemption always involved a human leader through whom the salvation reaches its destiny.[102] Becker's distinction between the Davidic monarchy and theocratic reign may thus be refuted, as the two are effectively merged and ultimately point toward the same goal.

However, this does not mean that a Davidic king in any way was considered divine or that his royal authority was considered equal with that of God. Such a notion would be blasphemous in Judaism. In fact the prophets relentlessly criticized individual kings for failing to live up to the idealized standard, but never do they criticize kings for claiming divinity for themselves. The Davidic king with all the great attributes given to him is merely a representative of God. This brings us to the final question of this section concerning the authority of David in relation to the Israelite notion of divinity and how this affects Matthew's unique perception of Jesus' messiahship.

It has been argued by some scholars that the idealization of David in the Psalms goes beyond human traits, and that David is portrayed as possessing power comparable to God Himself (Ps 89:6–19, 22–28). The characteristics ascribed to David in Psalm 89, for instance, resemble those ascribed to Yahweh, such as the designation of David as the "Most High" (v. 28), which leads to the conclusion that some degree of idealization of David into the realm of divinity was intended by the author. This idea may have been subsequently applied to Jesus by the New Testament writers.[103] However, any idealization of David in divine terms is incongruent with the biblical understanding of "son of David," as it is explicitly stated in Matthew 22:41–45 that the person of David is clearly subordinate to God and the deliberate placing of David under the authority of Jesus points against the notion of a Davidic king being deified. The scholars who argue in favor of the idea of a Davidic king in divine terms are likely to have been influenced by the generalized picture of king in the ancient Near Eastern context where the kings were

---

102. Horbury, "Messianism in the Old Testament Apocrypha and Pseudepigrapha," 412–13.

103. Heim, "The (God-)forsaken king of Psalm 89," 314–15; cf. also Tate, *Psalms 51–100*.

frequently ascribed divine power. Against this generalization, Roland de Vaux points out that it is not correct to say that the idea of a divine king was universally accepted by the people of the ancient Near East. No doubt the kings shared a privileged relationship with God from which their royal authorities were legitimated, but this does not mean that Israel was disposed to the idea of deified kings.[104]

The figure of David is essential in understanding Jesus' messianic kingship in connection with the Old Testament, which is the main theological concern of Matthew. In this respect, the Old Testament messianic texts, such as the royal psalms which deal with the figure of David and his descendents as the anointed Messiah for Israel's salvation, are particularly important in our discussion of Matthew's Christology. However, the evangelist explicitly places Jesus' authority above that of David (Matt 22:41–45) in conjunction with the statement above in order to demonstrate that the same God is operating consistently in the redemptive history of Israel. However, this time, the messianic king would far exceed his predecessors in his redemptive authority. The Gospel of Matthew primarily defines Jesus' messianic ministry in terms of its Davidic legacy, but it will also become clear that the evangelist wishes to portray Jesus in higher terms. It is this paradoxical aspect of Matthew's Gospel that makes it profoundly Jewish but at the same time distinctively Christian.

---

104. De Vaux, *Ancient Israel*, 112–13.

3

First-Century Jewish Christians and Their Interpretation of Scripture

PART ONE: WHY GO TO THE FIRST CENTURY?

Introduction

WE ESTABLISHED IN CHAPTER 1 that typology is the key to the overarching concept of Israel's redemptive history. Chapter 1 examined various theological themes that are prevalent in Matthew's Gospel which become intelligible only when it is placed within the framework of Israel's covenantal relationship with Yahweh and His ultimate redemptive purpose for the nation. The belief that God faithfully fulfilled the promises to Israel through Christ Jesus is the most crucial element which formed the foundation of the early Christian community as it sought to define itself within the Jewish legacy. In order to understanding Matthew and his Christology, it is important to go back to the first-century Christian understanding and seek to appreciate the historical context of the early Church and its psyche in its transitional phase of religious transformation. It is generally agreed that in order to grasp the theological purpose and emphasis which the evangelist stresses, it is crucial to have an awareness of the social and historical background in which the Gospel functioned. It is inevitable that history in one way or another has influenced and to a certain extent shaped the evangelist's understanding of Scripture, and, on the other hand, Scripture alters the way that Israel's history is perceived. In other words, historicity and theology should be viewed in a symbiotic relationship. This indicates that to gain a proper understanding of the theology of the Gospel, it is crucial to understand the history that has informed and shaped it. One of the distinct characteristics of Jewish religion is that the two dimensions of religion and political history were inextricably intertwined. In this vein, Anthony Gelston has pointed out that "it is pertinent to remember that there was a persistent tradition in Israel which thought of the secular and religious leadership as ideally in the same hands."[1] Since Matthew was Jewish in his mind-set and wrote for a Jewish audience, then it is plausible to assume that he also had this common perspective towards theology and history. This is a crucial point which we need to bear in mind as we approach the Gospel, since Matthew's message and conviction in Christ Jesus are made intelligible only within the historical context of Israel and her dealings with Yahweh. This will help us understand what the original intention of the evangelist may have been as he sought to justify the movement newly launched by Jesus and his followers, who sought to defend themselves against the accusations of its Jewish critics. The early Christians, that is, the Jewish Christians of Matthew's community, sought to maintain authenticity by insisting on the view that their ethos and spiritual principles were not aberrant from their Jewish roots. By emphasizing the continuity of the essence which is in accordance with his ancestral religion, Matthew displayed his affiliation to Judaism (Matt 10:5, 6; 15:24). By contrast, however, Matthew's Jesus condemns the Jewish authorities for failing to practice what they profess (Matt 23:1–36). Matthew's relationship with the Jewish tradition may seem paradoxical and at times contradictory if one neglects the volatile circumstances of first-century Christianity. For this reason, we need to explore the world of the early Christians and their mind-set. Matthew's use of the Old Testament is thus a literary phenomenon which should not be perceived in terms of a figurative construction of literary artifacts but essentially as spiritual and intellectual edification in the context of historical circumstances and the emerging contemporary needs.

The Jewish Character of the Early Christians.

In order to understand typology and how the New Testament authors utilized the Old Testament, we need to explore the world of the first-

---

1. Gelston "The Royal Priesthood," 152–63.

century social setting in which the Gospels were written. This is an important period for biblical theologians, one which to a large extent determines one's methodological presupposition. In other words, only when we have an appropriate understanding of the original context in which the Gospels were composed can we produce an exegesis that is sound and responsible.

There can be no doubt that in Matthew's Gospel Jesus and his followers are constantly at tension with the Jewish authorities, which may suggest that they had separated from mainstream Judaism to form a sectarian group called Christians. Consequently, their distinct and almost radical view of the Torah and their conviction that the kingdom of God was imminent are crucial factors for correctly interpreting the evangelist. Jesus and his disciples thus frequently engaged in debates which often led to conflicts. However, it must be noted that the reason for Jesus' harsh critique of the Jewish authorities was that they failed to practice what they preached and misused their power to satisfy their vainglory and pride (Matt 23:1–36). Jesus still upholds the identity which, according to E. W. Stegemann and Wolfgang Stegemann, "remained constitutively related to the central social institutions of the Israel of their time."[2] It seems that there was a fine balance between defining oneself within the Jewish tradition and at the same time repudiating its fundamental principle, which is what characterizes the social setting of the Matthean community. It seems that the dichotomy of the two entities had not fully taken place, and Matthew's community was caught in the transitional stage of rupture. Stegemann also notes that "it is evident that this eschatological, charismatic self-understanding of Jesus' followers also shaped their relationship with the institutions of Judaism and especially with Torah. Yet this is often interpreted to mean that already in the beginnings of the Jesus movement there was at least an implicit break with Judaism."[3]

The relationship between the early Christians and Judaism is somewhat paradoxical in that while their identity derives from the parent body of Judaism, their movement implies a certain level of deviance. This may be classified as the early stage of the emergence of the Jesus movement. However, as the movement progressed, under different circumstances, it developed a firmer sense of identity and self-consciousness which in

2. Stegemann and Stegemann, *The Jesus Movement*, 102.
3. Ibid., 206.

time extrapolated the Jewish context. This process must have taken place when the followers of Christ began to reach out to the non-Jewish population. As their message became increasingly missionary-oriented, they gradually detached themselves from the Jewish tradition and formulated an independent identity. However, this is the later stage of the religious and social development of the Jesus movement. For the first-century Christians, however, the distinction between Jews and Christians is not so apparent. Barry Schwartz explains the unique context of first-century Christianity by applying the theories of social memory.[4] He argues that "society changes constantly but social memory endures because new beliefs are superimposed upon—rather than replace—old ones."[5] This is in fact how the early Jewish-Christians defined themselves, as they did not seek to discard their Jewish heritage and thereby create a new religion of their own, but they continued to define their faith in Christ on the basis of their Jewish sacred text. According to the theory of social memory, one may surmise that the past memory of God's redemptive promise becomes a decisive driving force in the present reality of the early Christian setting. Even though the circumstances of the first century were evidently different from the original context in which the Old Testament texts were written, the Jewish ethos more or less maintained its relevance. Therefore, the memory of the past redemptive activity of God became a decisive element in the formation of early Christian identity, as the past memory was reinterpreted to "serve new power distributions, institutional structures, values, interests and needs."[6] This is demonstrated by the synoptic writers, who take it for granted that Jesus and his followers should attend synagogue on the Sabbath (Matt 4:23; 12:9–14; cf. also Mark 1:21, 39; 3:1; 6:2; Luke 4:15–16); the same is true of John, who records that Jesus celebrated the major Jewish festivals such as Passover, the Festival of Booths, and the Festival of Dedication (John 2:23; 5;1; 7:2–11; 10:22). Nowhere does Jesus deny the fundamental ethos of the Jewish religion and challenge Israel's status as God's elect.[7] Jesus' stance toward the law and the prophets makes it clear that

---

4. Schwartz, "Christian Origins," 44, 46, 53.

5. Ibid., 44.

6. Ibid.

7. Stegemann and Stegemann, *The Jesus Movement*, 208, write that "it is true that there are provocative arguments with the witness of Gentiles in the judgment, the participation of Gentiles in the Kingdom of God, and the exclusion of the 'sons of the

he affirmatively accepts the authority of the Torah (Matt 5:17–20; cf. Mark 12:28–34). However, as the early Christians began to evangelize the Gentiles, who presumably had very limited knowledge of Judaism, it became inevitable and indeed necessary that their image as an independent religious movement had to be clearly delineated. This is when they began to withdraw from formative Judaism into a separate religious entity.[8]

This naturally directs our attention to the Old Testament in our study of Matthew's Gospel. The first-century Christian use of the Old Testament, therefore, is the starting point in understanding the New Testament authors' view of the Christ. There are, however, scholars who rely on extracanonical sources to illumine their analysis of Gospel compositions. For instance, Bridget Gilfillan-Upton[9] employs a methodology of comparing Mark's Gospel with the Greek novel *Ephesiaca* in her examination of the first-century Christian writings that were fostered by Hellenistic culture. But such methodology is highly problematic, since

---

Kingdom,' as well as the exemplary faith of a non-Jew. This presupposes, nonetheless, the election of Israel. There is no programmatic turning of Jesus' attention toward non-Jews."

8. Ibid., 225. Also, the followers of Jesus would have been rejected outright by mainstream Judaism, which subsequently compelled them to create their distinct and independent religious identity. We discussed in chapter 2 the date of the composition of Matthew's Gospel, and it was presupposed that it is most likely to have been composed around 70 AD. Stegemann and Stegemann also date the Gospel to approximately the same date. With regard to the historical circumstances of 70 AD, they make the following observation: "The consequences of the first great war of the Jews against Rome were extremely far-reaching and can hardly be overestimated in their importance for the further history of Judaism. For Judaism in the land of Israel they meant crucial political, social and economic changes, but also lasting changes in the religious praxis from earlier eras." The destruction of the Second Temple meant that the Israelite sacrificial cult was brought to an end. This would have a profound impact on the office of the High Priest which was usurped by the pagan oppressors. Stegemann and Stegemann argue that "the composition of the Gospels of Matthew and John must be understood against the background of this conflict with the newly reoriented Judaism of the time after 70."

9. Gilfillan-Upton, *Hearing Mark's Ending*. In terms of her methodological approach, the only merit is her attempt to reemphasize the fact that the Jesus movement transported their traditions initially in oral form, and written traditions appear only after the movement was institutionalized. This will generate further methodological implications in the way one interprets the text, which was originally designed to be read aloud rather than silently. Holland, *Contours of Pauline Theology*, would highlight that such a form of delivery suggests it was read to the gathered congregation and was written with a corporate setting in mind. Its application is therefore to the church directly rather than individual believers.

the two writings differ in terms of their literary genre and historical purpose and were written for entirely different audiences. We should rather accept that the synoptic authors, although undoubtedly influenced in some ways by the surrounding Hellenistic culture, nevertheless regarded themselves as Jewish. Especially in the discussion of Matthew's Gospel, it will become clearer that various motifs, such as the New Exodus and the messianic expectation, cannot possibly be understood in isolation from the Old Testament. A point for further discussion is whether the other New Testament authors would have deviated from this fundamental principle to an extent that the readers of the New Testament are encouraged to draw parallels from the Hellenistic texts for clarification. We believe that this is highly unlikely in the face of the overwhelming evidence, which this volume seeks to demonstrate, that it is generally impossible to deny the Jewish mind-set of the New Testament writers.

The significance of the early Christian setting as the starting point for the analysis of the use of the Old Testament in the New is precisely the fact that this period offers insight into the historical setting which conditions the mind-set of the New Testament writers. As the Jewish religion always had a tendency to refer to the past redemptive event in revitalizing Israel's faith in Yahweh, the early Jewish-Christians, in the midst of oppression and conflict, looked to the promises of God that were originally made to Israel. This gave them a particular understanding of promises which they believed to have been fulfilled in Christ Jesus.[10] The revisitation of that past by Jewish Gospel writers is thus an act of re-validation of the history of Israel and of God's redemptive activity manifested in the Old Testament. It is necessary, therefore, to redirect our attention from the assumption proposed by the likes of Gilfillan-Upton to a more plausible theory that the early Christians sought to combat their opponents by validating the authenticity of the Old Testament and the redemptive history of Israel as the central theme. The primary source for the investigation of any New Testament text need not be documents derived outside the canon, but the Old Testament in which the Jewish tradition is rooted.

---

10. Schroter, cited in Kirk and Thatcher, eds., *Memory, Tradition, and Text*, 39.

PART TWO: SOCIAL SETTING OF MATTHEW'S COMMUNITY

Date of Composition

The general trend in contemporary scholarship is to assume Markan priority. Matthew is considered to have reworked the Markan material and expanded it according to his own theological concerns with the help of oral tradition that was available to him from the "Q Source."[11] According to R. T. France, Mark was composed sometime around 65 AD,[12] before the destruction of the Second Temple by the Romans and perhaps even before the Jewish revolt—or during the heat of an incipient tension between Israel and the Roman authorities. Jesus' prediction of the fall of Jerusalem in fact occurs in each of the Synoptic Gospels, but is more emphatically stressed in Matthew, which suggests that the Gospel was composed subsequent to the temple's destruction in 70 AD.[13] Against this late dating, R. T. France argues that the style of the language used in the Gospel is very much future-oriented, and as an example, he draws a passage from the parable of the wedding garment (22:1–14), which he believes to be a genuine prediction of political annihilation in the Jewish context which does not depend on specific knowledge of what in fact occurred in 70 AD.[14] He thus postulates that due to the entirely forward-looking nature of all of the references to the destruction of Jerusalem, the Gospel is more likely to have been composed before the event rather than after it.[15] However, it is not entirely convincing that the references to the political destruction of Israel are as forward-looking in nature as France argues. In fact, the parable of the wedding garment seems to portray a king who has initially displayed his generosity by inviting people to come to his feast, and the subsequent refusal causes the king to become enraged. It seems that the references to the destruction and burning of their city (Matt 22:8) and the final statement in verse 14 point to the definitive end rather than alluding to some distant future.

---

11. Hill, *The Gospel of Matthew*, 24–30, writes that it is best to speak of Q material (i.e., material found both in Matthew and Luke) as a common layer of tradition. Note that N. T. Wright challenges the existence of this Q source. Cf. Wright, *The New Testament and the People of God*.

12. France, *Matthew*, 83.

13. Ibid.

14. Ibid., 84.

15. Ibid., 88.

Moreover, the early dating of the composition of the Gospel does not fully explain the hostility between the community of Matthew and the Jewish authorities evident in the extreme anti-Jewish polemic of Matthew 27:25, which is better explained if the dating of the Gospel is put immediately after the destruction of the Second Temple, which would have undoubtedly intensified the struggle between Matthew's community and the Jewish authorities as they underwent the painful process of a final break from each other. Presumably, the tension between them would have gone from bad to worse, and the Jewish Christians would have been blamed for the disaster.

In conjunction with this assumption, Schuyler Brown also presupposes that "although both Mark 13 and Matthew 24–25 have a great deal to do with the Jewish War (AD 66) and the destruction of the temple (AD 70), Mark 13 was probably composed before these crucial events, whereas Matthew 24–25 are generally thought to have been composed afterwards."[16] According to Brown, Matthew could afford to be more explicit and definitive in his apocalyptic discourse than Mark because the Jewish War which the evangelist identified with the end of the world was a historical certainty. Brown further notes, "From Matthew's historical vantage point these verses are fulfilled prophecies, but he passes them on to his community as proof of the unshakable authority of Jesus' words (24:35)."[17]

This reinforces the view that the Gospel was composed after the Jewish War and that the author had full knowledge of the destruction of the Second Temple by the Romans. However, it must be noted that exact dating of the composition of the Gospel is impossible due to the lack of empirical evidence, and so scholars continue to debate this issue, which is by nature speculative. However, if we are to allocate a possible date for the composition of the Gospel, a dating immediately after the destruction of the Second Temple by the Romans, possibly AD 72–75, seems the most plausible assumption, since this was a period when the tension between the Jewish community and the Jewish-Christian community would have been at its worst before the eventual schism.

---

16. Brown, "The Matthean Apocalypse," 3, 5–6, also notes that "the intensity of the evangelist's hostility to the scribes and Pharisees suggests rather that persecution was a present reality for Matthew's readers and not simply a piece of past history."

17. Ibid., 8.

Offense and Defense

We have thus far witnessed Matthew's thorough knowledge of the Old Testament and his adherence to the Jewish tradition, as he advanced the claim that Jesus fulfills the prophecies of the Old Testament as the long-awaited Davidic Messiah. With regard to the Jewish nature of the Gospel, scholars have proposed the view that the Gospel fundamentally aims at the evangelization of the Jews. The new followers of Christ would continually have had unbelieving members of the synagogue debating with them in an attempt to persuade them to return to Judaism. Thus, the Gospel was written to enable them to demonstrate Jesus' legitimacy and possibly to win converts to their movement. Along this line of thought, D. R. Bauer and M. A. Powell suggest that in the context of incipient schism between the followers of Christ and the parent Jewish body, it is very unlikely, both psychologically and theologically, that the community of Matthew would have altogether forfeited the mission to their unbelieving Jewish members.[18] Rather, Matthew retained the mission and saw the redemptive ministry of Jesus primarily in the context of the Jewish evangelization.

Bauer and Powell note that the community of Matthew was, on the one hand, constantly at tension with their non-believing Jewish kinsfolk (from whom they were experiencing painful rupture), and, on the other, they had to cope with a Christian body populated largely by Gentiles and embrace them as their own. The fulfillment themes and formula quotations were functional tools which Matthew's Jewish Christians utilized in affirming that they were at home with the Jewish faith, thereby defending themselves against charges of disloyalty to the religion of Israel.

With regard to Gentile Christians, the community of Matthew was under subtle pressure to minimize their Jewish outlook (this is possibly displayed in the aforementioned anti-Jewish polemic against those who rejected their own Messiah), as their adherence to the Law and customs could easily cause a theological problem for those who presumably did not possess a thorough knowledge of the Old Testament and might impede the process of solidarity in the community.[19]

Concerning the social setting of Matthew, David Hill has stated that "the Jewish Christianity evidenced by the Gospel is a Christianity which

---

18. Bauer and Powell, eds., *Treasures New and Old*, 43.
19. Ibid., 46.

has just severed connection with the Jewish communities, but which expresses itself in forms and categories borrowed from Judaism."[20] It may be added that, for Matthew, the designation "Christianity" is premature, as the evangelist defines his community in the context of Jewish religion by adherence to the Law (5:17–20; cf. also 5:27ff.) and specific religious issues, such as fasting (6:16–18), the Sabbath (12:1–14; 24:20), temple offerings (5:23–24), and the temple tax (17:24–27),[21] which supports the idea that Matthew and his community regarded themselves to be within the boundary of Judaism.[22] The community is in the transitional stage of bitter separation, so on the one hand expresses concern (cf. 10:5ff.) for their Jewish brothers and sisters, but on the other hand shows extreme frustration in the form of polemic at their obdurate attitude.[23] A demarcation between Christianity and Judaism at this stage is thus anachronistic; rather, Christianity is still in the transitional stage of evolving to become an independent religious entity. Hill's statement that Christians "borrowed" religious elements from Judaism is therefore not an accurate description of the socioreligious setting of Matthew's community, who regarded themselves as the true remnant of Israel.

With regard to Matthew's apparent contradictory attitudes to Judaism, it is often surmised that a relatively conservative Jewish-Christian body of tradition has been worked over by a later Gentile writer, who saw any attachment to official Judaism as obsolete, explaining away

---

20. Hill, *The Gospel of Matthew*, 41. Cf. also Daniélou, *Theology of Jewish Christianity*, 7–11.

21. France, *Matthew*, 18.

22. Barth, "Matthew's Understanding of the Law," 159, 160, 164, argues that Matthew's adherence to the Jewish law indicates that the evangelist is protesting against the antinominians depicted as false prophets (Matt 5:17ff.; 7:15ff.; 24:11f.). He notes that "the enemies against whom Matthew fought have been regarded as a Pauline group." For Paul, Christ is the end of the Law (Rom 10:4), whereas Matthew's Jesus claims that he has come to fulfill the Law. This marked difference in attitude towards the Law has led Barth to conclude that "Matthew opposes a group who appeal in support of their libertinism to the fact that Christ has abolished the law; these opponents rely on their 'charismata,' their spiritual gifts. The constant exhortation to do God's will, to yield fruit, and the threat of judgment according to works have clear significance in Matthew."

23. The most extreme anti-Jewish polemic is the passage 27:24–25, which is found in the passion narrative at the trial of Jesus before Pilate, where the terrible cry of the Jewish people makes it clear that Israel as a nation has rejected Jesus and is responsible for his death. France notes the use of the term *laos* (people), which is used particularly for Israel in its privileged status rather than the term *ochloi* (crowds).

the religious conservatism and adherence to the Law, which is now presented along with the editor's outright animosity against non-believing Jewish counterparts (cf. Matt. 23:30, 35; 27:25).[24] First, assuming Gentile authorship solely on the basis of the hostile polemic directed against the Jewish community is failing to appreciate the extremely volatile social circumstances after the destruction of the Second Temple. The tension between Jewish Christians and Jews, intensified by the war, resulted in the former's fierce resentment of official Judaism and their immutable attitude to the acceptance of Jesus as their Messiah, and this led to the abrupt change of the evangelist's initial affiliation with Judaism and his concern for Israel into outright denunciation and bitter resentment. Furthermore, if the final completion of the composition of the Gospel is attributed to a subsequent Gentile author who apparently regarded any sort of connection with official Judaism as fundamentally incompatible and contagious, why present both accounts of Jewish favoritism and anti-Jewish polemic? Such a presentation would be illogical and haphazard. The textual evidence, in the light of theological analysis and some consideration of its social setting, is much more likely to point toward the idea of a Jewish author who initially expresses concern for his non-believing Jewish counterparts, but as his program of Jewish evangelization proves to be unsuccessful, he expands the kingdom to the Gentiles. In the context of such a "love-hate" relationship of Matthew's community with its parent body, and especially after the event of 70 AD, the tension subsequently became worse. The mutual indignation and belligerence between the two parties which evolved out of this historical context, therefore, account for the change of perspective inherent in the Gospel of Matthew.

However, this need not mean that Israel is completely obliterated from salvation history. The Gentiles included in the New People do not usurp Israel's privileged position, with Israel consigned eternally to the pit of darkness, but the Gentiles are the newly extended Israel in the age-old purpose of God's redemptive plan that fulfills Israel's destiny.

---

24. France, *Matthew*, 95. France presents this line of argument prevalent among certain scholars and offers a critique of his own. Here, I have used France's list and endeavored to give my own critique. The official form of Judaism at this date was likely Pharisaic, since the Sadducees' power base was the temple. It has been argued that the destruction of the temple had taken place when Matthew's Gospel was written, and therefore Pharisaic Judaism must have been the official form, as Pharisaic Judaism is synagogue-based.

It is the new covenant community which replaces Israel in which there are both believing Jews and Gentiles. G. N. Stanton has offered a useful parallel in his article "5 Ezra and Matthean Christianity in the Second Century," where Matthean paradox is exhibited in a Jewish-Christian environment, which reveals that this second-century Jewish-Christian tract developed the theme of the rejection of Israel which is replaced by "a new people to come." Stanton notes that this "coming people" is essentially in continuity with the Israel of the Old Testament, and in those people Israel's holy destiny reaches its culmination.[25] In other words, God's promise to Israel still remains intact, but being the true remnant of Israel does not necessarily entail ethnic origin from the nation, as John the Baptist warns in Matthew 3:9, but in repentance of sin and acceptance of her Messiah Jesus Christ. It is this paradoxical nature of Matthew's attitude towards the Jewish faith, that is, his dependence on the Jewish heritage but at the same time his Christological innovation, that must be grasped if a sound biblical exegesis is to take place. The diagram below illustrates this aspect of Matthew's attitude towards the ancestral religion.

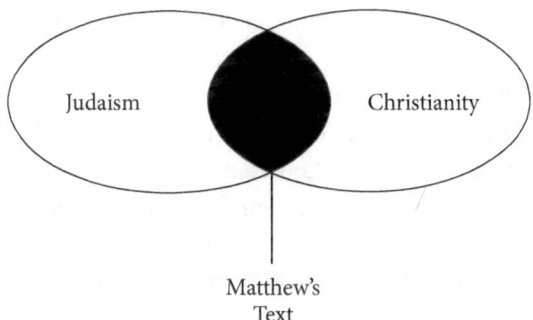

The above diagram recapitulates the social setting of the Gospel argued for thus far. Note that the dichotomy between the two circles representing both parties has not been completed but is at the transitional

---

25. Stanton, cited in France, *Matthew*, 104, 105, as an example supporting the view of Jewish authorship in contrast to the Gentile one. France adds on the basis of Stanton's observation that if an undeniably Jewish-Christian document can exhibit these characteristics, namely, the rejection of Israel and the introduction of the Gentiles to salvation—they constitute the new people of God—then it is not only necessary but also unlikely to assume that Matthew's Gospel must come from a Gentile author.

state of rupture. Therefore any tension, however harsh it may be, is to be seen as internecine strife rather than as two opponents confronting each other. The concept of a new phenomenon such as "Christianity" is clearly emerging, but its form is rudimentary; this places Matthew's Gospel in the region of overlap which contains traits common to both Judaism and Christianity. Hence, the description of Matthew's community as "Christian" is a misnomer at this stage, so the designation "Jewish Christian" is more appropriate.

The major opponents against whom the polemic is directed are the Pharisees and the Sadducees, who are sometimes grouped together with the scribes. Scholars often point out that Matthew appears to have mistakenly grouped the two Jewish parties together without realizing that they possessed a fundamentally different theological ethos and at times were involved in confrontational debate. However, it is highly doubtful that Matthew, who is evidently well acquainted with Jewish religion, was oblivious to this rather plain factual detail of his time. Rather, a more likely reason for the grouping of the two parties in the same category is that, regardless of their differences in theology, they are enemies of Christ, and both were clearly antagonistic to his message. It is in this respect that they were viewed homogeneously by the evangelist.

However, Noel S. Rabbinowitz argues that "Jesus does affirm the authority of the Pharisees and that for this reason he endorses their exposition of the Torah and their halakic teachings in principle."[26] According to Rabbinowitz, although Matthew is unrelenting in his criticism of the Pharisees for their hypocrisy and their failure to recognize Jesus as their Messiah, he never criticizes them for teaching the Law (cf. Deut 17:11).[27] This suggests that Matthew was not intending to present Jesus as a teacher who offered a radically innovative interpretation of the Torah; Matthew saw himself and the community to be within the broad spectrum of Judaism. On the basis of this evidence, Rabbinowitz contends that Jesus maintained a positive relationship with traditional halakah.[28] He also argues that far from repealing Jewish ordinances, Matthew displays a strong observance of the Law, and the Pharisees are condemned precisely because of their failure to practice what they profess and because they are more concerned with their ostensible religiosity than with

26. Rabbinowitz, "Matthew 23:2–4," 423–47.
27. Ibid., 434–35.
28. Ibid., 436.

keeping the actual content of the Law (Matt 15:1–4). Matthew does not denounce the authority of the Pharisees (Matt 23:2–4), but condemns them precisely for failing to practice what they preach (Matt 23:23).

The argument presented by Rabbinowitz is plausible in that it directs our attention to the Old Testament in the understanding of Matthew's Jesus and the state of "Christianity" which matches history. Matthew conveys his theological notions in accordance with Jewish Scripture, but he sees in Jesus something greater than the Law and "greater than the temple" (cf. Matt 12:1–14). For Matthew, therefore, halakah is meaningful only in the context of Jesus—whose authority is above halakah and in whom the Jewish Scripture reaches its fulfillment—and his ministry.

Sectarianism

G. N. Stanton's theory of "social conflict, boundaries and dissent"[29] aptly describes the social context in which Matthew's community is confronted by opposing groups. In this respect, Matthew's community is confronted by two antagonistic forces. Stanton points out that "in Matthew, there is strong condemnation of unfaithful members of the (internal) community; their rejection and judgment is referred to in several passages."[30] To support his view, Stanton draws on Matthew 24:51, where it is stressed that unfaithful "Christians" will equally share judgment with the hypocrites (i.e., the scribes). In conjunction with this apocalyptic worldview, Gunther Bornkamm states, "It would be difficult to maintain that the description of the judgment of the world, the whole construction of the discourse concludes, refers only to the judgment that is to come upon the Gentiles in distinction from the members of the community of Jesus. Rather it is typical for the end-expectation of Matthew that by means of a great picture already current among the Jews the judgment is announced as applying to 'all nations,' but now in such a way that no distinction is made between Jews and Gentiles, nor even between believers and unbelievers."[31]

On the basis of this observation it seems that the sectarian worldview in Matthew is not necessarily inclusive of Christians but that the nature of the apocalyptic thinking inherent in the Gospel applies even to

---

29. Stanton, *A Gospel for a New People*, 102.
30. Ibid.
31. Bornkamm, "End-Expectation and Church in Matthew," 23.

the Christians. Considering Matthew's acknowledgement of the validity of the Jewish Law and its importance, even though the tension with the Jewish authorities was evident, it can be deduced that the internal enemies referred to in the Gospel are not so much the apostates who are looking to abandon the faith altogether, but the Christian antinomian heretics who felt that faith and grace alone were sufficient to gain salvation without attributing value to the Law.[32] As we have seen thus far, Jewish Christianity, despite its "newness," still possesses characteristics in common with Judaism, and Matthew's community was not ready to accept any radical separation from its parent body or the perception of the Law as obsolete.

Stanton reasons that in such historical affliction and alienation from both external and internal worlds, the Jewish Christians naturally turned to apocalypticism.[33] In fact, the effectiveness of the polemic against the Jewish authorities is enhanced in the context of apocalyptic discourse, as the central content of the polemical treatise in Matthew is criticism of the unfaithful in the light of imminent judgment. In support of this view, Stanton points to the structure of Matthew's Gospel, where a seemingly incongruent sequence—chapter 23 (seven woes directed against the scribes) in correlation with chapter 24 (signs of the end of the age) and 25 (the parable of the ten virgins)—is in fact consistent, as both polemic and apocalyptic revelations are natural responses of a minority community experiencing alienation and rejection from the world at large.[34]

For Matthew and his community, such apocalyptic conviction was not some imaginative metaphor created to provide unrealistic hope or to alleviate distress, but a palpable reality in the wake of the trauma of AD 70, which would have been regarded as a divine demonstration of the end time. The judgment was visibly at hand, which would have reinforced the meaning and the force of apocalyptic writings and the worldview of the community, namely, that they were the exclusively elected remnant of Israel and that God would judge the nations on the basis of their treatment of His people.[35] These are a few of the most salient features of the so-called sectarian community. Theologians who employ

---

32. Ibid., 47.
33. Stanton, *A Gospel for a New People*, 162.
34. Ibid., 165.
35. Ibid., 224.

the social-scientific method to determine the social setting of the New Testament community[36] have constructed the model of "sectarianism" in order to comprehend the social issues in the early church. The following features aptly summarize the description of Matthew's community argued thus far: "Their (sectarian community) emergence under conditions of social tension and conflict; their initial stage as a protest group within a larger corporate entity; their gradual marginalization and their dissociation from their original body . . . their experience of social disapproval, harassment, and pressures urging conformity; their conception of themselves as an elect and elite community favored with special grace and revelation; a separatist response toward all 'outsiders'; and further related strategies for asserting their collective identity, assuring internal social cohesion and maintaining ideological commitment."[37]

This is not the place to go into a discussion of social-scientific criticism as biblical hermeneutics, but the analysis of a sectarian community and its typical features outlined above is useful for understanding the social setting of Matthew's community and his use of apocalyptic language. It is in this social context where longing for the messianic deliverer became fervent, and apocalyptic language helped to reinforce the truth about Jesus as the long-awaited Davidic King who would save his people from darkness. Everet Ferguson has stated that "in apocalypticism the future represents a radical break for there is pessimism about history and God must intervene from without and bring history to an end."[38] The origin of apocalyptic writings in the context of a sectarian community where oppression and alienation are prevalent functioned

---

36. Cf. Horrell, *Social-Scientific Interpretation of the New Testament*. Cf. also Elliot, *A Home for the Homeless*.

37. Elliot, *A Home for the Homeless*, 351. Cf. also Stegemann and Stegemann, *The Jesus Movement*, 245, who employ the "deviance theories" in understanding the process of the separation of messianic groups in the mainstream Jewish context. They also attempt a sociological interpretation of conflicts between Jews and followers of Christ by using "conflict theory," which helps to reveal that the early Christians still regarded themselves as within the Jewish religion. On the basis of this they argue that "the closer the relations of the groups are, the more intensive is the conflict; conflicts serve the definition and reinforcement of group structures" (356). This is reflected in the extremely polemical manner in which the Pharisees and the Sadducees are portrayed in Matthew's Gospel.

38. Ferguson, *Backgrounds of Early Christianity*, 448.

as a source of hope and encouragement, for God would soon intervene and deliver His people.[39]

PART THREE: THE ACT OF QUOTATION

Typology in the Early Christian Context

It should be noted that the evangelist's use of the Old Testament is embedded in the historical context of the first century. When we have a clear grasp of the contemporary setting of Matthew's community we can better understand the motifs of the evangelist in his use of the Old Testament as he justifies his Christological claims.

Let us now turn to the mechanism of the act of quoting which remains to be explored. Usually, the analysis is conducted within the boundaries of the literary dimension of the text, but it has been argued that the intended effect of these literary artifacts had a specific purpose in their contemporary historical circumstances. It is easy to think that the New Testament passages with explicit quotations should receive priority in the discussion, but studies of the use of the Old Testament in the New and its mechanisms suggest that the usage is wider than direct literal quotations. To limit oneself to the discussion of explicit quotations hardly explains how the writers of the New Testament understood the theology of the Old and the ways in which they appropriated these existing materials in order to assert and reinforce their beliefs in Christ Jesus. This limitation, according to Stanley E. Porter, may be justifiable if one simply wishes to discuss passages introduced by quotation formulas as literary artifacts, but this is different from discussing the subject of New Testament writers' use of the Old Testament in their unique historical setting.[40] The latter has much more profound implications and far-reaching consequences. However, a study of intertextuality needs to be narrowed down and specified, as the task of ascertaining how each writer

---

39. Ibid., 449. Against the view of sectarianism, Gunther Bornkamm argues that the divine judgment is not confined to the Gentiles and the people outside the community of Christ but is applicable to all nations in such a way that no distinction is made between believers and unbelievers. See Bornkamm, Barth, and Held, *Tradition and Interpretation in Matthew*, 23. While Bornkamm's universalistic argument has some degree of plausibility, Matthew's perception of salvation is derived from the belief that only the faithful followers of Christ have the prerogative and represent the legitimate remnant of Israel.

40. Porter, "The Use of the Old Testament in the New Testament," 89, 92.

of the New Testament viewed a certain passage would be overwhelming. This volume has capacity only for dealing with the key Christological passages of Matthew's Gospel and its use of the Old Testament not in its entirety but only of certain types of psalms. Therefore, we are attempting a discussion of a particular kind of use of the Old Testament text and how the material is refined and appropriated schematically in order to present Jesus as the messianic culmination of Israel's redemptive history. This presupposition naturally entails analyzing the specific uses of psalmic language and reconstructing the sociohistorical setting of the early Christian community in which they utilized their Jewish texts. We are attempting to discover how certain types of Psalms were perceived and used by the early Christians in their message concerning Christ Jesus. For this reason, literary analysis of the text needs to be firmly placed within its historical context, as both approaches are valid and necessary, although literary analysis seems to be the primary objective if one is attempting to understand the use of the Old Testament within the written corpus of Christian texts.[41]

It should nevertheless be noted that the Greco-Roman world during the first century was fundamentally an oral culture. This means that the texts as we now have them were not originally designed to be read silently but to be read out aloud for a listening audience. In an oral environment, a particular saying may be exaggerated or played down according to the mood of a speaker and of an audience in a particular situation and at a particular period of time. This is not to say that these sayings were prone to inadvertent distortions of the original meaning, but a speaker might expound a particular idea and offer interpretive insight to give the audience a deeper understanding of the Scripture.[42] Christopher D. Stanley refers to this liberal process of quotation in the new rhetorical context as a "controlled freedom of textual variation," which can be witnessed in the manuscript tradition of antiquity.[43]

To what extent the quoted passages may undergo changes from their original meaning and context is an important question at this point.[44] The primary function of the quotations in the biblical framework

---

41. Ibid., 95–96.

42. Stanley, "The Social Environment of 'Free' Biblical Quotations in the New Testament," 18–20.

43. Ibid., 25.

44. Ibid. See also Stanley, "The Rhetoric of Quotations," 44.

is to legitimize the new message by claiming the historical legacy of the archetypal form of its religious corpus so that it can assert authority and authenticity in its innovative beliefs and thoughts. In the process, it becomes inevitable that a quoted passage becomes qualitatively different from the original context of meaning. Meir Sternberg has noted that "however accurate the wording of the quotation and however pure the quoter's motives, tearing a piece of discourse from its original habitat and reconstructing it within a new network of relations cannot but interfere with its effect."[45]

When a word or a phrase is taken out of its original context in order to be quoted in a different habitat, a shift in meaning inevitably takes place. However, this does not mean that the newly constructed meaning usurps the original voice. The original meaning is not engulfed by the new phenomenon but, rather, a quotation produces "expressive repatterning."[46] S. V. McCasland, in "Matthew Twists the Scriptures," examines precisely this aspect of the evangelist's use of the Jewish Scripture. He uses the genealogical accounts in Matthew and Luke and demonstrates how Matthew freely adapts the material to achieve a unique theological perspective. He notes that the genealogy of Jesus in Matthew 1:1–17 is divided into three main sections, each containing fourteen generations, which gives a total of forty-two generations from Abraham to Christ Jesus. On the other hand, Luke's genealogy covering the same period (Luke 3:23–34) contains fifty-six generations. It is evident that Matthew omitted Ahazah, Joash, Amaziah, and Jehoiakim from the royal lineage of Judah (Matt 1:8, 11; 1 Chr 3:11–15) to obtain fourteen generations in the first division. McCasland also notes that "to get fourteen in the second and also the third, Matthew counted Jeconiah in both groups."[47] The difference in the presentation of the historical background of Jesus may be attributed to Matthew's theological emphasis on the Davidic legacy of Jesus. It is frequently presumed that the number fourteen is a Gematria of the name of David in Hebrew and that the number three in the division of the genealogical structure signifies the completeness of Israel's redemptive history, which reaches its fulfillment in Jesus who is the Son

---

45. Sternberg, "Proteus in Quotation-Land," cited in Stanley, 50, 51.

46. Ibid., 52.

47. McCasland, "Matthew Twists the Scriptures," 143–48, on the basis of Markan priority, also notes that "Matthew's account of the triumphal entry of Jesus into Jerusalem (21:1–11) radically changes Mark (11:1–11)."

of David. This is congruently implemented throughout the entire narrative where Jesus is presented as Israel's long-awaited Davidic Messiah.[48] Through the process of quotation the significance of the prototype event is revisited and indeed revitalized. By appropriating the old material and reinterpreting it in the light of newly emerging circumstances and needs, the meaning of the earlier event is reinforced in the context of the present which, in effect, sustains the validity of the original context of meaning in a creative tension between the old and the new.

This further leads to a presupposition that the evangelist was well acquainted with knowledge of the Jewish Scripture. When he quotes a passage from Psalms, for instance, he does so with full knowledge of its original context and meaning. Since the Gospel was primarily designed for a Jewish audience, Matthew would assume that his readers would recognize the source being quoted, even if the original wording had been slightly modified.[49] Against this view, F. V. Filson suggests "that the early Christians, who knew the Psalms and heard them sung, had a partial understanding of the nature of Hebrew poetry and composed Greek hymns which imitated it, but without mastery of its technique." This understanding completely fails to grasp the principle that overrides the use of the Old Testament text by Matthew and the first-century social setting which fostered the writing of the Gospel. Matthew was a faithful Jew who had a thorough understanding of the Jewish religious texts and used them creatively in delivering his Christological message without compromising the essence of the original meaning of the Old Testament text. Even though he lived in a Hellenistic environment, his mind-set was not diluted by the dominant culture.

This plain fact is also overlooked by scholars such as Gilfillan-Upton and Tolbert, who seem to assume rather naively that Jews in the Diaspora in the first century would have been thoroughly Hellenized due to the dominant surrounding culture. These scholars are so convinced of this that they regard any attempt to separate Jewish and Hellenistic strands in early Christianity to be futile, as the Gospels would have been intrinsically influenced by Hellenistic culture.[50] Gilfillan-Upton follows Tolbert's methodological assumption that the apparent similarity between the audiences of the ancient Greek novels and the Gospels leads

---

48. The genealogical account of Matthew is discussed in detail in chapter 5.
49. Cf. Filson, "How Much of the New Testament Is Poetry?" 132–33.
50. Tolbert, cited in Gilfillan-Upton, *Hearing Mark's Endings*, 11.

to comparing and contrasting these texts as a point of departure for an understanding of biblical texts as popular literature in the Greco-Roman world.[51]

There are two fundamental problems with this methodological presupposition. First, the assumption that living in a foreign culture would intrinsically alter the Jewish mentality and religious character implies that the Jews either consciously or unconsciously abandoned their historical heritage. But this is far from what we see through Matthew's use of the Jewish Scripture and how he insists on emphasizing the importance of the Jewish historical legacy in his presentation of Jesus' identity and his ministry. All New Testament writers, to varying degrees, seek to support their theology on the basis of the Jewish ancestral religion.[52] Incidentally, this is not unique to the world of the ancient Near East. In our modern contemporary world, especially in the cosmopolitan cities of Western civilization, one commonly observes that minority cultures (often thoroughly acquainted with Western culture) in closely bonded communities have their special ways of celebrating their own distinct cultural or religious festivals, thus preserving their own traditions and national identity. Even though they may be thoroughly integrated into the culture of a foreign nation, the roots of their identity are not so easily forgotten. This is more likely to have been the case with Jews in the Diaspora. When one considers the history of Israel in its entirety, one sees that the Israelites suffered a series of foreign invasions and deportations from their own homeland. However, they were able to preserve their religious tradition and national identity through their faith in Yahweh and His deliverance. Despite the turbulent nature of their history, the pivotal aspect of their Jewishness was never compromised. This further indicates that any scholarly attempt to gain interpretive insight into the Gospel by drawing inferences from foreign texts other than the Old Testament undermines the unique character of the early Christian texts.

Secondly, the assumption that there is an apparent similarity between the audience of the ancient Greek novels and the Gospels fails to appreciate the social setting of the early Christian community. Matthew's

---

51. Ibid., 16–17.

52. See also Holland, *Contours of Pauline Theology*. He argues persuasively that Paul relied entirely on the Old Testament in his Christological message as a "Jewish" theologian.

Gospel in its historical setting had a specific purpose and was intended for a specific audience. It was written primarily for Jewish Christians caught in the transitional stage of rupture from the Jewish community. The literary structure of the Gospel is designed for the purposes of evangelizing Jewish counterparts and embracing Gentiles. It is clear that the early Christian texts had a definite goal and were not composed simply for the entertainment of the general public, whereas the ancient Greek novels B. Gilfillan-Upton refers to were intended to entertain. The overwhelming evidence indicates that the debate of the Jewish mind-set versus the Hellenistic influence is becoming outdated, as the New Testament texts clearly direct our attention to the Old Testament tradition.

Matthew's Use of Old Testament Themes

Literary analysis is an essential tool in deciphering the use of Old Testament quotations and allusions in the Gospel narratives, but it must be stressed that these texts are not literary artifacts but texts written to appeal to specific historical circumstances.[53] Matthew's concern, just like other New Testament writers, is historical rather than purely expository. The evangelist's interpretation of Scripture, therefore, is not a commentary for the purpose of literary exposition of the religious text but a historical interpretation of the contemporary setting and the Messiah's work in the light of the sacred past.[54]

Exodus Theme

It has been argued that the use of Old Testament quotations by the early Christians had a historical interest in that the old passages have been interpolated into a new, emerging context in a way which preserves the original meaning, but at the same time appropriated to fit the contemporary setting in the light of the Christ event. By quoting the Old Testament, the early Christian writers revisited the historical past of Israel, which not only reaffirmed its ancestral faith but also witnessed that it was taking a new turn. The imagery of Exodus, the prototype redemptive activity of Yahweh in the history of Israel, is particularly relevant in our discussion of Matthew's use of the Old Testament because the word *Egypt* is found only in Matthew's Gospel within the synoptic tradition (Matt 2:13, 14,

---

53. Kelber, "The Works of Memory," 242.
54. See also Goldingay, *Approaches to Old Testament Interpretation*, 152.

15, 19). This supports the view that the evangelist fitted and interpreted the life of Jesus within the context of the redemptive history of Israel. This will be examined in more detail in chapter 4.

In fact, the theme is also strongly emphasized by Paul, who utilizes the pattern of the redemptive activity of Yahweh displayed in the prototype Exodus event as the paradigm for the New Exodus event manifested in Jesus.[55] Paul's use of the motif is interesting, since he utilizes the Exodus theme in order to encourage the Christian community to keep their faith in God's salvation, but he nevertheless subverts the later event of the Exodus, that is, the giving of the Law (cf. Gal 2:16, 21; 3:2, 10, 11, 12, 13).[56] Again, we encounter the paradoxical tension in the use of the Old Testament in the New by the early Christian writers. On the one hand, Paul displays his fidelity and affiliation to Jewish tradition, but on the other hand he radically debunks one of the central aspects of the story. Failing to observe the law wholeheartedly had devastating consequences which will result in the postponement of God's redemptive action.[57] Anyone trained as a Pharisee would certainly have been aware of this plain fact. However, it is evident in the Pauline Epistles that Paul believes the New Exodus to have already been established in Christ Jesus,[58] which consequently causes the validity of the law to become obsolete. It is Paul's conviction that through Jesus the New Exodus has been inaugurated which is also common in Matthew, who, by situating Jesus' life within the framework of the earlier Exodus event, wishes to convey that the redemptive history of Israel has come to its decisive fulfillment.

Enthronement Motif

It is indicated that the New Exodus will be established by the "Son of David,"[59] as it is prophesied that the covenant with David will be the basis of a new covenant with Israel (Jer 31:31–34). This is intertwined with Exodus imagery as the Lord God who once displayed His mighty act

---

55. Keesmaat, "Paul and His Story," 303. See also Holland, *Contours of Pauline Theology*.

56. Ibid., 310.

57. Ibid., 313.

58. Ibid., 314.

59. For the prophecies concerning the Son of David and his role in leading the exiles back from Babylonian captivity to the promised land, see Isa 11:11; 48:20; 61:1–2; 66:18; Mic 7:15.

of redemption will once again lead Israel through the wilderness (Hos 2:14; 12:9). It is foretold in Ezekiel 44–45 that a descendent of David would build and dedicate a magnificent temple and thereby establish the New Exodus (cf. Hag 1:13–14; Zech 3:8–9). In the prologue of Matthew's Gospel, the evangelist brings into focus the historical background of Israel in the context of the exile and claims that Jesus is the prophesied Son of David who would draw the redemptive history of Israel to a fulfillment. We seek to demonstrate in this volume that some crucial parts of this Davidic legacy are drawn from the Psalms, which are applied systematically to the key christological passages of the Gospel in order to assert that Jesus is the Son of David who fulfills the role of messianic agent in the New Exodus event. This will be examined more closely in subsequent chapters.

However, evidence suggests that Jesus was more than a mere Davidic king who was expected to redeem Israel from foreign oppression. Jesus is primarily identified as the Son of David, but in Matthew 16:27, we read that he is also the messianic Son of Man. Although the tone of the verse suggests his subordinate status to God the Father, he nevertheless seems to enjoy divine royal authority. Whether Jesus enjoys divine authority as God's appointed agent or is on par with God is an extremely important point, one which is subject to intense scrutiny. However, the Gospel ends with Jesus being endowed with divine function, and especially in the judgment scene (Matt 26:64) the Son is not necessarily portrayed as subordinate to God the Father but is an authoritative figure who shares the power of judgment with God; the Son of Man appears at the right hand of power in the presence of God judging the world (cf. Dan 7:13–14). This magnificent enthronement motif of Jesus in the apocalyptic discourse where the Son of Man is mentioned deserves a closer look. This enthronement motif, which elevates Jesus' status far above any ordinary human being, is well attested in John's Gospel. Mary R. Huie-Jolly notes this in her investigation of John's Gospel: "The relationship between Jesus and God is so exalted that no down-to-earth analogy is adequate to explain it; it pushes beyond familiarity with father and son relationships to a godlike image of divine sonship, which cannot be communicated except through myth."[60]

She notes in her study that although Psalm 2 is not explicitly cited in John 5, its mood—perhaps by way of conceptual allusion—implies

60. Huie-Jolly, "Threats Answered by Enthronement," 191.

that those who challenge the Son's authority are indicted by the sayings concerning the divine authority of his sonship.[61] When one refers back to the Psalms (cf. Pss 89:9–10, 26–29), it is evident that the Davidic king's enthronement is deliberately modeled on the enthronement of Yahweh and that this was applied by the early Christians to Jesus' Kingship.[62] This has far-reaching implications for identifying Jesus with Israel's messianic king in the line of David. We should understand the application of Davidic legacy to Jesus not for the purpose of comparison between Jesus and David, but to delineate the trajectory of divine redemptive activity that comes to its fulfillment in Christ. It must be stressed that while the Davidic heritage is the central element in the Christology of Matthew, David was never deified in Jewish tradition, which indicates that the application was made to demonstrate that the historical events leading up to Jesus through the covenant originally made with David (2 Sam 7:12–14) are all under God's redemptive purpose for Israel. Although the admissibility of using John's Gospel to interpret Matthew may not go unchallenged, since the former is much more emphatic in stressing Jesus' divine sonship, Huie-Jolly's observation may be applicable to Matthew's Christology to a certain extent, as it also seems that Matthew wishes to portray Jesus as someone more than just a Davidic Messiah. Matthew is certainly more subtle than John in this Christological aspect, possibly due to his Jewish audience, for whom the idea of divine Messiah is a premature and sensitive concept. However, the crucial problem with Huie-Jolly's statement is that she sees the application of the enthronement motif to Jesus in terms of "mythic" significance. She argues that through the mythic speech, the death threat by the authorities in John 5:18 is countered with the godlike authority of the Son in 5:18–27.[63] Whether the writers of the New Testament would have been satisfied with their message being limited within a figurative mythic dimension is certainly doubtful in the light of the early Christian setting. Rather, the use of the Old Testament imageries by the evangelist must be seen in their historical context, as he witnessed the words of the past being fulfilled in his contemporary context through Christ Jesus.

61. Ibid., 206.
62. Ibid., 205.
63. Ibid., 196.

Summary

In this chapter we have examined the social setting of the first-century Christian world in which Matthew's Gospel was written. On the basis of sociological models, it became apparent that the early Christians still regarded themselves to be within the broad spectrum of Judaism. This is acutely demonstrated by the way Matthew relies on the Old Testament and his emphasis on the fulfillment of the prophecies that were made between Yahweh and Israel in order to reestablish the covenantal relationship. Having a clear understanding of the first-century world of the early Christians generates methodological implications that are fundamental to the interpretation of New Testament Christology. If one concedes that Matthew's community was Hellenistic in their mind-set, as it was the dominant culture in the Greco-Roman world, then the use of the Old Testament by the New Testament authors becomes almost impossible to explain. This is why scholars such as B. Gilfillan-Upton draw analogies from Hellenistic texts and look for similarities in order to compare the texts and argue that Hellenism deeply influenced the New Testament writings. On the contrary, however, the early Christians regarded themselves as the true remnant of Israel, and their fundamental Jewish mind-set was neither compromised nor diluted. This ought to direct our attention not to these Hellenistic texts but to the Old Testament, to which Matthew explicitly refers.

We need to appreciate the extremely volatile historical circumstances of the first-century world, especially after the destruction of the Second Temple in 70 AD, when the tension between mainstream Judaism and the new movement launched by Jesus and his followers reached its boiling point. The movement of Jesus subsequently becomes an entirely separate and independent religious entity as the followers take a missionary approach to the Gentile population. However, when the Gospel of Matthew was written in roughly 70 AD, the movement is still at a transitional stage of rupture, and the process of separation from Judaism had not been fully completed. Therefore, Matthew exhibits characteristics that are common to both Judaism and Christianity as it subsequently emerged, which indicates that his Christology is thoroughly based on the Old Testament.

Against the unbelieving Jewish critics, the evangelist quoted the Old Testament, or sometimes alluded to these texts to assert and legitimize the claim that Jesus is the long-awaited messianic figure in fulfillment of the prophecies of Israel's redemptive history. The early Christians employed the Old Testament in support of their Christological message in a way that did not neglect the original context in Jewish tradition, but also in a way that met the emerging needs of the early Christian community. Typology, therefore, should be understood within the early Christian historical context. On the basis of this fundamental principle, Matthew utilizes biblical themes which are derived from the Old Testament concept of Yahweh's redemptive acts in his Christology to proclaim to his Jewish kinsfolk that the Messiah has finally come.

4

Psalms in the Context of Israel's Redemptive History

SECTION ONE: THE USES OF THE ROYAL-ENTHRONEMENT
PSALMS BY THE EARLY CHRISTIANS

*Part One: Significance of the Use of the Psalms
in New Testament Christology*

Psalms in New Testament Studies

A DISCUSSION OF THE uses of the Old Testament in the New Testament in general is not an innovative scholarly movement in itself, but the uses of a specific Old Testament book with its distinct character in a particular New Testament text have not been studied with the same level of intensity. In fact, the study of intertextuality between the Psalms and the New Testament has emerged as a relatively new phenomenon and is beginning to receive closer attention from the likes of Steve Moyise and M. J. J. Menken.[1]

In Matthew's Gospel, the book of Psalms clearly emerges as the key text in deciphering the christological significance, as the messianic title "Son of David" stands in the most prominent position among the

---

1. Watts, "The Psalms in Mark's Gospel"; Brooke, "The Psalms in Early Jewish Literature in the Light of the Dead Sea Scrolls." See also Mays, "Prayer and Christology," 322–31; Bateman, "Psalm 110:1 and the New Testament," 438–53; Jacobson, "The Royal Psalms and Jesus Messiah," 192–98; Johnson, "The Davidic-Royal Motif in the Gospels," 136–50.

synoptic tradition.[2] Here the connection between the Son of David and the Psalms is made due to the fact that in Matthew's Gospel certain types of psalms, especially the royal psalms, are quoted to support the claim that Jesus is the long-awaited Davidic Messiah. The genealogy starts by designating Jesus as the Son of David and narrates the founding of the Davidic dynasty (Matt 1:6) and the loss of it during the Exile (1:11). This is emphasized subsequently in the narrative of the triumphal entry: "The crowds that went ahead of him and those that followed shouted, 'Hosanna to the Son of David!' 'Blessed is he who comes in the name of the Lord!' 'Hosanna in the highest!'" (Matt 21:9).

The parallel is found in Mark's Gospel: "Those who went ahead and those who followed shouted, 'Hosanna!' 'Blessed is he who comes in the name of the Lord!' 'Blessed is the coming kingdom of our father David!' 'Hosanna in the highest!'" (Mark 11:9–10).

Matthew emphasizes the title "Son of David" by placing it in the initial part of the Hosanna acclamation. In comparison, Mark omits the title and instead has it in the latter part of the acclamation narrative, and there it points to Jesus' Davidic legacy rather than being used to emphasize Jesus' messianic identity.[3] This demonstrates that Matthew is keen on the Son of David in his Christology.

The title appears in Matthew's narrative with remarkable frequency: in Jesus' healing ministry (Matt 9:27; 12:23; 20:30), in the act of exorcism (Matt 15:22), and as his public name (Matt 21:9). When the title is applied to Jesus it causes indignation among the Jewish authorities (Matt 21:15), and in the passion narratives, scribes acknowledge that the Messiah is the "Son of David" (Matt 22:42). We have already established in chapter 2 of this volume that the anointed one (αξψμ) refers exclusively to the "Son of David," and therefore, the equivalent Greek term, χριστός, should be seen as another christological title which effectively means the same thing (Matt 1:1; 1:16; 11:2; 16:16, 20; 22:42; 23:10; 24:5, 23; 26:63, 68; 27:17, 22). More simply put, when Jesus is referred to as the Christ, he is identified as the Son of David.

All these textual evidences strongly suggest that the "Son of David," which is identified primarily with the book of Psalms, plays a crucial

---

2. In the Synoptic Gospels, Matthew cites the name David fifteen times, Mark seven times (2:25; 10:47, 48; 11:10; 12:35, 36, 37), and Luke twelve times (1:27; 1:32; 1:69; 2:4, 11; 3:31; 6:3; 18:38, 39; 20:41, 42, 44).

3. Bassler, "A Man for All Seasons," 164–65.

role in the Christology of Matthew's Gospel. Although the importance of the Psalms for Matthew cannot be decided simply by the number of quotations and allusions he uses, it nevertheless plays an indispensable role in the entire New Testament; one third of the Old Testament quotations in the New Testament are from the Psalms, which underlines the importance of the Psalter for early Christianity.[4] This may suggest that the early Christians were very familiar with the Psalms in their entirety, as they depended on them in their claims for the Messiah. The defining moments in terms of revealing or reaffirming the divine messianic identity of Jesus and the crucial events of his ministry cannot be fully understood without appreciating the importance of the use of Psalms.[5]

The ways in which the Psalms are utilized in the New Testament, then, deserve closer scrutiny. Incidentally, in today's academic world, there has been an increasing concern regarding plagiarism, and so an author is expected to provide full information in the acknowledgement of the source being quoted or paraphrased. However, in the literary world of the early Christians, it seems to have been a common practice for authors to blend the quoted material with their own words without proper acknowledgement of the original source. Such conduct would be seen as a travesty by modern standards, but when we consider the intellectual and spiritual matrix of the early Christian writers, who were thoroughly Jewish in character, and that the originally intended audience was primarily their Jewish counterparts, it is not far fetched to assume that the New Testament writers expected their readers to recognize the quoted materials without having to explicitly acknowledge the source. The Psalms are particularly significant for the New Testament authors; the sheer number of quotations indicates that they must have been widely known by the Jewish people, perhaps because they were believed to have been composed by David, who was their national hero.[6]

A. M. Harmon's study of Paul's use of the Psalms provides abundant evidence for the concept of quotation in the ancient context. He concurs

---

4. Day, *Psalms*, 137–38.

5. McCann, *A Theological Introduction to the Book of Psalms*, 166.

6. Harmon, "Aspects of Paul's Use of the Psalms," 2–3. Modern acknowledging conventions are only a relatively recent requirement; until only a few hundred years ago it was standard practice to quote an entire section without any acknowledgment, even in scholarly works.

largely with the definition constructed by H. B. Swete which regards passages as formally cited on the basis of the following criteria:

a. Those which are cited with an introductory formula: (e.g., in Matthean context; "this was to fulfill what was spoken by the prophets" [Matt 1:22–23; 2:15; 2:17–18; 2:23; 4:14–16; 8:17; 12:17–21; 13:35; 21:4–5; 27:9–10]).

b. Those which, though not announced by a formula, appear from the context to be intended as quotations or agree verbatim with some context in the Old Testament.[7]

Both of the above points are relevant in our discussion concerning Matthew's Gospel, but it is the second point which deserves a closer look in this discussion. It is noted that even if the passages are not directly quoted with a formal introductory formula, if the overall context and wording of the passages are conceptually related to the Old Testament themes by allusion, then they should also be included within the category of Paul's use of the Psalms. A modern exegete is often faced with difficulties, as Paul, at times, accurately quotes from the LXX but also deviates considerably from the original material.[8] However, Paul is not distorting the original meaning of the old scriptural texts in order to force them into the overall scheme of his work, but, as G. T. Purves points out, Paul is fulfilling the role of a creative theologian who could extract a certain passage from the Scripture and offer an interpretive insight. Purves correctly notes that Paul's exegetical method was determined by his practical purpose, which supports the view that Old Testament quotations have a historical interest, since the primary goal of the New Testament writers is not necessarily confined within the expository dimension of texts. Hence, the writers were at liberty to change the phraseology when the occasion required it.[9] This is why appreciating the first-century context is vital if one is to fully grasp the use of the Old Testament by early Christians and their intentions in terms of scriptural quotations. This is far from discarding the original context and meaning of the quoted passage, as the common Jewish mind-set shared by all New Testament authors would naturally sustain the validity and authenticity of the Old

---

7. Cited in Harmon, 2–3.
8. Ibid., 7.
9. Purves, cited in Harmon, 8.

Testament tradition. Like Paul, Matthew, who indubitably displays adherence to the Jewish tradition, would not be interested in the infringement of the original meaning of the Old Testament. Rather, his intention is much more likely to preserve the authenticity of the Jewish Scripture by applying it to the Messiah who brought the prophecies of Israel to a decisive fulfillment.

In the same manner, the Psalms are thoroughly integrated into the overall theological substructure of Matthew's Gospel in a way that transcends mere literal quotation as "proof texts" and forms the backbone of the message revealing God's redemptive purpose as fulfilled in Jesus the Son of David.[10]

Earlier, we presupposed a connection between the title Son of David and the Psalms; however, not all the Psalms are exclusively attributed to David. Herman Gunkel has demonstrated that the book of Psalms contains various genres and different historical settings, and their identification must be prudently distinguished from one another. We need to bear in mind, however, that the New Testament writers had no such neat understanding of different types of psalms. For Matthew, they were just the Psalms of David! The categorization is a modern scholarly attempt to better understand the settings of various psalms with their unique emphases. However, the distinction of the Psalms is useful for a modern contemporary reader seeking to identify what effect was intended by the evangelist, who was clearly keen to use these texts in the defining moments of his story. The sole purpose of discussing different types of psalms, as Gunkel demonstrated, is to discern and isolate certain types of psalms, at which point it becomes more feasible to understand the specific purpose and intention of the evangelist, who employed these texts to support his Christology.

Identification of the Royal Psalms and Their History

We have established that Son of David (as the royal messianic agent of divine salvation) is the key christological title in the Gospel of Matthew; now we turn to the type of psalm identified primarily with the Davidic figure, namely, the royal psalm.[11] The royal psalms describe the covenant-

---

10. Doble, "The Psalms in Luke-Acts," 90.

11. Cf. Grant "The Psalms and the King." See also Johnson, "The Role of the King in the Jerusalem Cultus"; Johnson, *Sacral Kingship in Ancient Israel*. Fairman, "Worship and Festivals in an Egyptian Temple," 165–203; Bentzen, *King and Messiah*; Frankfort,

al relationship that the Davidic king shares with Yahweh and that has a direct impact on the welfare of the nation as a whole. The royal psalms are prayers concerning the king (Pss 2:6ff; 20:7ff.; 101:1, 4), declaring that the king is adopted as the son of Yahweh on the day of his enthronement (2:7ff.). The fundamental traits of the relationship between the king and Yahweh prescribed by the royal psalms later became the basis for the expectation of the ideal royal figure, the eschatological King.[12] This indicates that the royal psalms were considered to be prophetic in nature by the early Christians, as they constitute the foundation of later messianic expectation. The early Christians saw in them a supplication of the then-enthroned king, who longed for the reign of the ideal King who would exceed him in redemptive authority. The belief that the sole purpose of the Psalms is christologically oriented is what underlines the religious ethos and historical perspective of the early Christians. The Psalms are meaningful insofar as they offer interpretive insight into the events surrounding Jesus. Contemporary scholars of the history of religion would regard such a line of thought as historically inaccurate, and would thus emphasize the original context of the text under consideration.[13] The early Jewish-Christian use of the Old Testament tradition reveals that they utilized the Psalms not as plain predictions; rather, they used the texts as the basis of prophecy and fulfillment in the realm of the continuing act of divine salvation manifested in Israel's historical reality.[14] It is highly unlikely that the community, who firmly believed that they represented the true remnant of Israel, would discard the original context of Jewish tradition. It is difficult to believe that Matthew's Jewish-Christian community was oblivious to the historical facts illustrated in the Psalms—such as the central figure, a reigning king of Judah, depicted in the royal psalms—as the Psalms portray the place that the office of the king had in the spiritual/political welfare of Israel.[15] The use of the Psalms in the New Testament is thus paradoxical: it preserves the

---

Kingship and the Gods; Sanders, *The Psalms Scroll of Qumran Cave 11*; Sanders, *The Dead Sea Psalms Scroll*; Whitelam, *The Just King*; Mettinger, *King and Messiah*.

12. Hempel, "Royal Psalms," 947.

13. See Mowinckel, *The Psalms in Israel's Worship*. Cf. Mays, "Prayer and Christology."

14. Cf. Cooke "The Israelite King as Son of God," 202–25. See also Eaton, "The King's Self-sacrifice," 141–45; Childs, "Psalm Titles and Midrashic Exegesis," 137–50.

15. Mays, *The Lord Reigns*, 110.

original historical context in which these texts were written, and yet, at the same time, by taking into account their prophetic character, we discover the crucial function the Psalms had for the early Christians. In other words, the perception of the Psalms must have evolved during the course of Israel's history without relinquishing the fundamental ethos of the original text.[16]

Any biblical scholar who attempts to discover which royal psalms in particular were utilized in the Gospel immediately faces difficulties, as various Old Testament scholars have somewhat different notions regarding what constitutes a group of royal psalms.[17] A detailed discussion of which psalms should be classified within the category of royal psalms stretches beyond the boundary of this volume. However, the most widely accepted criteria in classifying certain psalms as royal is that the king is mentioned as Yahweh's anointed, and those psalms that clearly refer to the king either in the second or third person are, in general, considered to be royal by Gunkel. In contrast, some of J. H. Eaton's royal psalms (Pss 28; 61; 63) are disputable, since the mention of the king is not entirely evident.[18] Gunkel's royal psalms (Pss 2; 18; 20; 21; 45; 72; 101; 110; 132; 144:1–11; cf. 89:47–52) are grouped on the basis of the internal unity of the common subject of royal entity, which seems appropriate especially in our discussion of Matthew, as he espouses Jesus' kingship with the psalmic language.[19] We shall see subsequently that Matthew utilizes the royal psalms in his key christological passages to support the claim that Jesus is the legitimate Messiah of Israel in the line of David.[20] In this

---

16. Cf. Engnell, *Studies in Divine Kingship in the Ancient Near East*. See also Frankfort, *Kingship and the Gods*. Cf. Gadd, *Ideas of Divine Rule in the Ancient East*.

17. Gunkel identified the following as royal psalms: 2; 18; 20; 21; 45; 72; 89:47–52; 101; 110; 132; 144:1–11. The following are less clear examples: 5; 11; 16; 31; 36; 42/3; 51–52, 54. Cf. Day, *Psalms*, 88. See also Eaton, *Kingship and the Psalms*, 17; Engnell, *Studies in Divine Kingship*. Gunkel's irreducible minimum is adequately sufficient in our discussion of Matthew's Christology. While other scholars' addition to Gunkel's classification offers elaborate understanding of the underlying theme of royal psalms, they are often superfluous for the discussion of the evangelist's use of the Psalms. Cf. also Wilson, "The Structure of the Psalter," 230–35.

18. Croft, *The Identity of the Individual in the Psalms*, 76.

19. Cf. Durham, "The King as 'Messiah' in the Psalms," 425–35. The psalms that can be classified primarily as royal psalms in Durham's view are 2, 18, 20, 21, 45, 72, 89, 101, 110, 132, and 144. He notes that "though some scholars have argued for a much larger group of Royal Psalms, there is little evidence for such an expansion."

20. Cf. Whitelam, *The Just King*.

volume, Gunkel's classification will be adopted as the standard paradigm of the royal psalms for the discussion of the key christological passages of the Gospel.[21] While Gunkel's identification is useful in defining the genre of the psalms under discussion, he argues strenuously against regarding the royal psalms as inherently messianic. Although he acknowledges their prophetic character, the prayers and oracles depicted are intelligible primarily within their own historical context.[22] This is correct insofar as one is endeavoring to preserve the authenticity of the text by discovering the original meaning, but limiting the interpretation within its historical timeline often leads to a partial understanding of the full capacity of these ancient sacred texts. As mentioned above, we need to place the New Testament use of the Old Testament within the context of Israel's redemptive history. When we appreciate how the covenantal relationship between Yahweh and Israel progressed in the historical setting of the early Christian community, we grasp how the perception of the Psalms evolved without relinquishing the fundamental character of the text in its original context. The Psalms became the basis for later historical understanding of Israel's standing in the overall redemptive scheme of Yahweh. Royal psalms were thus originally attributed to the ruling native kings of Judah, but through the history of Israel, the theology of the Psalms has also become the model for the ideal messianic king of Israel.[23]

The Model of the Suffering Messiah?

One of the chief characteristics of Jesus' messianic ministry is that of the vicarious Suffering Servant. Even though it seems evident that Matthew's christological concern is to proclaim that Jesus is the Son of David, that is, the Messiah who fulfills the redemptive history of Israel, the evangelist is in agreement with Mark and indeed also with Luke in emphasizing the crucial part of the Messiah's ministry, which is the suffering and death of Jesus Christ. Even though the suffering and death of Christ should be seen in the light of the subsequent glory of resurrection as he is vindicated by God, there are explicit features within the Synoptic Gospels which point to the necessity of suffering prior to the triumph of resurrection. For instance, Jesus issues a "command to silence" to the

---

21. Gunkel, *An Introduction to the Psalms*, 99.
22. Ibid., 119–20.
23. Cf. Miller, *Interpreting the Psalms*. See also Brueggemann, *Message of the Psalms*.

disciples concerning his identity in the Transfiguration scene (Matt 17:2; Mark 9:2). The command of Jesus to keep his true identity a secret has didactic implications in that Jesus' identity as the glorious heavenly Son of God cannot be fully grasped without appreciating the necessity of his suffering and death. The disciples only become privy to this knowledge when they accompany Jesus in the pathway of self-sacrifice and bear the cross of humility and obedience. For the synoptic writers, the divine sonship is intimately related with the crucifixion, which is paradoxically revealed through it (cf. Mark 15:39). The crucial question here is the reason for the Messiah's suffering and his sacrificial death.[24] Why was it necessary that the Messiah should endure suffering and willingly take up the cross of his death? More importantly, can this portrayal of Jesus as the suffering Messiah be justified on the basis of the Old Testament? In the birth narrative, Matthew defines the purpose of Jesus' redemptive function as the saving of his people from their sins (Matt 1:21). Indeed, Jesus' healing ministry was characterized as the forgiveness of sins (Matt 9:2, 6). As the Gospel reaches a climax, the ultimate reason for Jesus' death and shedding of blood is revealed by Jesus himself, and it is precisely for the forgiveness of sins (Matt 26:28). At a glance, perhaps the only parallel is found in the Old Testament sacrificial system, where the priest slaughters a scapegoat and offers it as atonement for the people whom he serves and represents (cf. Lev 1:4; 4:20, 26, 31, 35). In a similar manner, Jesus assumes the role of the scapegoat by being imputed with the sin of humanity, and later God vindicates him by raising him from death in order that the divine redemptive purpose should be fulfilled. This is where the New Testament's conception of the Messiah in the light of Jesus' suffering and death is seen to differ from the messianic belief of the Jewish tradition. In the entire synoptic tradition, the impression is that the early Christian belief was that Jesus was the long-awaited

---

24. This is known as "messianic secrecy" in Mark's Gospel. See Winn, *The Purpose of Mark's Gospel*. Another feature concerning Mark's Gospel is the theory of "corrective Christology." The later evangelist found the concept of Jesus as the "divine man" problematic in conveying the proper understanding of Jesus' messiahship. The Hellenistic divine man Christology was considered to be flawed because it focused solely on the divine power of the Son of God. The evangelist restricted this by reinterpreting the life of Jesus as a whole in the light of the cross. The evangelist employed the "Son of Man" title in the context of suffering and death in order to correct the "Son of God" title, which only seemed to concentrate on the glory and miraculous power of Jesus. Corrective Christology argues that it is the passion story of Jesus that dominates the whole of the Gospel. Cf. Kingsbury, *The Christology of Mark's Gospel*.

Messiah who was reprehensible in the eyes of the scribes. The most likely reason for this treatment is that the Jewish authorities did not see how Jesus could be the Messiah whom the prophets had foretold. We have briefly encountered that this is one of the most intensely debated areas in biblical studies: whether Jesus' messianic claim is, indeed, in conformity with the Old Testament.

If our understanding of the Psalms as prophetic texts which subsequently became the model for the future eschatological messianic king is correct, then the claim that Jesus' messianic identity in terms of his suffering is essentially aberrant from the Jewish tradition can be refuted. A closer examination of the Psalms reveals that Jesus' ministry of vicarious suffering is modeled on the pattern depicted in the Psalter. Throughout the book of Psalms, we see contradictory images of the king: he is portrayed in lofty terms in enthronement rites, and yet we witness him entreating Yahweh in such a manner that no reference is made to his exalted royal status.[25] This is evident in the royal psalms, where we see the status of the king on the day of his enthronement elevated to the extent that he is called Yahweh's son (Ps 2:7), but we also witness the king's lowliness in his painful lamentation (Ps 89:38–51). John Day argues that this lamentation is most likely to have been written during the time of the Babylonian exile in the sixth century BC, for this would bring a feeling of finality and utter rejection of the Davidic covenant.[26] It was a period of historical chaos and sheer disappointment at the failure of the Israelite monarchy to live up to the standard prescribed in the Psalms. This has led Joachim Becker to contend that the initial hope in Davidic kingship died out during this period, and consequently, Israelite faith was centered in Yahweh alone. In other words, Yahweh's kingship effaces the kingship of the Davidic Messiah. We have argued earlier that this is far from what happened, as Davidic hope did not simply dissipate, but the pejorative attitude towards the monarchy during the exilic period re-intensified the Israelite hope in the promised eschatological King. Therefore, the context of lamentation is not merely an incident of the historical past, but the rekindling of hope in an ideal messianic figure in the postexilic period indicates that these psalms were interpreted in an eschatological sense.[27] This is certainly the case in the first-century

---

25. Eaton, *Kingship and the Psalms*, 19–25.
26. Day, *Psalms*, 95.
27. Ibid., 133.

Jewish-Christian context, as they believed that the Messiah whom the psalmist was pointing to had finally manifested himself in fulfillment of Israel's redemptive history.

Identification of the Enthronement Psalms: Yahweh as King— a Dominating Theme in the Old Testament?

Gunkel's classification of the various psalms indicates that the history and genre of the royal psalms must be distinguished from that of the enthronement psalms, which were written to celebrate Yahweh's Kingship (in contrast to those written to celebrate Davidic kingship).[28] The two types of psalms differ in terms of literary style and ideological function. However, it is doubtful whether such distinction is helpful or indeed of any value for understanding the early Christian use of the Psalms in supporting the messianic fulfillment of Jesus. This will be discussed in more detail later.

Again, there is no unanimous agreement with regard to what constitutes the enthronement psalms. Day lists the psalms proclaiming Yahweh to be King as follows: 24:7–10; 29:10; 48:2; 74:12; 93:1; 95:3; 96:10; 97:1; 98:6; 99:1. In these psalms, one may observe that the style of language in describing Yahweh as the glorious King is remarkably similar to that of the royal psalms, which were designed to affirm the enthronement of the Davidic monarchy and its everlasting covenant with Yahweh, which will guarantee the kingship of Davidic descendents throughout the generations. He also argues that the images of Yahweh as shepherd (cf. Pss 23:1ff.; 80:1) and judge (Pss 82:1; 96:13) are alternative ways of referring to His Kingship.[29] However, it is the latter, that is, the authority of Yahweh as judge, which is the major theme in this particular type of psalm. The threat of the impending judgment and the glory of exaltation which will vindicate the righteous ones of Israel are the foundational elements of the enthronement psalms.

The dominant theme in the divine kingship ideology portrayed in the enthronement psalms primarily consists of the function of the judge, which is directly connected to divine kingship. Yahweh displays His might by destroying the enemy nations of Israel with His "strong right

---

28. Cf. Morgenstern, "The Cultic Setting of the Enthronement Psalms," 1–42. See also Westermann, *The Praise of God in the Psalms*.

29. Day, *Psalms*, 125–26. To the category of enthronement psalms, Gunkel adds Ps 47:3, 8, 9. Cf. Gunkel, *An Introduction to the Psalms*, 68.

arm" and, as the triumphant victor, pronounces judgment upon the incapacitated kings of the nations. S. J. L. Croft concurs that the theme of judgment plays a prominent role in the enthronement psalms (Pss 96:10, 13; 97:2, 8, 10f.; 98:9; 99:4ff.). We believe that this theme is later absorbed into the Son of Man sayings by the evangelist (cf. Matt 24:39; 24:44; 25:31; 26:64), a possibility which we shall examine more closely in subsequent chapters.[30]

Those who favor Yahweh's Kingship as the dominant factor in the Old Testament, especially after the exilic period, would be inclined to the think that since Yahweh's Kingship usurps the place of the Davidic Messiah, the enthronement psalms should be considered the kernel of the Psalter, that which supplanted the royal psalms in later Jewish tradition. However, such a view will prove to be dissonant with the early Jewish-Christian understanding of their ancestral religion and their Messiah.

Royal and Enthronement Psalms: Conjoined?

It has been argued in the discussion on "Messianic Expectation of the Old Testament" that hope in a Davidic Messiah as an agent of salvation did not dissipate during the exilic period, but it gave rise to an intensified messianic expectation. In referring back to the prototype Exodus event, Becker contends that the Israelite faith sought consolation in Yahweh alone. In contrast, however, we have learned that the "New Exodus" would be established by Yahweh. This entailed the messianic function of the Davidic king, which suggests that Yahweh's reign and Davidic kingship in Jewish thinking are not in conflict, as Becker argues, but are complementary.

We may thus infer from this observation that the royal psalms, celebrating the Davidic kingship, and the enthronement psalms, which celebrate Yahweh's Kinghsip, should be viewed as one entity rather than as two groups of psalms with opposing ideological interests. This is certainly true of the early Jewish-Christian understanding of the ancestral tradition, as the unification of the divine reign and the expectations of a royal messianic figure was believed to have been realized in Christ Jesus. For instance, in the Gospel of Luke, a heavenly messenger appears to shepherds to announce the birth of Christ (Luke 2:8–12), which is immediately joined by "a multitude of the heavenly

---

30. Croft, *The Identity of the Individual in the Psalms*, 84.

host" (Luke 2:13) proclaiming "glory to God in the highest heaven." Although this is not a direct quotation, it certainly alludes to the enthronement psalm 96:11–13, which affirms Yahweh's kingship as the judge and which in turn indicates that Jesus' kingship as the Messiah embodies the reign of God.[31] In the same manner, Matthew begins his Gospel with the genealogy which designates Jesus as the Son of David (Matt 1:1), but we soon discover in the birth narrative that Mary is "found to be pregnant through the Holy Spirit" (Matt 1:18), which demonstrates the divine involvement in Jesus' birth.

The ultimate question is whether this characteristic of Jesus' identity can be claimed typologically on the basis of the Old Testament. According to S. J. L Croft, the combination of the divine and human kingship, which is expressed in the binary character of Jesus' identity both in terms of its divine nature and its Davidic origin, was not uncommon in the ancient Near Eastern religious context, where the renewal of the earthly kingship was not only closely connected with the affirmation of divine kingship in the annual festival, but the style of the earthly enthronement rite was modeled on the ceremony of divine coronation.[32] This is also attested in the royal psalms, as Yahweh not only proclaims the king as His son (Ps 2:7), but also the divine prerogative as the judge is conferred upon the king that he may rule with His righteousness (Ps 72:1–2) and all his enemies will be utterly destroyed by Yahweh (Ps 110:1–7). In return for divine favor, the king displays loyal submission by proposing to build "a dwelling place for the Mighty One of Jacob" (Ps 132:1–5). The solidarity between the divine reign and Davidic kingship forms the central theological emphasis in the Psalter, and the cultic role assumed by the king not only forms a crucial part in the relationship between Yahweh and Israel but the political welfare of the nation also depended directly upon the religious righteousness of the king.[33]

Gunkel's classification of psalms according to their genre and historical setting is useful in determining the original context of textual composition, which helps in understanding the intended meaning behind the Psalms and how they were incorporated into the New Testament

---

31. McCann, *A Theological Introduction to the Book of Psalms*, 164.

32. Croft, *The Identity of the Individual in the Psalms*, 84. Cf. also Gunkel *The Psalms*, 36.

33. In Ps 110:4, Yahweh confers upon the king an everlasting priesthood after the order of Melchizedek.

text. What is problematic, however, is the presupposition which lies behind such classification. Are the royal and enthronement psalms categorized into different groups because Israel had conflicting notions about the Davidic messianic king and Yahweh? It seems that this was at least what Gunkel must have thought when he presented his case on the categorization of the Psalms. In this line of thought, Becker would certainly argue that there was a conflict between the messianic expectation of the Davidic Messiah and Yahweh's Kingship. However, when it comes to the royal and enthronement psalms, it is doubtful whether the early Christians regarded them as separate ideological entities that should be distinguished from each other. Gunkel makes the observation regarding the enthronement psalms (Pss 93; 97; 99) that these poems, in addressing Yahweh in royal terms, imitate the motifs from the royal poems of David and carry them into the spiritual realm.[34] This effectively means that the songs that celebrate the monarchy and the ones for the cult of a god have close affinity in terms of ideology and genre. Gunkel's strong emphasis on distinguishing different genres of psalms is inadvertently contradicted by his own statement that ideas and customs which were originally used in reference to the earthly king have been transferred to God.[35] The ideology of both groups of psalms in a complementary relationship and the remarkable homogeneity in terms of the style of royal exultations used for both Yahweh and the Davidic king suggest that both the royal and enthronement psalms should characteristically be viewed as one entity. The idea that these two types of psalms are interchangeable may have a far-reaching ideological implication when Matthew constructed his Christology with the language of the Psalms.

This will become evident in our discussion of the christological significance of the Psalms, as both royal and enthronement psalms are used by Matthew in order to present Jesus not only as the long-awaited Davidic Messiah but also as the manifestation of the divine reign which brings the redemptive history of Israel to a decisive culmination. The typological use of the Psalms in Matthew's Christology can only be properly grasped in the context of Israel's redemptive history. Therefore,

---

34. Gunkel, *An Introduction to the Psalms*, 66–67.

35. Ibid., 73 However, this should not lead to an understanding of dual kingship of Yahweh and the Davidic king, as the latter is clearly subordinate to the deity. The relationship is better explicated in terms of vassal kingship under the authority of divine rule.

we shall now turn to a discussion of the biblical concept of redemptive history and its significance, which lies behind the use of the royal-enthronement psalms in the Gospel of Matthew.

SECTION TWO: REDEMPTIVE HISTORICAL PERSPECTIVE

Part One: Trajectory of Redemptive History of Israel

Introduction

Discussion of the redemptive history of Israel is closely connected with the messianic expectation of the Old Testament, which we explored earlier in chapter 2. The historians of the Old Testament—of the Deuteronomistic History, for instance—present a rather turbulent picture of Israel's constant rebellion and the infringement of the covenantal relationship with Yahweh. The consequence of Israel's sin is painfully experienced, as she is repeatedly dominated and conquered by foreign powers and is eventually forced out of the promised land which Yahweh has given to her. Sin and rebellion prevent Israel from moving forward into the blessings promised in the Mosaic covenant, and they are pushed back into the darkness of punishment, of the covenant curses in Deut 28:15-68.[36] Even though Israel has strayed from Yahweh and has often deviated from the stipulations of the Law, the covenants of Abraham and David once again bring the hope of restoration and blessing upon Israel. The prophets vividly describe the threats of the impending judgment which will befall Israel if she does not repent of her sin and surrender to Yahweh in order that the covenantal relationship may be restored. The prophets proclaim that God's promise to Abraham will be brought to fulfillment, and there will be a New Exodus which has far greater significance than the original event and which will be marked by the Davidic Messiah, who would be anointed with the Spirit to achieve the redemptive mission and establish the New Covenant (cf. Hos 12:9; Isa 11:1-13; 19:19-25; 40:5; 44:3, 23; 48:20; 52:1-12; 58:8; 61:1-3; 66:18;

---

36. Olson, "The Jagged Cliffs of Mount Sinai," 229-76, notes: "The Book of the Covenant is found within a larger literary context associated with the Covenant God makes with Israel at Mt. Sinai (Exod. 19-24). This Sinai narrative stands between the other key narrative events in the Book of Exodus: 1. The Exodus of Israelite slaves out of Egypt (chs. 1-15) 2. Israel's idolatrous worship of the golden calf and its aftermath (chs. 32-34)." He also posits that "the laws of the Book of the Covenant function as an interpretative extension of the Ten Commandments into various details of the community's life."

Ezek 36:24–28; 37:1–4; 44–45; Mic 7:15; Joel 2:28; Jer 33:19–22; Mal 3:1). This theme of redemption is intensified through their painful experience of exile, and the messianic hope is rekindled as they eagerly anticipate the coming of the Messiah, who will far exceed David in terms of his authority and redemptive impact. The people of Israel constantly looked for the coming of the descendent of king David (Hag 1:13–14; Zech 3:8–9). However, none of these prophecies had been fulfilled by the time of the coming of Jesus. The New Testament is the epitome of such messianic hope, as the writers convey their conviction that the prophecy has now been fulfilled in the person and ministry of Christ Jesus.[37] There are evidences in the New Testament which show that the New Exodus has occurred in the death and resurrection of Jesus. For instance, both John the Baptist and Jesus began their ministries by quoting Isaiah 40:3–5: "He went into all the country around the Jordan, preaching a baptism of repentance for the forgiveness of sins. As is written in the book of the words of Isaiah the prophet: 'A voice of one calling in the wilderness, "Prepare the way for the Lord, make straight paths for him. Every valley shall be filled in, every mountain and hill made low. The crooked roads shall become straight, the rough ways smooth. And all mankind will see God's salvation""'" (Luke 3:3–6).

By quoting Isaiah, the writer is showing that the prophecy of the New Exodus is now fulfilled in Christ Jesus. Likewise, later in the story, when John the Baptist sent messengers to Jesus to determine if he was the Christ, Jesus replied by pointing to the signs of Isaiah. They were the evidence of the inauguration of the New Exodus:

> When the men came to Jesus, they said, "John the Baptist sent us to you to ask, 'Are you the one who was to come, or should we expect someone else?'" At that very time Jesus cured many who had diseases, sicknesses and evil spirits, and gave sight to many who were blind. So he replied to the messengers, "Go back and report to John what you have seen and heard: The blind receive sight, the lame walk, those who have leprosy are cured, the deaf hear, the dead are raised, and the good news is preached to the poor. Blessed is the man who does not fall away on account of me." (Luke 7:20)[38]

---

37. Pate et al., *The Story of Israel*; see chapter 3, "The Historical Books: Sin and Exile."

38. Jesus also commended John, saying that he fulfilled the prophecy of the one sent before the Lord to prepare His way (Luke 7:27).

Along with the inauguration of the New Exodus through the coming of the Messiah, the New Testament writers also say that the New Covenant has been established through the death of Christ (cf. Luke 22:20; 2 Cor. 3:6; see also 2 Cor 5:17; 6:16–18; Heb 8:8–13).[39]

The historical background of Israel is crucial if we are to explain the way in which the Old Testament texts were utilized in the early Christian setting. This section of the chapter seeks to show how the Psalms in particular are thoroughly embedded within the historical thinking of the early Christian community. Indeed, as we will see, this was a natural outcome of the Church's understanding that the Psalms had a prophetic function. They were used by the early Christian writers as proof that the messianic promise had finally been fulfilled in Christ Jesus. It is, therefore, important to examine the concept of history portrayed in the Old Testament biblical tradition and whether such an understanding helps to illumine the significance of the Psalms for the Christology of Matthew's Gospel. A discussion regarding the redemptive history of Israel is therefore necessary since Matthew, along with the other synoptic writers, who do not stress it in the same way, is particularly keen on the fulfillment theme of Jewish messianic history in the person and ministry of Jesus (cf. 1:22–23; 2:15; 2:17–18; 2:23; 4:14–16; 8:17; 12:17–21; 13:35; 21:4–5; 27:9–10).

The early church's recognition of Jesus as the fulfillment of messianic prophecy is indissolubly connected with the Old Testament concept of salvation history. Without this historical background, the early Christians' claim regarding Jesus as the Messiah and the subsequent development of their Christology quite simply have no foundation. The inferences drawn by the early church from the Jewish Scriptures are not an infringement of their ancestral legacy but demonstrate a continuity of its essence, which provided a way for the early Christians to draw

---

39. Goldingay, *Approaches to Old Testament Interpretation*, 69, notes the importance of the story of salvation in the Old Testament, as he comments that "the major overt emphasis of much of the Old Testament is that Yahweh has created, acted, acts and will act in Israel's history for her salvation. The importance of this emphasis should not be lost in the course of recognizing complementary features of Old Testament faith." Cf. also Mack, "The Innocent Transgressor," 135–65; Root, "Dying He Lives," 155–69, focuses on the use of irony and paradox in the Christology of the Gospels, as he notes that "the submissive redeemer is redeemer only as his submission is somehow also his conquering activity." In other words, Jesus is the powerful redeemer only as the crucified Messiah.

evidence from their Jewish tradition for the emerging theological challenges facing them.[40]

Biblical Concept of History

Since the presupposition that the use of royal-enthronement psalms in Matthew's Gospel conveys the notion of fulfillment of Israel's messianic expectation by the intervention of Yahweh through the Davidic Messiah, it is crucial to examine the biblical concept of history. The way in which the early Christians perceived history is directly connected with the way in which the Old Testament texts were used. This fundamental principle also applies in the way the Psalms were incorporated in Matthew's Christology, which is set within the frame of Israel's redemptive history.[41]

Walther Zimmerli argues that the promise and fulfillment theme is what drives the biblical story forward. This is also prevalent in Matthew's Gospel, as the fulfillment of the Old Testament promise is manifested in a concrete historical context. This makes Israel's religion unique in comparison with neighboring ancient Near Eastern religions, which were much more prone to a mythical understanding of deities.[42] Zimmerli highlights that the "biblical perception of deity firmly anchored in historical reality guarded Israel against every flight into a timeless, mythical understanding of God's activity." This is an important point, since many people who lack a sufficient level of biblical awareness would say

---

40. Wolff, "The Understanding of History in the Old Testament Prophets," 352. Cf. also Pannenberg, "Redemptive Event and History," 323. The past and the new are comprehensively held together only by the awareness of the redemptive history which brings the eschatological community of Jesus and ancient Israel into the realm of "promise and fulfillment."

41. Cf. van Groningen, *Messianic Revelation in the Old Testament*. See also Carter, "Evoking Isaiah," 503–20, who points out that "an audience elaborates the gaps of a text to build a consistent understanding not by supplying whatever content it likes but by utilizing the tradition it shares with the author. The common traditions provide the audience with a frame of reference, the 'perceptual grid,' for its interpretive work." This view is plausible in the context of Matthew's community. When the evangelist quotes the book of Psalms, he expects the readers to understand its origin and its meaning, since the audience was most probably Jewish. Senior, *What Are They Saying about Matthew?* 42, presents a three-stage progression of redemptive history in Matthew's Gospel: "1. A time of preparation. This encompasses the history of Israel prior to Jesus. The patriarchs and prophets point forward to Jesus. 2. The time of Jesus. His message is directed exclusively to Israel. 3. The time of the Church"; see also Meier "Salvation History in Matthew," 203–15.

42. Cf. Walton, *Ancient Israelite Literature in Its Cultural Context*.

that Scripture is somehow *ahistorical*. In other words, the biblical writers were unconcerned with historical development, as they sought to define God's identity and activity primarily within a spiritual dimension. However, when we begin to appreciate the Jewish understanding of Yahweh, which was thoroughly based in a concrete historical setting, we soon discover that biblical exegesis cannot be conducted from an individualistic perspective without historical awareness in a corporate sense.[43] In other words, God's revelation in the Old Testament and its fulfillment in Christ are made intelligible only within the context of Israel's communal history. This encourages readers of the Bible to seek to determine how the story was understood by the first audience.[44]

However, it should be noted that the understanding of history as presumed in Scripture does not refer directly to the facts of world history in a way that satisfies the modern standard of objective analysis of factual information. The history of Israel is interpreted in a certain manner, in which historical events convey the relationship between God and His people by way of "narrative-theological structures."[45] This indicates that the core events of Israel's history are made intelligible through her faith in Yahweh and His redemptive purpose. The narratives concerning the promise of the Davidic covenant (2 Sam 7), for instance, maintain their force in subsequent history in a definite sense, which Gerhard von Rad refers to as "theological historiography." He notes that "the realism with which the anointed is depicted, and the secularity out of which he emerges and in which he moves, are without parallel in the ancient East."[46]

On the same note, the kerygmatic proclamation of the Gospel and its witness are intelligible only when it is based in this understanding of history. Ridderbos explains that "the redemptive history of Israel not only bears witness to facts in terms of historicity but also the theological perception of the meaning and truth of a particular event."[47] This unique

---

43. Zimmerli, "Promise and Fulfillment," 96–115. Cf. also Holland, *Contours of Pauline Theology*. He argues that Scripture was designed for the community at large in a corporate setting, which means that God speaks to the community of believers as opposed to individuals.

44. See chapter 3, "First-Century Jewish-Christians and Their Interpretation of the Scripture."

45. Ciampa, "The History of Redemption" 255.

46. von Rad, *Old Testament Theology*, vol. 1, 316.

47. Ridderbos, *Redemptive History and the New Testament Scriptures*.

perspective of history departs from an accepted standard of historical investigation of our modern world. The modern historical-critical scholars would seek after factual details, and often in biblical theology this leads to frustrating outcomes. Rather than isolating the historical facts from the religious spiritual dimension, the writers of the Bible must have viewed the historical facts and theological truth as one and the same entity. This is what is meant by "redemptive history." Israel hoped for divine intervention in their historical atrocities—for example, conquest and exile. Therefore, unlike modern definitions of history where any biased religious preconception would be unacceptable in the evaluation of history, ancient Jewish writers understood history precisely in the light of their religious faith in Yahweh.[48] It seems that this attitude was common among the early Christians, as they viewed the witness to facts and theological truth as one and the same phenomenon, which indicates that the Gospel presents a historical revelation in the context of "redemptive history."[49] This is thoroughly in agreement with our discussion of the messianic expectation of the Old Testament (see ch. 2), as Israel's hope of divine salvation was manifested in the historical context of exile (see also Isa 5:13; Isa 27:8: Jer 13:19; 24:1; 27:20; 29:1–16; 52:15–31).

The biblical concept of history, therefore, was not understood in a figurative sense, but the authors of the New Testament wanted to delineate the trajectory of the covenantal relationship of Yahweh with Israel in a definite historical perspective, which suggests that religious elements such as eschatological expectation were not abstract, spiritual concepts but were firmly anchored in historical reality. In other words, in the mind-set of the early Christians, the concept of divine salvation is intelligible only in the context of Israel's historical circumstances with a definite beginning and end.[50]

Biblical Concept of Redemptive Event and Its Significance

The history of Israel and Yahweh's promise of deliverance in the Bible evolves around redemptive events that shape the relationship between

---

48. Israel always looked back to the prototype redemptive event of Exodus in reaffirming her faith in Yahweh's faithfulness. Cf. Fretheim "'Because the Whole Earth Is Mine,'" 229–76; see also Fretheim, "The Reclamation of Creation: Redemption and Law in Exodus," 355–57; Gowan, *Theology in Exodus*; Nicholson, *God and His People*; Childs, *The Book of Exodus*; Fishbane, *Biblical Interpretation in Ancient Israel*.

49. Ridderbos, *Redemptive History and the New Testament Scriptures*, 56–67.

50. Cf. Cullmann, *Christ and Time*.

Yahweh and His people. We have seen how the events of Exodus and Exile in the Old Testament have shaped the mind-set of the early Christian writers in their understanding of Jesus' messianic role in establishing the New Exodus.

However, one might assume a critical stance and raise questions over such a heavy emphasis on these events. In other words, is it reasonable to assume that the major redemptive events shape the later understanding of and faith in Yahweh's redemptive purpose? Do they function as a lens through which we define and interpret the redemptive history of Israel?

In response to this, Oscar Cullmann argues that not all fragments of ongoing time carry equal significance and constitute redemptive history, but rather specific points (καιρός) that are singled out from time as a whole. They represent what would be designated as the decisive redemptive event. These are not brought about by human deliberations but by divine execution, which stand in a special place in the history of God and His people. To illustrate this point, it is significant that Jesus himself, according to the synoptic witness, characterizes his passion as καιρός (Matt 28:18, 41, 42, 44). This surely marks one of the major events of Jesus' earthly ministry. More significantly, the passion and crucifixion take place during the time of Passover, which is surely one of the most commemorated and representative redemptive events in the history of Israel (cf. Matt 26:18).[51] It may thus be suggested that not all events

---

51. Ibid., 39–41 Cf. von Rad *Old Testament Theology*, vol. 2, 102–3. Von Rad points out that "any description of the concept of time in the ancient world in general and in Israel in particular would be perfectly inadequate unless something was said of the significance of the festivals. The festivals, not time, were the absolute data, and were data whose holiness was absolute." Cf. also Holland, *Contours of Pauline Theology*. It is argued that the paradigm of the Passover event and the related themes are decisive elements in Paul's Christology. With regard to the significance of the Passover in Israel's religion, cf. Wood et al., eds., *New Bible Dictionary*: "Abib, later called Nisan, the month of the ripening years and of the first Passover, was made in honor of the first month of the Jewish year (Ex. 12:2; Dt. 16:1; cf. Lev. 23:5; Num. 9:1–5; 28:16)." The month of the Passover being placed right at the beginning of the year underlines the representative role the Passover, i.e., the Exodus event played in the mind-set of the Jewish people. See also Segal, *The Hebrew Passover from Earliest Times to AD 70*; Stewart, "The Jewish Festivals," 149–61. It is assumed that the Last Supper coincided with the statutory Passover. Mann, "Passover: The Time of Our Lives," 229–76, also notes that "the Passover narrative is arguably the most important section of the entire book because it is primarily here that the experience of Exodus is communicated not simply as a moment in historical time but as a perennially recurring moment in the

in the history of Israel carry an equal level of significance, and certain representative redemptive events do function as defining moments in shaping the perception of God's dealing with Israel.

While it is crucial to appreciate the significance of the redemptive events of the Old Testament in the New Testament proclamation of Jesus as Israel's Messiah, the early Christian writers nevertheless understood these redemptive events only as precursors to the fuller realization of salvation in Christ Jesus. We cannot read the New Testament into the Old Testament texts (as if the earlier Jewish writers were aware of later events). However, it is justifiable to read the Old Testament into the New Testament, as the early Christians certainly viewed the life of Jesus in the context of Old Testament prophecies. For instance, Aage Bentzen points out that the term *messiah* may be used of the preexilic Israelite sacral king and also of the eschatological Son of David. There can be no doubt that the term originally referred to a historical figure of the Israelite monarchy. To argue that the Messiah in the Old Testament prefigures Jesus would be the result of the Christianization of the Jewish text, which is not a plausible exegetical practice in biblical theology. Of course, the prophecies point to the coming of the Messiah who would surpass David in his redemptive authority, but to argue that they point to Jesus is beyond the textual evidence. In other words, it is crucial to draw a clear line of distinction between the Savior, the Divine King of eschatology whom the early Christians believed to have been revealed in Jesus, and the Davidic sacral king, the royal entity as depicted in the Psalms (cf. 45:7). Even though both figures are commonly designated the Messiah, the term did not have equal meaning for the early Christian community. The difference should be recognized, as the early Christians regarded the Old Testament prophecies to be messianic, which, while thoroughly retaining their value, are nevertheless incomplete in nature. The fulfilled concept of the Messiah is realized only in Jesus (cf. Matt 16:16).[52] Cullmann states that "the preservation of the Old Testament

---

present life of those for whom the story is sacred." See Theiss, "The Passover Feast of the New Covenant," 17–35; Carmichael, "David Daube on the Eucharist and the Passover Seder," 45–67, highlights the significance of the communal event of redemption, as the Passover Eve was thought to be the very night when the people would be redeemed by the Messiah. In the New Testament, the echoing motifs can be seen in the Eucharist, as the ritual initially constituted by Jesus commemorates a true deliverance which is reminiscent of Israel's Passover in the prototype Exodus tradition.

52. Bentzen, *King and Messiah*, 37–38.

has its inner justification in the fact that it is regarded as a 'preparation in time' for the Christ-event, not in that it is regarded as a parallel presentation of the same thing in another form."[53]

Similarly, Wolfhart Pannenberg argues that "the advocacy of a typological exegesis of the Old Testament is based on a concern to find in the Old Testament and the New Testament not only a common 'doctrine' or 'spiritual content,' but to regain reference to the facts attested in the New Testament: That is, to discover the connection between the Testaments in the historical process itself . . . So long as the connection between the Christ event and the Old Testament is sought primarily in structural agreements, the primary realization in Christ necessarily depreciates the shadowy preliminary representation in Old Testament history."[54]

While Matthew is thoroughly embedded within the Jewish tradition (cf. Matt 5:17, 18; 7:12), he also makes it clear that the Old Testament is subordinate to Jesus' authority (Matt 12:6, 8). Since ultimate salvation is won only through the death and resurrection of Christ, the center of redemptive history no longer lies in the future but is now a historical certainty.

Although divine salvation has been decisively revealed through Christ, the final consummation of Parousia is still expected in the future, as indicated in the finale of the Gospel of Matthew (28:16–20). It should be emphasized, however, that the future is no longer, as in Judaism, the τέλος, or "end," that defines the meaning as a whole. Primitive Christianity certainly retains an eschatological view of history, but it no longer thinks in an exclusively eschatological manner where the future is uncertain (cf. Acts 17:31).[55] On the same principle as Matthew, Paul also says that Jesus ends the era of the law (Rom 10:4), but the transformation of believers—that is, being clothed with the new spiritual body—remains the object of hope for the future, since resurrection for individual believers is possible only at the end of days (Cf. John 11:24; Acts 24:15).[56]

Jewish Perception of History

If it is correct that the use of the Psalms by the evangelist indicates the thorough Jewishness of the early Christian mind-set, then the percep-

---

53. Cullmann, *Christ and Time*, 134.
54. Pannenberg, "Redemptive Event and History," 326–27.
55. Cullmann, *Christ and Time*, 140.
56. Ibid., 237.

tion of history in terms of messianic promise and its fulfillment is also to be seen as Jewish in nature. The use of the Old Testament as proof texts in supporting Jesus' identity and ministry clearly indicates that the New Testament writers did not deviate from the Jewish concept of history. In fact, their mind-set was completely immersed in the Old Testament tradition.[57]

Contrary to this understanding, Rudolf Bultmann relies on the presupposition that the mind-set of the New Testament writers was Hellenized, as they employed the Hellenistic method of "allegorizing" the Old Testament to enforce messianic promises. This indicates that the themes of prophecy and fulfillment are nothing more than an artificial construction of the later followers of Christ, who read into the Old Testament in order to support their ideological agenda.[58] However, the early Christian perception of history clearly shows that their mind-set and spiritual identity were thoroughly Jewish. These Jewish believers saw in Jesus and his ministry not a radical departure from their ancestral tradition but the continuity of its essence in a fuller sense.

Bultmann's presupposition undermines the Jewishness of the New Testament writers, which also leads to an eschatological understanding that is inconsistent with the Old Testament ethos. He argues that the dimension of the new covenant lies outside the historical reality, and he regards the notion of fulfillment as the consequence of historical development to be an absurd idea.[59] However, a figurative understanding of biblical salvation fails to appreciate the intimate relationship between Yahweh and His people manifested in concrete historical reality. The Jewish people sought to interpret and secure their faith through historical awareness of God's redemptive activity in Israel. Redemptive history, therefore, denotes a historical understanding of divine revelation in the context of a religious community.

---

57. Cf. Holland, *Contours of Pauline Theology*; Ellison, "Typology," 158–66; Legarth, "Typology and its Theological Basis," 143–54. See also Dodd, *According to the Scripture*.

58. Bultmann, "Prophecy and Fulfillment," 51, 54.

59. Ibid., 63, 69, 73.

Part Two: The Divine-Royal Formula and the New Exodus Motif

Introduction

A unique concept of Israel's redemptive history is displayed in the way the Old Testament text was utilized by the early Christians, and the same paradigm applies to the use of royal-enthronement psalms in Matthew's Christology. We have argued that the Son of David who represents divine authority is the long-awaited messianic agent in the New Exodus. We have noted above that the Exodus centered on Moses, and the covenant was based on the giving of the law at Mount Sinai. In the New Exodus, however, God makes a covenant with David which will be the basis of a new covenant with Israel: "I will save my flock, and they will no longer be plundered. I will judge between one sheep and another. I will place over them one shepherd, my servant David, and he will tend them; he will tend them and be their shepherd. I the LORD will be their God, and my servant David will be prince among them. I the LORD have spoken" (Ezek 34:22–24).[60]

The promise of the Davidic Messiah in the New Exodus naturally directs our attention to the royal psalms in particular, which vividly describe the enthronement of the king of Israel. This also indicates that there exists a textual, historical, and theological connection between these psalms and Israel's redemptive history in the way Matthew's Christology is presented. The Exodus tradition, in particular, lays the foundation of the future expectation of the Messiah in a prophetic vision concerning the salvation of Israel as a state. This is in no way to disregard other preceding biblical themes such as the creation motif, which lays the foundation of the universal aspect of the Bible which addresses the whole of humanity. However, the community to which Matthew writes his Gospel is predominantly a Jewish one, and it would make perfect sense for him to use themes from Scripture that would have been familiar and also appealing to the Jewish mind. In this regard, the deliverance of the nation from Egypt would no doubt have been one of the most significant redemptive acts of Yahweh and would have resonated in Israel's mind throughout the ages. The use of the royal-enthronement psalms in the christological message of the Gospel would show that the promise of the New Exodus has now finally been fulfilled in Christ, which signifies the revelation of the power and glory of God. This claim, as we

---

60. See also 2 Sam 7:12–14; Jer 31:31–34.

shall see in more detail in subsequent chapters, stands on the prototype redemptive event of Exodus. Whereas the first Exodus event revealed the awesome power of Yahweh by the overthrow of the Egyptians in the Red Sea, the New Exodus will achieve greater salvation by defeating the kingdom of darkness through the Son of David. The centrality of the Exodus motif and its redemptive significance are pervasive not only in Matthew's Gospel but also in the bedrock of the New Testament kerygma as a whole.[61]

Psalms and the Exodus Motif

The presupposition of this volume is that the use of the Psalms by the early Jewish Christians was deeply embedded within Israel's redemptive historical consciousness. In order to understand the principle behind the use of the Psalms by the evangelist, we have reviewed the biblical concept of history and the eschatological consciousness that would condition the way certain types of psalms are used to assert the early Christians' belief in Jesus as their Messiah. All of this is originally rooted in the concrete historical reality of the exile (568–538 BCE). A rekindling of the fervent expectation of the Messiah from the exilic period to New Testament times is modeled on the Exodus, during which Yahweh's mighty act of deliverance was first manifested to Israel as a nation (cf. Isa 11:16; Jer 2:6; 7: 22, 25; 11:4, 7; 16:14; 23:7; Ezek 20:6–10).

The centrality of the Exodus motif is also clearly visible in the Psalms, where it reinforces eschatological belief by recalling the redemptive event, as evidenced by the recurring expression "the day I brought you up out of the land of Egypt" (cf. Pss 78:12, 43, 51; 80:8; 81:5, 10; 105:23, 38; 106:7, 21; 114:1; 135:8; 136:10). The event provided for the psalmist the imagery and the reality of the eschatological "day of the Lord."[62]

---

61. Ciampa, "The History of Redemption," 295, 296, 299. Mark begins the Gospel with a composite quotation from Exodus 23:20, Malachi 3:1, and Isaiah 40:3, which serves to indicate that the understanding of the New Exodus in terms of God's postexilic forgiveness and restoration is based on the first Exodus event, and it telegraphs the inauguration of the fulfillment of the prophecy in the coming of Jesus (Mark 1:2). Luke also begins with the hope of the mighty Davidic savior (Luke 1:69ff.) who will liberate Israel from the exile. Paul, likewise, refers to the Davidic promises in the scheme of Israel's redemptive history, which begins with the establishment of the covenant at Sinai and the subsequent exile due to Israel's sin and the prophecy of restoration that follows the exile (cf. Rom 1:1–5). See also Strauss, "The Davidic Messiah in Luke-Acts."

62. Motyer, *Look to the Rock*, 169. Cf. also Howard, "Christ Our Passover," 97–108.

Heinz Kruse, in his study of Psalm 132, notes that although the atmosphere of David's covenant lingers over the whole Psalm, the covenant expressly mentioned as a condition for the continuity of the Davidic monarchy must be regarded as pointing to the covenantal establishment at Sinai: "The LORD swore an oath to David, a sure oath that he will not revoke: 'One of your own descendants I will place on your throne. If your sons keep my covenant and the statutes I teach them, then their sons shall sit on our throne for ever and ever'"[63] (Ps 132:11–12).

Even though the covenant with David replaces the old covenant at Sinai, it seems that the new covenant is at least based on the statutes originally given to Moses. This shows how the Exodus event deeply influenced Israel's historical consciousness and faith in Yahweh, which is reflected in the language of the psalmist.

The internal textual nuance of the royal psalms (Pss 2; 18; 20; 21; 45; 72; 101; 110; 132; 144:1–11; cf. 89:47–52) clearly shows historical awareness of Yahweh's mighty act of salvation demonstrated most probably from the memory of the Exodus, since this was the major redemptive event which undergirded faith in the God of Israel and his promise for the coming of the Messiah.[64]

---

63. Kruse, "Psalm 132 and the Royal Zion Festival," 286.

64. Piper, "Unchanging Promises," 3–22, argues that if excessive emphasis has been placed upon Genesis and the creation, then it would have rendered religion on a mythical realm. Cf. Mettinger, *In Search of God*, 21. It was in the time of Moses that the revelation of the name YHWH came into focus and introduced a new major chapter in the history of the people of God, prior to which God was the deity of individuals (Exod 3:6; 6:2–3). Cf. also von Rad, *Old Testament Theology*, vol. 2, 322. Jahwism was preceded by a phase which is called the religion of the God of the ancestors; this was adopted by the Jahwism which followed. This incorporation, von Rad argues, did not lead to merging or coalescing; on the contrary, it was for long remembered that the revelation of the name YHWH involved a fresh start (Exod 3:1ff; 6:3). This implies that the Exodus was the beginning of the redemptive history of Israel. However, this need not mean that there is a discontinuity with the pre-Mosaic worship, as the primitive form of the religion in a very remarkable way anticipates the Jahwism which succeeded it; von Rad, *Old Testament Theology*, vol. 2, 337, 338, 339. The Deuteronomist's theology of history is also worth noting here, as it reflects the event of the Babylonian exile when the prophecy of the New Exodus was proclaimed. The Deuteronomist, like the rest of the Old Testament, ascribes to the monarchy the crucial key-position between Yahweh and Israel. Von Rad notes that this did not depend only on the kings' religious devotion to or apostasy from Yahweh, but upon their attitude to the revelation of the Mosaic law. The Torah of Moses and the dynasty of David were powerful historical realities. Thus, the Deuteronomist sees the main problem of the history of Israel as lying in the question of the correct correlation of Moses and David.

The quotations from the Psalms are intended to characterize Jesus as the messianic agent in Israel's redemptive history, and the internal progression of the Psalms makes it clear that expectations regarding the fulfillment of the Davidic promises were superimposed on the New Exodus prophecies out of the conviction that they spoke of the universal Davidic kingdom which was to be established at the time of postexilic restoration (cf. Pss 14:7; 53:6). The themes of exile and restoration based on the Exodus thus play a major role in the theology of the Psalms. In the same manner, the later use of the Psalms by the evangelist also displays a belief in the continuing redemptive act of God for Israel, which is consummated in Christ Jesus.[65]

Jesus, the Royal or Divine Messiah?

The state of the exile for Israel transcended mere tangible experience in a physical world to a state of spiritual crisis and abandonment, and the need of divine intervention was desperately felt.[66] For Israel, the exile was a direct consequence of her sin, which means that the covenantal relationship with Yahweh had to be set right before she could hope for restoration.

Matthew takes this into account, and he makes it abundantly clear in the genealogical account (Matt 1:1–18) that the answer to the problem of the exile is the Son of David who will bring about the ultimate salvation from sin (cf. Matt 26:28). Jesus is thus identified as the Davidic Messiah who will end Israel's exile. However, Jesus' identity as the Son of David is immediately complemented by the divine origin of his birth, as the virgin conception by the Holy Spirit shows (Matt 1:20). Matthew takes up the promise of the virgin Mary's child, whose birth was to have profound significance for Israel's well-being. This designated child was to be of the Davidic line (Isa 7:14).

Although Jesus is primarily identified as the Son of David, the prologue of the Gospel suggests that the Christ cannot be confined within the legacy of David. From the beginning, he is portrayed to be someone far greater. According to our survey of the messianic expectation of the Old Testament, both Yahweh and his Davidic agent are eagerly awaited

---

65. Ciampa, "The History of Redemption," 277, 281.

66. N. T. Wright argues that many postexilic and Second Temple Jews believed that they were still living in a state of exile, which forms the paradigm for christological assertion by the community of Jesus.

to save the people of Israel from exile and restore the kingdom of Israel.[67] Since it was *both* the Messiah and Yahweh, we have questioned whether the evangelist would have been satisfied with quoting just the royal psalms, which are written primarily to celebrate the Davidic king in various royal ceremonies. We believe that Matthew wished to portray Jesus to be someone far greater than a mere Davidic king. He achieved this by utilizing themes that are inherently characteristic of the enthronement psalms, which are written to celebrate Yahweh's Kingship and His reign. Therefore, we believe that both the royal and the enthronement psalms, as categorized by Gunkel, must have had an important function in the overall New Exodus motif as they are applied to the Christology of Matthew's Gospel. These two types of psalms (as will be argued in more detail in subsequent chapters) have a crucial christological function, as they support the evangelist's claim about Jesus in royal, Davidic messianic terms, as well as in language that was normally reserved for Yahweh.

Such hope in the deliverance of Yahweh is not purely metaphorical or spiritual in nature but is grounded in a concrete historical reality with a definite beginning and end. The people of Israel as a nation first experienced divine salvation from the bondage of slavery in Egypt. Because of the historical nature of the Exodus, this event always played a critical role in the minds of the Israelites and exerted a strong influence on the mind-set of the Old Testament writers.

Even during the turmoil of the Babylonian exile, Israel consolidated her faith on the basis of the Exodus. Yahweh's redemptive act for Israel in the past provided hope for the people facing uncertainty over the future, as they could revisit their history of redemption and have their faith in Yahweh revitalized. In fact, one could argue that the messianic hope of Israel in the great Son of David was made possible only because they had already experienced God's deliverance in the past.[68]

Despite the differences in scholarly opinion concerning the messianic expectation of the Old Testament (see ch. 2), it seems that the early Jewish Christians believed that the ultimate salvation of Israel would be

---

67. It should be stressed that this dual kingship in terms of heavenly and earthly reign does not detract from the monotheistic belief of Israel or even deify David, but rather it reinforces the belief that Yahweh is intimately involved with the history of the world.

68. Old, "The Psalms of Praise in the Worship of the New Testament Church," 25.

wrought by God, whose divine authority is manifested in His messianic agent. The hope for the ideal Davidic Messiah and the establishment of divine reign are consistently exhibited in Christ Jesus, as he embodies the fulfillment of both divine and Davidic kingship.

It follows therefore that the "divine-royal formula" in Matthew's Gospel is both textually and theologically evident, which justifies our claim that the evangelist uses the royal-enthronement psalms as one ideological unit. These two types of psalms, therefore, are crucial texts for early Christian belief in Jesus as the Messiah from the line of David in the redemptive history of Israel.

It seems viable, then, to suggest that the redemptive historical perspective inclines us to properly appreciate the unique character of the theological thinking which the Old Testament text imparts to the christological message of the Gospel in terms of supernatural and historical dimensions.[69] In broader terms, the use of the Old Testament in the New Testament can only be grasped when we appreciate the importance of the ongoing nature of Israel's redemptive history, which finds its fulfillment in Christ Jesus. The royal-enthronement psalms in the Christology of Matthew therefore should be viewed on the basis of this historical awareness of Yahweh's redemptive dealing with Israel. We shall now put this methodological presupposition to the test in the light of what are believed to be the key christological passages of Matthew's Gospel.

SUMMARY

We have argued that the Old Testament quotations have historical interest, and the use of the royal psalms supports the messianic claim of Jesus in terms of his Davidic legacy. Gunkel's classification of the Psalms according to genre and historical setting establishes the original context in which these texts were first written. Although such distinctions between the Psalms would be irrelevant to the early Christians (since the categorization is a modern scholarly artifact), it nevertheless helps us understand a motif behind Matthew's Christology, as he incorporated certain types of psalms to support his claims concerning Jesus. There can be no doubt that the subject mentioned in the royal psalms is the king of Israel, but later the text also became the prophetic model for the ideal Messiah in the community of the early Jewish Christians. Such

---

69. Ridderbos, *Redemptive History and the New Testament Scriptures*, 75.

understanding is upheld because we find that Matthew, in addressing the Jewish community, regarded the Old Testament texts as a foundation to the fulfillment of prophecies manifested in Christ Jesus.

It is argued that the Psalms were used to support the view that the Old Testament promise of salvation through the Davidic agent has finally been realized in Jesus. In terms of which types of psalms were particularly useful in the Christology of Matthew, we have suggested that the royal psalms, which were written to celebrate the Davidic kingship, were of major importance for the early church.

Moreover, the enthronement psalms, which were written to celebrate Yahweh's Kingship, provided imagery crucial to revealing Jesus' identity as a being far greater than David ever could be. We shall examine this more closely in our exegesis of the christological texts in Matthew with particular attention to the Son of Man sayings.

It is interesting to note that not only is there structural correspondence between the royal and the enthronement psalms but that our review of the messianic expectation of the Old Testament strongly indicates that Israel regarded the dual kingship of Yahweh and the Davidic Messiah as complementary. In effect, they anticipated that both would intervene to bring about salvation. This makes Gunkel's presupposition of the royal and enthronement psalms as ideologically incompatible of dubious value in the context of the early Jewish-Christian setting. It is the presupposition of this volume that in Matthew's Gospel both types of psalms are used in the christological statements because the early Christians expected both the Davidic Messiah and Yahweh to intervene in Israel's salvation.

In conjunction with the analysis above, we have reviewed the biblical concept of history, which is essential if one is to grasp the principle behind the evangelist's use of royal-enthronement psalms. The use of these psalms presupposes a "divine-royal formula" in Matthew's Christology which identifies Jesus primarily as the Son of David, but it also places him above this category. He exhibits characteristics that are exclusively attributed to Yahweh.

Also, an examination of Israel's redemptive history allows us to appreciate the unique perspective of Israel's history as defined by Yahweh's redemptive promise and fulfillment in the Psalms, which is based upon the Exodus tradition.[70] As these texts were utilized by Matthew,

70. See Pss 78:12, 43, 51; 80:8; 81:5, 10; 105:23, 38; 106:7, 21; 114:1; 135:8; 136:10.

the whole picture of Israel's redemptive history came into view, as the evangelist sought to convey to his Jewish counterparts that the Messiah had finally come. This man whom Matthew came to believe to be the Messiah would accomplish a salvation that far outweighs the Exodus or even liberation from foreign oppression (cf. Ps 137:1, 8). He would indeed inaugurate the New Exodus, as foretold by the prophets, and establish the New Covenant. He would be the eschatological King of the New Exodus.

The early Jewish-Christian use of the royal-enthronement psalms, therefore, supports the thesis that in Christ Jesus the divine reign and Davidic kingship are wholly manifested, and that he brings the redemptive history of Israel to a decisive culmination.

5

Christology in the Gospel of Matthew

EXEGESIS OF THE KEY CHRISTOLOGICAL PASSAGES

Introduction

THERE IS GENERAL AGREEMENT that the primary concern of the author of Matthew's Gospel is to reveal Jesus' identity and his ministry as the fulfillment of God's promise of the Messiah in the Old Testament.[1] In order to examine how Matthew achieves this effect in his Gospel, we need to isolate the key passages where the claim concerning Jesus' identity is decisively revealed. However, deciphering what constitutes the key christological passages in the Gospel is subjective and therefore debatable. Nevertheless it can be argued that it is the entire narrative structure of the Gospel which progressively discloses the truth concerning Christ Jesus. Indeed, in seeking to read the Gospel and understand its intention it is important to keep the whole literary context in mind when we focus on particular passages. However, there are certain passages where Matthew's literary skills are used to point to Jesus' identity; these require closer attention.

The question as to which constitute the key christological passages has been raised by the pioneering scholars in the field of the literary criticism of the Gospel. J. D. Kingsbury argues: "The literary-critical

---

1. Fuller, *The Foundations of New Testament Christology*, 15. Fuller defines Christology as the doctrine of the person of Jesus Christ. He states that in traditional dogmatics, Christology precedes soteriology. It was because of Jesus' identity that his actions became meaningful.

recognition that Matthew tells a story in which he posits God's evaluative point of view as normative is of paramount significance for the study of the Christology. If it be granted that God's evaluative point of view is normative in the First Gospel, it follows that the center of Matthew's Christology must lie with God's understanding of Jesus, i.e., with the way in which God thinks about Jesus . . . The task is to ascertain both how God thinks about Jesus in Matthew's story and what place Matthew gives to this understanding of Jesus as he moves the reader through the plot."[2]

In a somewhat contrary manner, David Hill argues that Jesus rather than God is the focus of interest. He states: "Jesus fulfills the Old Testament and his messianic status is confirmed therefrom, and it is Jesus who proclaims and makes effective divine judgment."[3]

In the baptism and transfiguration narratives, Hill contends that it is not God's voice that is the dominant concern, but Jesus' identity. It is Jesus' identity Matthew emphasizes throughout the Gospel. He further states that this is not to say that Jesus' perspective does not align with God's concerns, but in Matthew's story it is not the latter which is being presented as normative or determinative, but rather Jesus' own self-consciousness.[4]

Both arguments, in our judgment, are indisputable, as both God's and Jesus' points of view are what determine the meaning of the story. However, it is misguided to set up an argument that implies, even if inadvertently, Jesus' perspective to be in any way different from God's. This is in fact what Kingsbury and Hill are implying, as if God's point of view precedes Jesus' and vice versa. We suggest that it is best to avoid such interpretation where Jesus' perspective is somehow not in complete agreement with that of God. Both scholars mentioned above would probably concede this point, but once the exegete separates Jesus' point of view from God's, he is most likely to run into conclusions that are entirely different from what Matthew intended to convey. The person of Jesus in Matthew's Gospel is an extraordinary character whose authority is far above anyone Israel has ever come across before. His authority in issues of salvation and judgment bears such a close resemblance to that of Yahweh in the Old Testament that any attempt to distinguish

2. Kingsbury, "The Figure of Jesus in Matthew's Story," 3–36.
3. Hill, "The Figure of Jesus in Matthew's Story: A Response," 37–52.
4. Ibid., 40, 42.

Jesus' perspective from that of God could not have been the intention of the evangelist. We shall see in more detail later that Jesus embodies both the royal Davidic claims in human terms as well as possessing the status of the divine person. This is an indication that the divine status has been invested in Jesus which means that anything he does or says is a reflection of God's presence on earth. This is consistent with the messianic expectations of the Old Testament in that Israel anticipated not only Yahweh but also the Davidic Messiah in her ultimate redemption from the exile. If we accept the thesis that Matthew is genuinely Jewish, could he have intended that the Messiah's point of view is somehow at variance with that of God?[5] On the basis of the messianic expectation of the Old Testament, it is much more plausible to presuppose that what God says regarding Jesus' identity is surely accepted by Jesus himself and vice versa. The passages where Jesus' identity is declared or confessed involve the use of the royal-enthronement psalms. The decision to focus on these types of psalms is derived from the fact that Matthew is presenting a "divine-royal" Christology. The passages in which these psalms are used set the image of Jesus in both royal Davidic terms as well as in divine status. This fundamental aspect of Matthew's Christology is consistently reflected throughout the Gospel even if the use of these psalms is absent. We have chosen specific passages where the use of the royal-enthronement psalms is reasonably explicit for the sake of clarity in argument, but we believe that the "divine-royal" Christology which is formed by these psalms can readily be detected elsewhere in the narratives. For instance, in Matthew 12:1–8, where the Son of Man is declared to be Lord of the Sabbath, Jesus' authority over religious regulation is portrayed to be something that no man can resemble. John Nolland raises a few possibilities with regard to the implication of the passage in question: Is David appealed to as an interpreter of the Law? Or is Jesus claiming to be, like David and beyond David, the one who is entitled to arbitrate in the interpretation of the Law? Or is David viewed as "above" the Law? David and, even more so, Jesus as the Christ are free from the restraints of the Law because of their special places in the purposes

---

5. The Jewish nature of the New Testament is also emphasized by Marshall, *The Origins of New Testament Christology*, 16, who notes that "many of the concepts in the New Testament have been taken over from the Old Testament and it is necessary when we are examining any passage in the New Testament to look for passages in the Old Testament which may have influenced the writer to think in the way he did. It would be folly to neglect the impact of Judaism on the early Church."

of God. Nolland feels that the best option is the appeal to David as an interpreter of the law, since David was "a man after God's own heart who will do all [God's] will" (Acts 13:22) and further notes that a christological claim shows that Jesus is the antitype to David in this respect.[6] We would not necessarily disagree with Nolland's view here, as it is certainly part of what Matthew wishes to convey in his Christology. However, we believe that Matthew is not only merely presenting Jesus as the antitype to David. Rather, Nolland asserts that Jesus is in fact claiming to be the antitype to David but he is also above David in his authority. He is the Lord of the Sabbath, and no religious regulations can bind him or restrict him from doing what he desires. When we take the Son of Man into consideration and the authority that is attributed to this title, it is difficult to conclude that Jesus is a mere antitype to David. However, it is doubtful whether the Old Testament would warrant the claim that David is viewed as "above" the Law. There is no doubt that David has a special role in the redemptive history of Israel, but his authority is not comparable to that of the Son of Man in that his authority clearly surpasses human power. Therefore, we believe that Nolland's second option above best explains the meaning of the passage under discussion, namely, that Jesus is the Son of David but also beyond him in his redemptive authority, whose power also surpasses the Law. In this regard, it may be argued that the "divine-royal" Christology is also consistently employed in this christological statement.

Another christological passage which also brings this aspect of Matthean Christology into the discussion is 14:22–33. Here, Jesus is seen walking on the lake, which causes the disciples to become terrified. Nolland notes that "the response in 14:33 builds on the question posed in 8:27, where the wording of the question has left no doubt for the readers that Jesus acts as God acts. The disciples are now conscious that they are in the presence of God, and they worship."[7] He also notes the use of the verb προσκυνεῖν, which is typically used in the context of bowing down to kiss someone's feet and in the New Testament is used when a subject worships or venerates a divine object. In conjunction with this, the same verb has also been used at the beginning of the Gospel in Jesus' infancy narrative in Matthew 2:2 where the Magi come to pay homage to the king of the Jews. Here, Nolland points out that the verb is used "in

6. Nolland *The Gospel of Matthew*, 483.
7. Ibid., 603.

a manner which seems designed to blur the distinction between deferential respect and religious worship."[8] However, in the present context of Jesus walking on the lake, which is clearly extraordinary, it is most likely that the verb used is pointing to the latter. This christological passage reveals Jesus' divine-royal status; "Truly you are the Son of God." This statement is not merely an expression of Jesus' identity but the disciples' confession of faith in Christ. Through this remarkable incident the disciples encounter God's presence manifested through Jesus, and in that moment they worship Jesus and confess him as the Son of God.[9]

On this note, the confession of Peter in Matthew 16:13–20 picks up on Jesus' identity as the Son of God and expands Mark's "You are the Christ" (8:29) into a more exalted designation, "You are the Christ, the Son of the living God." Again, Matthew's high Christology is displayed in Peter's confession of Jesus as the Christ who is worthy of worship "as one in whom God is immediately encountered."[10]

We have decided to focus on the royal-enthronement psalms because we believe that the divine-royal motif, which these particular types of psalms presuppose, is prevalent in Matthew's Christology. The key christological passages in this volume have thus been chosen on the basis of how Matthew presents his divine-royal Christology through the use of the royal-enthronement psalms, which defines the most fundamental aspect of his Christology. It cannot be stressed enough that the importance of Old Testament texts in the New Testament cannot be determined simply by the number or the frequency of the passages quoted or alluded to. By using royal-enthronement psalms elsewhere in the Gospel, Matthew creates an image of Jesus as the Davidic Messiah whose authority resembles something of a deity.

The key christological passages in this volume have been selected on the basis of where Jesus claims his identity, which is then affirmed by God as he reveals the Father's redemptive purpose in a mutually complementary manner.[11] Also importantly, it is not so much what Jesus

8. Ibid.

9. Nolland also notes that "the worship of the disciples prefigures the worship of the Church." Also, Jesus' divine-royal status is made explicitly clear in Matthew 11:27, where "a capacity to transmit knowledge of the Father and to exercise the Father's authority comes into focus."

10. Ibid., 665. "Matthew's language in 16:16 has its closest parallel in the high priest's words in 26:63."

11. Cf. D. W. K. So, *Jesus' Revelation of His Father*. He argues persuasively that the crucial character traits of Jesus portrayed in Matthew's Gospel are his radicalism, his

does that defines the Christology of the Gospel but who he is declared to *be* in the narrative that precedes the ministerial function. This is in no way to disregard Jesus' general ministerial activities. But what we are concerned to establish in this volume is a fundamental foundation of Matthew's Christology upon which Jesus' ministerial function is made intelligible. D. A. Hagner also notes that "Matthew's doctrine of Jesus as the Christ is fundamentally important to every theological emphasis in the Gospel, for it is the *identity* of Jesus that determines such things as fulfillment, authoritative exposition of the law, discipleship, ecclesiology, and eschatology."[12]

We have thus identified the key christological passages as the ones which reveal Jesus' identity that is in clear alignment with God's perspective. These, we believe, are the genealogical account (Matt 1:1–17), the baptismal scene (Matt 3:13–17), the transfiguration (Matt 17:1–13), the passion narrative, including the trial scene in particular (Matt 26:57–68), and finally the Great Commission (Matt 28:16–20).

Genealogy (Matthew 1:1–17)

It has been noted that the use of the Old Testament in the New Testament extends beyond mere literal quotation (see ch. 3). To limit oneself to discussion of the direct quotations hardly explains how Matthew understood the Old Testament text and its theology in the context of the Christ event.[13] In this regard, the genealogical account in Matthew, although it is not supported by direct scriptural quotation, encapsulates the history of Israel from the time of Abraham up to Jesus in its entirety. The fact that Matthew begins with such an account indicates that Matthew

---

lordship in exercising his authority in teaching and mighty works, his freedom, his integrity, and his humility. In these excellences, Jesus reveals his Father.

12. Hagner, *Matthew 1–13*, 1xi, also notes that "Matthew heightens the Christology of the material drawn from Mark, making it more explicit (cf. Mk. 8:29 & Matt. 16:16; Matt. 19:17 & Mk. 10:18; Matt. 9:3 & Mk. 2:7)."

13. Menken, "The Psalms in Matthew's Gospel," 61, notes that "in describing Matthew's use of the Old Testament, and thus his use of the book of Psalms, a distinction should be made between marked quotations, unmarked quotations and allusions." Marked quotations denote a series of clauses from Scripture, introduced by a formula. The unmarked quotations are the ones without an introductory/concluding formula. The allusions denote vague ways of making use of the Old Testament. The use of the Old Testament by the New Testament writers in general shows that the Jewish Scripture was an authoritative text and that the events surrounding Jesus are in accordance with God's redemptive plan.

is particularly keen on the fulfillment theme and the continuity of the redemptive history of Israel.[14]

The royal-enthronement psalms are not quoted in the genealogy, but the theological and historical themes in terms of the New Exodus which are generated by these psalms seem to be present. The royal-enthronement psalms intimate the messianic expectation in terms of both the royal Davidic Messiah as well as Yahweh's salvation from the state of exile. In the same manner, the genealogy portrays Jesus as the Son of David who represents Yahweh's reign by establishing the New Exodus.

The beginning of the genealogy states clearly that Jesus is the anticipated Messiah who is the descendent of David. The mention of Abraham is in conjunction with the expectation of the royal Messiah, as Abraham is promised that kings shall come from him. The covenant of Abraham is established by Yahweh in the manner of addressing the royal founder of a nation: "I will make you into a great nation and I will bless you; I will make your name great, and you will be a blessing. I will bless those who bless you, and whoever curses you I will curse; and all peoples on earth will be blessed through you" (Gen 12:2-3).

What is significant is the overarching motif behind the mention of the name Abraham. In Genesis 15:13-14, Yahweh foretells the future enslavement of Abraham's descendents under foreign oppression, which points to the Exodus. However, Yahweh promises that he will punish the nation that has enslaved Israel and bring Israel to great prosperity. God's redemptive activity is thus rooted in his promise to Abraham that he would deliver his descendants from the bondage of slavery. The fulfillment of God's promise to Abraham points to the Exodus when, through Moses, the covenant with Israel as a nation will be created and the revelation of the power and glory of God will be manifested to Israel through the overthrow of the Egyptians. By mentioning Abraham, the evangelist is in effect drawing the readers' attention to the redemptive history of Israel from the very beginning. Nolland notes that Matthew draws on Ruth 4:18-22, which is supplemented by 1 Chron 3:10-19. The

---

14. Mark begins his Gospel with the proclamation of John the Baptist, followed by Jesus' baptism. Luke begins with the dedication to Theophilus, shortly followed by the birth of John the Baptist.

Cullmann *The Christology of the New Testament*, finds a basic unity in the New Testament presentation of Jesus with the messianic expectation of the Old Testament, and this unity is explained in terms of "salvation history." He affirms that Christology arises out of meditation upon salvation history.

intention is that "by evoking important aspects of the story of Israel's history the genealogy functions as a compressed retelling of the Old Testament story."[15]

R. E. Ciampa notes that this anticipates the later biblical material about the ideal Davidic king.[16] As we have discussed, the redemptive event of Exodus will be relived by the greater salvation which will be brought about by the Son of David (cf. Ezek 34:22–24). Matthew is clearly interested in the Davidic sonship of Jesus in the overall structure of Israel's redemptive history, which will become clearer later, as he takes up the messianic expectation of the Old Testament in the royal Davidic figure who will liberate Israel from the exile.[17]

The mention of the two great names of the Old Testament, according to Kingsbury, is to be seen as mutually complementary, as the title Son of Abraham points to Jesus as the one in whom the nations are to find blessing in a more universal sense, whereas the title Son of David points to Jesus as the one in whom Israel is to find blessing.[18] However, it is interesting to note that the title Son of David is mentioned first even though Son of Abraham should come first if the evangelist was thinking in chronological order. This implies that, in Matthew's mind, the Davidic heritage of Jesus precedes the Abrahamic heritage. This further implies that the Gospel is primarily designed for Israel and that the Old Testament tradition is of great importance to the evangelist. Of course, there is no doubt that for a Jew, God's covenant with Abraham is the foundational historical event, but the Davidic connotations are much more prominent in the prophetic traditions pointing to the New Exodus of Israel (cf. Ezek 44–45; Hag 1:13–14; Zech 3:8–9; Isa 9:6).

---

15. Nolland, *The Gospel of Matthew*, 34.

16. Ciampa, "The History of Redemption," 265. Cf. also von Rad, *Old Testament Theology*, vol. 1, 133. The mention of Abraham also implies that the redemptive history of Israel is in view, as the covenant with Abraham and the covenant with Moses are connected with one another. It has been argued that the Exodus is possibly the most representative redemptive event for the nation of Israel. Von Rad notes that this shows the whole course of the saving history from Genesis to Joshua.

17. Cf. Menken, "The Sources of the Old Testament Quotation in Matthew 2: 23," 451–68. In his article, Menken points out that Matthew's "Nazarene" refers to the "shoot" from the stump of Jesse in Isaiah 11:1. In early Judaism, Isaiah 11:1–10 was considered a significant messianic passage, and Matthew is clearly interested in the Davidic sonship of Jesus (Matt 1:6, 17, 20; 9:27).

18. Kingsbury, *Matthew*, 100.

Because Matthew was undoubtedly keen to demonstrate the continuity of the Old Testament in the time of Christ, then the question of why he did not include the creation theme of Genesis must be asked. Indeed, as D. R. Bauer points out, if Matthew wished to emphasize the theme of creation, he would no doubt have begun his genealogy not with Abraham but with Adam.[19] This is an interesting and also a very important point. Matthew is not primarily concerned with the matters of creation but is focusing upon the history of Israel. The evangelist nowhere presents Jesus as the "representative human being" or the essence of the "new creation." His main concern is to show the continuity of God's faithfulness in his promise of salvation for the people of Israel. By taking his readers all the way back to Abraham via David, and by claiming that Jesus is the descendent of these forefathers, Matthew firmly places Jesus in the scheme of Israel's redemptive history.

The positioning of Jesus *before* these great names also deserves an explanation. D. R. Bauer's study of the genealogy reveals that in the Old Testament, the headings to genealogical lists normally identify the genealogy with the forefather rather than with the final descendent (Gen 10:1).[20] This is significant in our discussion of Matthew's genealogy; Bauer notes that "the descendants gained meaning and identity from their forefathers. The unusual practice here of entitling a genealogy according to the name of the last descendant serves to subordinate the forefathers to this last descendant and indicates that they gain their meaning and identity from the last progeny, i.e., from Christ."[21] Bauer adds that "the genealogy points to the paradox of Jesus as the Christ: He is of Israel and yet beyond Israel, a product of history and yet also of God's transcendent action."[22]

By positioning Jesus' name before these great ancestral figures, Matthew is placing the Christ's authority above them, which suggests that while Jesus is primarily identified with David, he cannot be confined within the boundary of Israel. Matthew is implying that he is far more

---

19. Bauer and Powell, eds., *Treasures New and Old*, 136. Cf. also Hill, *The Gospel of Matthew*, 74, 75. The Lucan genealogy (Luke 3:23–38) traces Jesus' origin all the way to Adam, "the son of God." Hill points out that the considerable differences between the Matthean and the Lucan genealogies may be explained on the basis that Luke provides a pedigree of actual descent, whereas Matthew presents the throne succession.

20. Bauer, "The Literary and Theological Function," 140.

21. Ibid.

22. Ibid., 143.

authoritative than David or Abraham. Although the royal-enthronement psalms are not explicitly quoted in the genealogy, the divine-royal motif which these psalms presuppose is likely to be in the mind of the evangelist in this part of the Gospel. Jesus' identity, therefore, is firmly embedded within the history of Israel, but his redemptive function also transcends it.

The emphasis on Jesus' identity as the Davidic Messiah is further reinforced when we consider the structure of the genealogical account. Matthew summarizes the structure in verse 17: "So all the generations from Abraham to David are fourteen generations; and from David to the deportation to Babylon, fourteen generations; and from the deportation to Babylon to the Messiah, fourteen generations" (Matt 1:17).

D. R. Bauer notes that the number fourteen may represent a gematria on the name "David," and the reference to three periods may signify fullness brought about by God.[23] Another important element is the historical reference to the exile in Babylon, as the genealogy mentions the exile four times (v. 11, v. 12, and twice in v. 17).[24] Bauer also notes that "the only event Matthew mentions in the genealogy is the deportation to Babylon for this event most accurately depicts the essential character of Israel's history."[25]

It seems evident that Matthew portrays Jesus as the Son of David who fulfills God's promise of Israel's salvation from the exile, thereby bringing forth the New Exodus.[26] Jesus achieves this as the Davidic Messiah through whom the divine reign is established. This, we have argued, is consistent with the messianic expectation of the Old Testament, as Israel longed for both Yahweh and the Davidic king to intervene in the salvation from the exile.[27] It may be suggested that Jesus embodies

---

23. Ibid., 151. Bauer also points out that just as the mention of the Gentile women in the genealogy supports that Jesus is the Son of Abraham who brings salvation to Gentiles, so the emphasis upon the number fourteen supports the claim that Jesus is the Son of David who brings salvation to Israel.

24. Cf. Ciampa, "The History of Redemption," 292.

25. Bauer, "The Literary and Theological Function," 146.

26. Bauer, "The Kingship of Jesus in the Matthean Infancy Narrative," 306–23. He notes that Matthew emphasizes that Jesus is a Davidic king, for Matthew repeatedly associates Jesus with Bethlehem, the city of David (2:1, 6; 8), and in the fulfillment quotation of 2:6, Matthew joins together Micah 5:2 and 2 Samuel 5:2, both of which refer to the Davidic king.

27. Ibid., 309. Bauer points out that it is important to note that in 1:18–25, Matthew

in himself the Davidic heritage as well as the divine status. This view is reinforced in the narrative of the birth of Jesus Christ (1:18–25), which is placed immediately after the genealogical account. Here, the emphasis is upon the divine nature of Jesus' conception, which distinguishes Mary and Joseph from the rest of the list.[28] J. D. Kingsbury concurs with this view, as he states that "although Matthew makes direct reference to the Davidic sonship of Jesus Messiah in the genealogy that precedes 1:18–25 but not to his divine sonship, in 1:16b, he employs the passive voice in connection with the verb ἐγεννήθη which may well be indicative of a circumlocution for divine activity. This passive verb points the reader forward to the passive participle γεννηθέν (that which was conceived) in 1:20, which is also suggestive of divine activity."[29]

This is indicative of the fact that the divine-royal motif which the royal-enthronement psalms presuppose is present in the genealogical account. In other words, while the evangelist outlines the origin of Jesus firmly within the context of the Davidic monarchy, the redemptive significance of Christ as the Son of God is extended beyond Israel.[30]

On a slightly different but complementary note, one influence in Matthew 1:18–25, especially in verses 20–21, Nolland argues, "is likely to come from haggadic tradition about Moses' infancy, here alluded to in order to draw a connection between the two figures in terms of their respective roles in salvation history."[31] The connection with Moses is more closely felt in the subsequent narrative (Matt 2:13–23), which reminds

---

connects Jesus' Davidic sonship with his divine sonship, and subordinates it to his divine sonship.

28. Bauer, "The Literary and Theological Function," 149. Bauer points out that the differences between the four women mentioned (Tamar, Rahab, Ruth, and Bathsheba) and Mary should be taken into account. He concurs in that the narrative of the birth of Christ (1:18–25) emphasizes neither Mary's role nor her character but rather the divine origin of Jesus. Cf. also France, *Matthew*, 74. It is also interesting to note that the four women mentioned in the genealogy are in the strictest sense non-Jews (Tamar is a Canaanite, Gen 38:11, 13–14; Bathsheba was the wife of a Hittite). This may indicate that Jesus' divine salvation is universally extended to include the Gentiles.

29. Kingsbury, *Matthew*, 43–44.

30. However, it should be stressed here that the idea of the "preexistence" of Jesus as Son of God and that of the divine conception of Jesus by the Holy Spirit, strictly speaking, are not compatible. Cf. Wainright, "The Confession 'Jesus is God' in the New Testament," 274–99. See also Machen, *The Virgin Birth of Christ*; Soares-Prabhu, "The Formulary Quotations"; Brown, *The Birth of the Messiah*.

31. Nolland, *The Gospel of Matthew*, 37.

the reader of the Pharaoh who had ordered a massacre of the Israelite infants in order to eliminate a threat to his control of the state. While we would not necessarily dismiss Nolland's observation here two things come up which need to be clarified, since they may affect the direction of Matthean interpretation. First, his link with haggadic tradition is somewhat surprising, since the allusion can perfectly be accounted for in connection with the Exodus tradition of the Old Testament. It seems evident that Matthew intends to draw a parallel between Jesus' birth and that of Moses; both Jesus and Moses were born under tyranny, but God's redemptive plan would not let human action jeopardize His ultimate purpose. They both survive the terrible ordeal and go on to fulfill their special destinies in the redemptive history of Israel. If anything, we would suggest that Matthew is referring to the Old Testament in which the Exodus tradition figures as possibly the most decisive redemptive event. Secondly, the allusion to the Exodus tradition in Matthew's infancy narratives is undeniable, but it is doubtful whether the evangelist intended to designate Jesus as the new Moses, which Nolland seems to assume. If it were so, it becomes difficult to explain why Matthew did not explicitly make the designation "the new Moses" in the prologue of the Gospel. Matthew is not timid in alluding to the great figures of the Old Testament in formulating his Christology, and if he wanted to present Jesus as the new Moses, he would probably have done so in the manner of Matthew 1:1. However, this designation never appears in relation to Jesus throughout the Gospel, although one may argue that there are structural/literary implications that support Mosaic reference, which indicates that Matthew is in tune with the messianic expectation of the Old Testament that has the Son of David as the messianic agent in establishing the new Exodus (cf. chapter 2).

Historical Reliability of the Genealogy

Another question regarding the genealogy remains, which is concerned with its historical reliability. Are we to understand the genealogy as an accurate historical account? Or are we to accept it as the product of a religious community that was not primarily interested in the exactitudes of historical data? Perhaps Matthew was more interested in promoting faith in Christ as their Savior than tracing the origin of Jesus with critical historical awareness. The questions regarding its authenticity and historical accuracy need to be critically examined in the light of the first century Jewish-Christian context. David Hill raises a number of factors which arouse skepticism on the historical value of the genealogical account of Matthew. For instance, he points out the evident artificiality of the genealogy, which claims the fulfillment of Old Testament prophecy in the events surrounding Jesus. He points out that the emphasis on the prophetic fulfillment indicates that the story was deliberately designed to fit scriptural quotations.[32]

Such theological/literary practice which quotes the prototype material without properly acknowledging the original context seems to have been prevalent among the first century Jewish-Christian believers. Today, this would be regarded as serious misconduct of literary practice. Nevertheless, the early Christians must have felt quite at home with appropriating certain Old Testament materials to support their religious views. Taking this into account the Jewish character of the genealogy is likely to indicate that the genealogical account should be interpreted from a redemptive historical perspective. Hill also points in a similar direction, if not the same direction, as he argues that the character of the genealogy of Matthew is unlikely to be from the mythological thinking of the first-century Hellenistic world. Rather, he sees it as typical of the first-century Jewish-Christian understanding of Scripture and history: "The unmistakably Jewish atmosphere of the prologue suggests that its contents should be treated as examples of Christian or Jewish-Christian midrashic activity; the literary genre to which they belong is 'haggadah,' an illustration which, by emphasizing the marvelous and supernatural, underlines the theological significance of historical events. They are neither simply history, although they deal with a historic fact, the birth of Jesus, nor apologetic or polemic, but rather confessions of a faith. This means that it is not primarily didactic but kerygmatic."[33]

This somewhat paradoxical character of the genealogy indicates that the account is historical in nature, but it also seeks to draw out theological significance in the events that surround Jesus. Caution might be in order in that any extreme view of regarding the genealogical account solely as a statement of faith undermines its historical essence. This is in fact consistent with our understanding of the redemptive history of

---

32. Hill, ed., *The Gospel of Matthew*, 77.
33. Ibid., 77.

Israel. The events only become *historically* meaningful when they are viewed through the faith that God is actively operating and is in control.[34]

In summary, although there is no apparent quotation of the royal-enthronement psalms in the genealogy as such, the explicit mention of the Son of David and the events surrounding the exile do have crucial methodological impact in the way these psalms are used to support Matthew's Christology throughout the Gospel. Without the understanding of the evangelist's concern to present Jesus within the context of Israel's redemptive history, which is firmly anchored by the opening genealogical account, any Old Testament quotation in the Gospel cannot be properly appreciated.

The Baptism of Jesus (Matthew 3:13–17)

Introduction

The Gospel of Matthew begins the story of Jesus by introducing the genealogy which brings the Old Testament history to a decisive culmination in the birth of Jesus Christ. The birth of Christ complements the genealogy, as Jesus' Davidic ancestry takes on a wider universal significance in divine terms (1:18). It is interesting to note that the Magi are presented as worshipping Jesus at his birth.[35] This clearly implies that Jesus' birth is no ordinary event. Whether they have come in acknowledgment of Jesus' divine identity is difficult to say at this stage. However, they are certainly presented as appreciating the significance of Jesus' birth for Israel (Matt 2:2). This, in turn, aroused King Herod's fear of a potential rival who would seek to threaten his royal status. As a result, Jesus and his family were forced to leave their hometown and to flee to Egypt as refugees, where they stayed until the death of Herod (Matt 2:19). The connection here may well be Exodus 4:19–20 where Yahweh commands Moses to return to Egypt to carry out the redemptive task.[36] We have discussed elsewhere that the Exodus formed the bedrock of the messianic expectation of the Old Testament as the

---

34. France, *Matthew*, 70. He supports the historical reliability of the events surrounding Jesus' birth and infancy. The details narrated in the Gospel, such as the cult of astrology, Herod's character, and his political vulnerability, as well as the rule of Archelaus and the choice of Egypt as a place of refuge by a suspect Jewish family are entirely probable.

35. Cf. Pannenberg, *Jesus*. See also Robinson, *The Human Face of God*.

36. Nolland, *The Gospel of Matthew*, 126.

prototype redemptive event, and it is entirely probable that Matthew here links Jesus' return with the words of Yahweh addressed to Moses. W. D. Davies and Dale C. Allison also point out that "in ancient Jewish sources concerned with eschatological matters, the redemption from Egypt often serves as a type for the messianic redemption, and the prospect of another exodus is held forth: before the consummation, the pattern, exodus/return, will repeat itself (cf. Isa. 40:3–4; 42:14—55:13; Ezek. 20:33–44; Hos. 2:14–15; 1 Macc. 2:29–30; 1 QS 8:12–18; Mt. 24:26; Acts 21:38; Rev. 12:6, 14; Josephus Ant. 20:97"[37] Nolland's comment that Matt 2:13–23 recalls Moses in Exod 4:19–20 certainly has some value which may be complementary to our understanding of the passage under discussion. But the link is based on literary implication rather than on a solid reference of the evangelist who, as we have argued, makes the clear link with David in the prologue of the Gospel. For this reason, it is more likely that the reference here is to the exile in which the New Exodus is eagerly anticipated. In this regard, Davies and Allison's comment deserves further attention. They argue that given the typological equation of Jesus with Israel (cf. 2:15; 4:1–11), the evangelist could readily have seen the fulfillment of Jeremiah's prophecy of Israel's return from the exile.[38] The words of the prophet had originally been addressed to Israel but the connection is made since the Messiah was the representative of the Israelite nation. We believe that it is the promise of the New Exodus from the exile that is relived here in this passage where Jeremiah 31 could well be in the mind of the evangelist, as Davies and Allison argue, which is in conjunction with the messianic expectation of the Old Testament as we have discussed elsewhere (cf. chapter 2, part 2).[39] In reinforcement of this view, Davies and Allison suggest that "just as the Jews, amid lamentation and grief, left Ramah to go into exile, so Jesus, amid lamentation and grief, left Bethlehem to go into exile. The departure of the Messiah to Egypt recapitulated the deportation of the people to Babylon—an event to which Matthew, significantly, calls attention thrice in the genealogy (1:11, 12, 17)."[40]

37. Davies and Allison, *A Critical and Exegetical Commentary*, 263.
38. Ibid., 267.
39. Ibid., 268.
40. Ibid., 269, 271. Cf. also Matthew 2: 20. It is also noted that "the language of Exod 4:19 has been retained without perfect grammatical adjustment, in order to make the

The Israel typology here sets the stage for the subsequent baptismal narrative which should also be viewed within the overarching New Exodus motif. In the account of his baptism, Jesus first appears as an adult just before his public ministry, which is preceded by the mention of John the Baptist's ministry.[41] Before we focus on the account of the baptism of Jesus, it is worth briefly examining the purpose of John the Baptist's ministry.

John the Baptist

It is interesting to note that Luke has John the Baptist preaching repentance to the "crowd" (Luke 3:7), whereas Matthew specifies the audience as the Pharisees and Sadducees (Matt 3:7). This supports the view that the Gospel of Matthew is designed to be read primarily by Jewish counterparts whose longing for the Messiah has finally been answered in Christ Jesus.[42] However, the failure in realizing the fulfillment of the promise in Jesus leads the Baptist to utter a direct rebuke against Israel's leaders.[43] Geerhardus Vos points out that "the very fact that John

---

parallel with the sentence from the story of Moses unmistakable." In response to this observation we have noted that the view is certainly complementary, as the allusion to the Exodus tradition is undeniable. However, the link between Jesus and Moses should be viewed as of minor christological significance compared with the more prominent Son of David in Matthew.

41. Mark begins his Gospel with the proclamation of John the Baptist which leads to the baptism of Jesus, thereby indicating the importance of the event for the ministry and person of Christ (Mark 1:1–11).

42. Meier, "John the Baptist in Matthew's Gospel," 383–405. The unlikely grouping of the Pharisees and the Sadducees should not be seen as an error by the evangelist but as an indication that Matthew is addressing the whole of Israel for her disbelief and unfaithfulness in her Messiah.

43. Ibid., 390. Meier notes that the epithet "brood of vipers" is repeated by Jesus in 12:34 against the Pharisees and in 23:33 against the scribes and Pharisees. Moreover, the saying of the Baptist in Matthew 3:10—"every tree not bearing good fruit is chopped down and thrown into the fire"—is repeated word for word by Jesus in the Sermon on the Mount (7:19). This further indicates that John the Baptist effectively prepares the way for the Messiah; his ministerial perspective is in alignment with that of Jesus. Cf. Charles, "The 'Coming One'/ 'Stronger One' and His Baptism," 37–50, notes in Matthew 3:11 that "the significance of another aspect of fire should not be lost sight of: its theophanic use. The presence and appearance of Yahweh was most akin to fire. Fire and glory become virtually synonymous (Exod. 13:21; 19:18; 24:17; Lev. 9:23, 24; Deut. 4:11; Ps. 50:2)." In Exodus 3, Yahweh initially reveals Himself to Moses through the burning bush. It is further noted that the two elements which characterize Jesus' baptism, i.e., "fire" and "spirit," could be interpreted as God's self-revelation (40). Fire and spirit are common elements in the prophecies of Joel, who "prophesied of a thorough purging

announces the judgment of Israel as the most important result of the approaching crisis, and that he warns against false pride and reliance on natural descent from Abraham, proves that his ideas concerning the Kingdom of God were radically different from those of contemporary Judaism."[44]

What is important about John the Baptist in Matthew is that the evangelist includes his ministry within the frame of Jesus' ministry, thereby showing continuity from the time of the prophets to the era of messianic fulfillment. This is interesting in comparison with Luke 16:16, where the author seems to draw a clear demarcation between the time of the prophets represented by John and the good news of the Kingdom of God proclaimed by Jesus.[45] The positioning of Matthew's Gospel at the very beginning of the New Testament tradition may also be perceived in the same light, as the sense of continuity and fulfillment of the Old Testament is of paramount importance for the community of Matthew. J. P. Meier argues along the same lines regarding John the Baptist: "The supreme privilege of John is, as we have already seen in Matt. 11 vv. 9–10, that he no longer stands in the period of prophecy as one of a line of prophets; the prophetic figure of the Baptist stands in the time of fulfillment alongside Jesus. Instead of Luke's 'the Law and the prophets (lasted) until John,' Matthew boldly turns the Old Testament canon on its head and makes John part of the period of fulfillment toward which the whole of the Old Testament pointed."[46]

This supports the thesis that Matthew, compared with other synoptic writers, is particularly keen on the aspect of the fulfillment theme, as the realization of the Old Testament messianic promise is very much a palpable reality. This indicates that John's ministry of repentance, his

---

and repentance in view of the plagues which had beset Yahweh's people and that the Day of the Lord was approaching as a vast fire, while gracious blessings and the Spirit on the other hand would be poured out (Joel 2). As depicted in Isa. 11:1–5, Israel's ideal ruler was to possess the fullest endowment of the Spirit of God."

44. Vos, *Redemptive History and Biblical Interpretation*, 300.

45. Flender, *St. Luke*, 123. He points out that ἀπὸ τότε clearly separates the two periods, but at the same time expresses continuity between John the Baptist and the preaching of the kingdom of God. Clearly, Luke's perspective towards the redemptive history of Israel is in alignment with that of Matthew. However, the emphasis of the argument is that Matthew is more explicit in conveying the theme of fulfillment and its reality in the person of Jesus.

46. Meier, "John the Baptist in Matthew's Gospel," 396.

rebukes, his threats, and finally his martyrdom, as Meier argues, are the continuation of the redemptive history of Israel which is brought to a decisive culmination by Jesus Christ.[47] Even though Matthew presents John the Baptist within the time frame of the New Exodus inaugurated by Jesus—and indeed John plays a prominent part in ushering in the new era—it should be noted that he does not partake in revealing the new truth but functions merely as a preparatory figure who recapitulates the Old Testament prophetic tradition before the manifestation of the Messiah. John's words in Matt 3:3, citing Isa 40:3, clearly show his role in preparing for the New Exodus as the Messiah's forerunner. The significance of the ritual performed by John cannot be underestimated, since Jesus is officially introduced into his public ministry through baptism, which may also symbolize the messianic anointing of Christ. Nevertheless, it is made clear that Jesus submits to the ritual "not for the confession of sin but rather for the fulfillment of righteousness (Matt. 3:15)."[48] This may be explicated in a way that even though Jesus himself is without sin, he nevertheless identifies with unbelieving Israel on whom the divine judgment is impending, and it is through Jesus that the New Covenant is ratified.

Jesus as Israel or Davidic King?

This leads us to the question of whether Matthew regarded Jesus as the true Israel or as the Davidic Messiah. There is dispute regarding which Old Testament passage is quoted in the voice from heaven when Jesus

---

47. Ibid., 404.

48. Freeman, "Matthew 3:13–17," 285–89, notes that the "baptism of Jesus signifies the dawning of a new age in the history of salvation." Different Jewish sects had somewhat different expectations of the Messiah. "The Zealots proposed a militaristic option of a Messiah-led revolt against the established Roman order. The Pharisees exemplified a pietistic solution, believing that the kingdom would come through strict adherence to the Torah." Cf. Beasley-Murray, *Baptism in the New Testament*, 64–67. See also Cullmann, *Baptism in the New Testament*, 18–19; Best, "Spirit-Baptism," 238–39; Wallace-Hadrill, "A Suggested Exegesis of Matt. 3:9, 10." The metaphor of washing, which is equated with the purging of sin, can be found in Psalm 51, where David pleads to Yahweh to wash him from his iniquity. The prophet Isaiah also warns Israel to be washed from sin which has become like scarlet. If Israel does not turn from evil ways, she will be devoured by the sword. Moreover, the destruction of the Egyptian soldiers and the salvation of the Israelites at the Red Sea (Exod 13:17—15:21) point to the image of water as an instrument of divine judgment. In the same way, the flood in Genesis 6–8 was a divine punishment.

was baptized and came out of the water: "And a voice from heaven said, 'This is my Son, whom I love; with him I am well pleased' (Matt 3:17)."

Nolland points out that the meaning of the voice from heaven is determined by which Old Testament text was quoted or alluded to. He argues that the voice from heaven in Jesus' baptism is from Isa 42:1. However, the only concern is that Isaiah is explicitly referring to a servant, whereas Jesus is designated as the son in his baptism. Nolland also acknowledges that "since the key word 'servant' is missing from the allusion to Isa. 42:1, the point of connection is not likely to be to identify Jesus as the Isaianic servant as such."[49] According to Nolland, what links the baptism to Isa 42:1 is the verb εὐδοκέω, which means "take pleasure, delight, be glad in." We are not disputing the fact that Isa 42:1 may well be one of the contributing factors in interpreting Matt 3:17, but whether this is the most prominent allusion in the baptismal account is doubtful, especially if the major link is considered to be only the verb "take pleasure, delight, be glad in," which is clearly a secondary factor in the composition of the voice from heaven.[50]

J. A. Gibbs argues that it is Isa 42:1—"Behold, my Servant whom I have chosen . . . I have put my spirit upon him"—which is quoted at Jesus' baptism. Since this passage from Isaiah is dealing with the servant figure, who is subsequently identified with Israel, the voice from heaven is addressing Jesus as the Servant of Yahweh.[51] Gibbs further argues that in the context of Matthew's narrative, an allusion in Matt 3:17 to Psalm 2:6 and the resulting royal Davidic Christology is unlikely. He advances the argument that the Old Testament theme of Israel as God's "Son" is the background for the Father's words from heaven.[52] Since Isaiah subsequently uses the term *servant* in relation to Israel (cf. Isa 49:3), the voice from heaven is not addressing Jesus as servant and Davidic King but, rather, as servant and Israel.[53] Gibbs states that "the first and primary

---

49. Nolland, *The Gospel of Matthew*, 157.

50. Ibid., 158. It is suggested that ἀγαπητός (beloved) in Matthew 3:17 is based on ἐκλεκτός (chosen) in Isaiah 42:1. However, Nolland does leave room for the conflation of Psalm 2:7, as well, but regards it as secondary to the Isaianic passage.

51. Cf. Marshall, "Son of God or Servant of Yahweh?" 326–36.

52. Gibbs, "Israel Standing with Israel." His argument is that Jesus is addressed as the servant of Yahweh, which is identified with Israel. This view is shared by Allison, "The Son of God as Israel," 74–81; Meier, *The Vision of Matthew*; and Bretscher, "Exodus 4:22–23 and the Voice from Heaven," 301–11.

53. Gibbs, "Israel Standing with Israel," 512.

'son of God' was the nation and not the king. If there is, along with the allusion to LXX Jer. 38:20, also some allusion to Ps. 2:7 in Matt. 3:17, one would necessarily regard it as subordinate or secondary."[54]

His argument is that even though Jesus was sinless, he nevertheless received John's baptism of repentance in order to identify himself with sinful Israel. Therefore, Jesus' baptism shows that Israel's existence and her history are summed up in Christ. Whereas Israel in the past was rebellious and unfaithful, Jesus as the true Israel in his baptism symbolizes Israel's turning away from sin in perfect obedience to God.[55]

Even though there is certainly a corporate identification, as Jesus represents Israel in his person and ministry, the servant in Isa 42:1 and elsewhere refers also to the Son of David (1 Kings 1:26; 3:6, 7; 1 Chron 17:4, 7; Pss 18:1; 78:70; 89:19–20; Isa 37:35; Jer 33:21; Ezek 34:23). These are only select examples that show the use of the word *servant* in the Old Testament. The terminology is widely used throughout the Bible and refers to various prophetic figures and kings. Some of the servant sayings are about Israel as well as the king, indicating that the two concepts are related to each other. Therefore, when the term refers to Israel, we need to bear in mind that it is also referring to the nation's representative figure, namely, the Davidic king.

Gibbs' skepticism against Psalm 2:6 and the royal Davidic Christology thus stands on tentative ground, since the terms *Israel* and *David* were, in effect, interchangeable. Although it is undeniable that there are references to Israel as a nation, the presence of Davidic promises and fulfillment cannot be overlooked. The evangelist begins the Gospel by stating that Jesus is the Son of David, which makes it highly probable that the quotation in Jesus' baptism also has Davidic background in mind. David represents the Israelite kingdom, and the nation's welfare in terms of political security and spiritual relationship with Yahweh is directly dependent upon the king's reign (cf. Isa 9:7; 37:35; Jer 21:12; 23:5; 33:15; Ezrk 37:25). The concept of servant which is identified with Israel in Isaiah 42:1, therefore, can also be directly related with the Davidic king whose relationship with Yahweh represents Israel's relationship with her God. The servant, therefore, is eventually shown to be Israel's king (cf. Isa 55:3).

---

54. Ibid., 520.
55. Ibid., 521.

In the New Testament, the concept is applied to Jesus in Acts (3:13, 26; 4:25; 4:27) where Jesus is described as the servant. In particular, Acts 4:27 combines the terminology with ἔχρισας, which means that Jesus as the anointed Davidic Messiah functions as the servant for the salvation of Israel even though she has rejected her own Messiah. It seems that in the early Christian setting, the servant can be interpreted as Israel as well as the anointed Davidic king who acts on behalf of the nation. This corporate understanding is then applied to Jesus the Son of David, who as the faithful servant of God has come for the salvation of Israel and the Gentiles.[56]

With this in mind, it is most probable that Matthew quotes Psalm 2:7 (categorized as one of the royal psalms) in connection with Isaiah 42:1, conveying the fulfillment of the Old Testament in Jesus' baptism. Davies and Allison concur with this argument; they state that "Matthew saw in Matt. 3:17 a confirmation of the truth of Jesus' divine sonship as proclaimed in Ps. 2 and the truth of his being the spirit-endowed servant of Deutero-Isaiah."[57] They identify four major Matthean themes in 3:13–17: "Jesus as Son, Jesus as Servant, Jesus as the inaugurator of the New Exodus and New Creation, and Jesus as the one who fulfills all righteousness."[58] However, since Matthew makes it explicitly clear in his prologue that Jesus is the Son of David, it is most likely that Psalm 2:7 takes precedence in terms of significance in Matthew's Christology.

Jesus as the Son or Servant?

Although "servant" is clearly a very important title in describing the nature of Jesus' ministry, it is doubtful that Matthew's primary intent is to portray Jesus in such a way.[59] In the account of Jesus' baptism, Matthew

---

56. Cf. Hill, *The Gospel of Matthew*, 98. It is also suggested that it was traditional in the early Christian community to think of Jesus the Messiah at the same time as the servant in whom the Lord had pleasure.

57. Davies and Allison, *A Critical and Exegetical Commentary*, 338, 339.

58. Ibid., 344, 345, notes that "probably the idea of new creation is also present, for in Jewish thought exodus motifs and creation motifs were intertwined with one another and with eschatological expectation."

59. Cf. Mawhinney, "Baptism, Servanthood, and Sonship," 35–64. It is argued that the titles servant and son have a significant degree of semantic overlap. When King Ahaz was threatened by Syria, he sent a message to Tiglath-pileser of Assyria affirming his vassal and vice-regent status with the words "I am your servant and your son" (2 Kings 16:7). It is also noted that this use of the words *servant* and *son* together as a description of a vice-regent is also found in extrabiblical texts. Moreover, Mawhinney

very clearly designates him as the "Son," and it is the sonship of Christ which stands out in the narrative. The earlier argument dealing with Isa 42:1 has "servant," which, even if it is argued that Matthew combines it with Ps 2:7, is not quoted in the baptismal account. Those scholars who argue in favor of the servanthood of Jesus in the baptismal account are inclined to tolerate the suggestion that an original παῖς was possibly replaced by υἱός as a result of Hellenistic influence.[60] However, we have already established that Matthew was thoroughly Jewish in his mind-set, and any evidence to substantiate the claim that Hellenistic influence led to replacing the original word *servant* with *son* is simply absent, so the argument is purely speculative in nature. It is very unlikely that engaging in a debate concerning the passages' authenticity will bear any tangible result that is significant in the study of Matthew's Christology.[61]

To contend that Isa 42:1 is the only background for the heavenly voice, which has servant as the primary object, is unwarranted in the text. There is no doubt that the content and the nuance of Isa 42:1 resemble the revelation of Jesus' divine sonship in the baptismal account, but the subject addressed by God is clearly intended to be the servant. We are not disputing the fact that Matthew at least makes an allusion to Isa 42:1, but discerning the key text for his Christology is not transparently obvious in Isaiah. The scholars who advocate the use of Isaiah in Matthew's baptism story have no other choice but to depend upon the view that at some stage of textual development, the original *servant* was replaced by *son*. The primary reason for such editing is due to the Hellenistic influence; *son* would be more appealing for readers in a Hellenistic environment. However, we have established that Matthew's mind-set is uncompromisingly Jewish, which makes it highly improbable that the

---

points out that in Ps 89:20, Yahweh calls David "my servant" and goes on to say that David "shall cry to me 'Thou art my Father'" (Ps 89:26), implicating the sonship of His servant David.

60. Lee, *From Messiah to Preexistent Son*. Cf. also Mawhinney and Gibbs.

61. Ibid., 166–67. The opening of heaven recalls the vision of Ezekiel 1:1 during the exile. Also, Isaiah's prophecy that the spirit of the Lord shall rest upon him might be in the mind of the evangelist (Isa 11:2). Lee argues that "the two components of the theophany (i.e., the endowment of the Spirit and the heavenly revelation of Jesus' divine sonship) could well derive from Jesus' own experience. The Gospel traditions suggest that Jesus attributed his power in ministry to a special endowment of the Spirit (Mt. 12:27–28 / Lk. 11:19–20; Mt. 12:31–32 / Mk. 3:28–29 / Lk. 12:10; cf. Lk. 4:16–21) and was conscious of the special relationship with God as his Father (Mt. 26:39 / Mk. 14:36 / Lk. 22:42; Mt. 11:25–27 / Lk. 10:21–22)."

evangelist shows signs of Hellenistic influence in a passage as important as the one under discussion. Lee points out that the evidence for an earlier παῖς Christology in the baptismal setting is patently lacking, as there is no textual evidence that υἱός at a later stage replaced παῖς in this account.[62] If it is granted that the passage is authentic, since there is insufficient evidence or reason to substantiate the change of original servant Christology to the divine sonship of Jesus, it is not Isa 42:1 but Ps 2:7 that is of greater importance for Matthew's Christology. For the evangelist, it is Jesus' unique status as God's Son that is of prime importance rather than his status as God's servant. Moreover, it becomes increasingly evident towards the climax of the Gospel that the sonship of Jesus receives christological emphasis, as Matthew associates the forgiveness of sins and the crucifixion with Jesus as the "Son of God," not as servant (Matt 27:38–54). The evangelist stresses the fact that Jesus dies on the cross as the "Son of God" because it is only the death of God's perfectly obedient and loving Son that achieves the ultimate salvation through the forgiveness of sins.[63]

Therefore, the use of Psalm 2:7 in the baptism of Jesus not only declares him to be the long-awaited Davidic Messiah but also the "beloved" Son whose unique relationship with the Father has redemptive significance for Israel as well as the Gentiles.[64]

New Exodus Motif

The Davidic king whom Yahweh addresses as His Son (Ps 2:7) is expected to deliver Israel from the exile, thereby bringing about the New Exodus and the restoration of the covenant (cf. Jer 23:5–6; 33:14–18).[65] The Exodus theme is prevalent in the baptismal account as well as the narratives surrounding it. G. L. Balentine also notes that Matthew has given special emphasis to the Exodus associations surrounding Jesus' baptism. The baptism in the Jordan illustrates the escape of the Israelites

---

62. Ibid., 170.

63. Cf. Hill, "Son and Servant," 2–16.

64. Ibid., 174. Lee also argues that the baptismal saying goes beyond a purely functional or messianic use of the title by the use of the qualifying adjective ἀγαπητός, which indicates the unique relationship of Jesus to his Father. The allusion to Ps 2:7 in the baptismal account has as its main purpose to declare Jesus as God's Son rather than simply the Messiah.

65. Again, it is evident that the Davidic reign represents Yahweh's righteousness in Israel. The two kingships are mutually complementary.

in their crossing the Red Sea, and the succeeding temptation narrative clearly has in mind Israel's sojourn in the wilderness for forty years. He also notes that the Sermon on the Mount resembles the establishment of the covenant on Mount Sinai.[66]

The promise of the prototype Exodus event is the foundation upon which the Israelites later, in the Babylonian exile, sustained their faith in Yahweh and the expectation of messianic deliverance. Jesus' birth is the response to such expectation in the history of Israel as the fulfillment of Yahweh's promise of the Messiah. In fact, Matthew sees the period of the exile as the pivotal point in the ancestry of Jesus, as the genealogy recapitulates the major events of the history of Israel.

W. J. Dumbrell notes that allusions to the Babylonian exile are frequently made in the Gospel of Matthew. For instance, the massacre of the infants (Matt 2:16) evokes the trauma of the Babylonian exile, where Rachel bitterly wept over the plight of Israel at Ramah and the loss of her children (Jer 31:15), which is the point of departure for the exile of 586 BC. Consequently, Jesus' exile in Egypt and the subsequent return after the death of Herod resembles the return of the Israelites from Babylon. However, unlike the disappointing return from Babylon of 537 BC, Jesus' return meant the good news of the potential end of Israel's exilic plight, thereby establishing the New Exodus.[67] It is also noteworthy that Jesus commences his public ministry in Galilee of the Gentiles (Matt 4:15). Dumbrell writes: "His ministry begins in the despised Galilee of the Gentiles; in the tribal areas formerly occupied by Zebulon and Naphtali, who were the first of the North to go into exile. It was appropriate that the ministry of Jesus, which could mean the end of the exile for Israel, began at the point where the dislocation of Israel had begun."[68]

It seems plausible to suggest that Matthew quotes Ps 2:7 as the major component in Jesus' baptism, which functions as a decisive key point which connects the three great events in the redemptive history of Israel.

---

66. Balentine, "Death of Jesus as a New Exodus," 27–41. Marshall, *The Origins of New Testament Christology*, 47, notes that the determining factor in the narratives of the Sermon on the Mount is the words *ego de lego* (But I say), which embody a claim to the Mosaic authority. Marshall argues that "anyone who claims an authority rivaling and challenging Moses has *ipso facto* set himself above Moses; he has ceased to be a rabbi, for a rabbi's authority only comes to him as derived from Moses." Cf. also Guelich, *The Sermon on the Mount*; Kissinger, *The Sermon on the Mount*.

67. Dumbrell, *The New Covenant*, 21–22.

68. Ibid., 29.

Firstly, the choice of Ps 2:7 clearly indicates that the anointing of the Davidic king is in mind, as Jesus is portrayed as the Messiah. Secondly, the Exodus motif reinforces the view that Jesus represents the true Israel. Unlike Israel in the past, who has constantly disobeyed and has fallen into temptation, Jesus enacts the true Israel that Yahweh initially called her to be. Thirdly, a combination of the Davidic kingship and the Exodus motif indicates that Yahweh's redemptive act is continuing through Christ Jesus, who will finally liberate Israel from the traumatizing era of the exile.[69]

William R. Stegner, in his study of the use of Scripture in the narratives of Matt 4:1–11, suggests that the use of the Exodus motif (such as the wilderness theme) shows that the evangelist was working with an Urzeit/Endzeit (beginning/end time) theology of history. In other words, Matthew's primary concern was christological in the context of the redemptive history of Israel.[70] He correctly discerns that Matthew places Jesus' ministry in the overall framework of Israel's redemptive history, but his argument that the selection of types from Moses achieves this effect is somewhat tentative. Nowhere in the Gospel of Matthew is Moses presented in relation to Jesus' identity or his ministry, and, even if such allusion is remotely made (see B. W. Bacon, "The Five Books of Matthew against the Jews"), the evidence of the Mosaic Christology is simply lacking to substantiate such a view.[71] Matthew mentions Moses in Matt 8:4; 17:3, 4; 19:7, 8; and 22:24, but the evangelist never makes a link between Moses and Jesus. However, Matthew makes an explicit link between David and Jesus (Matt 1:1, 20; 9:27; 12:23; 15:22; 20:30, 31; 21:9, 15), who is also understood to be the Christ/Messiah (Matt 1:1, 16, 17, 18; 16:16, 20; 22:42; 26:63). As the quotation from Ps 2:7 shows in Jesus' baptism, Matthew is consistent with the Old Testament view of the messianic expectation that it is the Son of David who will liberate Israel from the exile and bring the redemptive history of Israel to a decisive culmination.[72]

---

69. Cf. also Dumbrell, *The New Covenant*, 21–22.

70. Stegner, "The Use of Scripture in Two Narratives," 109.

71. Cf. Barth, "Matthew's Understanding of the Law," 58–164, esp. 93–95. See also Banks, "Jesus and the Law in the Synoptic Tradition," 226–42; Meier, *Law and History in Matthew's Gospel*; Johnson, "Reflections on a Wisdom Approach," 44–64 in reply to M. J. Suggs, *Wisdom, Christology, and Law in Matthew's Gospel*.

72. Moses is mentioned only four times in Matthew, who never makes a comparison with Jesus (Matt 8:4; 17:3–4; 19:7–8; 22:24). Cf. also Jer 31:32–34: "It will not be like

The Divine-Royal Motif in the Baptism of Jesus

It is evident that Matthew wishes to portray Jesus in his baptism as the long-awaited Davidic Messiah whom Yahweh addresses as His son in Psalm 2:7. However, it is interesting to note that later in the Gospel (Matt 22:41–45), Jesus seems to refute the Davidic title, since the Son of David is higher in authority than his ancestral forefather.

Although Psalm 2:7 is classified as one of the royal psalms, it has been argued that its literary structure, style of language, and ideology are closely connected with the enthronement psalms. On the fundamental principle that Israel longed for both Yahweh and His Davidic vice-regent to appear for her salvation, it is highly probable that when the early Christians utilized the Psalms, they viewed these two types of psalms as one entity in their christological statements (cf. ch. 4, part 1). We believe that it is not just the royal psalms but also the enthronement psalms that were used in Matthew's Christology. This explains Matthew's emphasis on Jesus' Davidic heritage but at the same time his reluctance in portraying Jesus solely in terms of the Davidic line. In other words, Matthew's quotation of Psalm 2:7 in Jesus' baptism need not be viewed as a paradox in 22:41–45. In fact, Matthew is consistent with the Old Testament expectation of the Messiah, as he would embody the Davidic heritage as well as represent Yahweh. Viewing the royal psalms as one ideological entity with the enthronement psalms in the key christological passages thus helps to illumine the fact that Jesus is the long-awaited Davidic king prophesied in the royal psalm, but he also embodies Yahweh's reign in his messianic ministry.

D. W. K. So takes a leap forward from this observation and argues for the divinity of Christ with special reference to Matthew's Gospel. In his analysis of Matt 3:3, he points out that "in contrast with John 1:23, Matthew, as in Luke and Mark, deliberately takes the verse away from the lips of the Baptist so that Matthew is not presenting the Baptist's understanding of the fulfillment of Isaiah 40:3 here. Rather, Matthew is presenting his own understanding of the fulfillment, which could be

---

the covenant I made with their forefathers when I took them by the hand to lead them out of Egypt, because they broke my covenant, though I was a husband to them. This is the covenant I will make with the house of Israel after that time. For I will forgive their wickedness and will remember their sins no more." The prophecies concerning the reestablishment of the Davidic kingdom are Isa 9:6–7; 11:1; Jer 23:5; 33:15–17; Amos 9:11; Zech 12:8.

different from the Baptist's, so that it is possible that Matthew might have identified Jesus with Yahweh the Lord."[73]

So proposes that Matthew could have quoted Isa 40:3 entirely verbatim from the LXX.[74] However, Matthew modifies Isaiah's τοῦ θεου (of our God) into genitive masculine singular αὐτοῦ (his), which refers to Jesus. This indicates that the evangelist did not wish to make a distinction between the deity and Jesus by quoting Isaiah in its exact form. So argues that if the passage has been quoted verbatim from Isaiah, Jesus would not be identified with "the Lord" either, since "the Lord" and "our God" are parallels.[75]

Despite the fact that the narratives of Matt 3:3 are primarily concerned with the proclamation of John the Baptist and the nature of his ministry, the passage quoted from Isaiah is narrated by the evangelist himself. This indicates that Matthew wants to make sure that Jesus is identified with the Lord Yahweh in Isa 40:3. However, it is doubtful whether Matthew identifies Jesus as God at this early stage of his Gospel. We are not disputing the fact that the evangelist may very well intend to portray Jesus in such a way, and the baptismal narrative is certainly not in disagreement with this view. In fact, in comparison with other Synoptic Gospels, Matthew's is the only Gospel that records John's reaction as Jesus comes to be baptized by him (Matt 3:14). The Baptist immediately recognizes Jesus' status, as he prevents him and says that it is he that needs to be baptized by Jesus. In this regard, Matthew's high Christology stands out distinctively compared with the baptismal accounts in Mark (1:9–11) and Luke (3:21–22). Caution might be in order, however, in stating that Jesus is here identified as God, which is a premature conclusion at this stage of the narrative development. When we consider the narrative structure of the Gospel in its entirety, we then may be able to argue in retrospect that the earlier narratives support such a claim about Jesus, as his identity is *progressively* disclosed. However, at this point, it would be stretching beyond the evidence to say that Jesus is identified as God in his baptism. Rather, he is identified as the Davidic Messiah who marks the decisive turning point in the redemptive history of Israel as

---

73. So, *Jesus' Revelation of His Father*, 29.

74. Ibid. Cf. also Jobes and Silva, *Invitation to the Septuagint*.

75. Ibid. So emphasizes that in the context of Isa 40:3, "the Lord" refers to Yahweh. Hence, Matthew's identification of Jesus with "the Lord" would naturally indicate that Jesus is identified with God.

the era of the Old Testament prophetic tradition comes to its fulfillment. The divine voice declares Jesus to be His beloved Son who represents the true Israel through his obedience and humility.

To sum up, the importance of the royal-enthronement psalms for Matthew's Christology should not be decided simply by the quantity or the frequency of the quotation. Matthew is clearly keen on conveying the identity and the redemptive ministry of Jesus by using the royal psalms at the decisive points of his Gospel. However, he is also cautious not to exploit the use of these psalms to an extent that Jesus is defined solely in terms of the Davidic kingship. This will become more evident later in the Gospel. Not only does Jesus fulfill Israel's redemptive history as her long-awaited Messiah who will bring the exile to a closure but there are also hints in the narratives surrounding Jesus' baptism, as D. W. K. So argues, which point to Jesus' nature that transcends such confinement. He is of David in his genealogy but is divinely conceived by the creative power of the Holy Spirit (Matt 1:20). In his baptism, Jesus is the beloved Son who is the greater Davidic Messiah foretold in Psalm 2, but it also points to his identity as someone who embodies the fulfillment of Isaiah 40:3 in formulating a divine-royal motif of Matthew's Christology.

The Transfiguration of Jesus (Matthew 17:1–13)

Revelation of Jesus' Messianic Identity

The transfiguration narratives are another crucial part of the Gospel story where Jesus' identity is once again revealed. He was confirmed by God's voice from heaven when God's presence was visibly manifested in the form of a cloud. In this regard, the content, nuance, and literary style of the passage bear close resemblance to the baptismal scene. However, unlike the baptism, where the revelation seems to be restricted to a private encounter with God and Jesus, presumably with John the Baptist as a witness, the transfiguration involves the three representative disciples: Peter, James, and John the brother of James. We see a progressive disclosure of Jesus' identity in the Gospel, as the disciples are exposed to this epiphany. From a private encounter between Jesus and God the Father in the baptismal narratives, the experience is now extended to a small number of his disciples. Not only that, but Matthew's Christology is reinforced, as the evangelist mentions perhaps the two most important figures of the Old Testament, Moses and Elijah, conversing with Jesus.

In exactly the same manner but with enhanced tone and urgency, God's command seems to take on a sharper penetration, as the addition of the phrase "listen to him" to Ps 2:7 indicates. Clearly, there is a literary as well as theological connection with the baptism of Jesus in terms of the development of Christology.[76]

Davies and Allison have suggested a possible chiastic arrangement of the transfiguration narrative as follows:

  a. Narrative introduction (v. 1)
    b. Jesus transfigured (vv. 2–3)
      c. Peter's response (v. 4)
        d. The divine voice (v. 5)
      c. The disciples' response (v. 6)
    b. Jesus speaks (v. 7)
  a. Narrative conclusion (v. 8)[77]

If such a literary structure was intended by the evangelist, then the above serves to highlight the centrality of the divine voice (Matt 17:5) in the same manner as in the baptismal account. The preceding narratives portray a remarkable epiphany in which Jesus' appearance is described as the shining sun and his clothes as white as the light, which is reminiscent of Moses' appearance in Exod 34:29–35. This observation has led some to think that Jesus' image as a New Moses is at the heart of the transfiguration narrative.[78] Indeed, throughout the Gospel narratives, Jesus' ministerial function had been something that closely resembles the ethical teacher, which Moses was for the people of Israel. Nolland affirms this in that the abiding role of the Mosaic law for moral guidance is clearly attested in Matt 5:17–20.[79] The link with Moses is reinforced

---

76. Cf. Synge, "The Transfiguration Story." See also Ziesler, "The Transfiguration Story and the Markan Soteriology"; Trites, "The Transfiguration of Jesus"; Penner, "Revelation and Discipleship in Matthew's Transfiguration Account," 201–10, posits that "Matthew's account centers on a revelation of Jesus as the Son of God and the impact of that revelation on the disciples."

77. Davies and Allison, *A Critical and Exegetical Commentary*, 685.

78. Kwon, *The Reception of Psalm 118 in the New Testament*, 145. He notes that Mark does not mention anything about Jesus' face (Mark 9:3), and Luke states only that his face was changed (Luke 9:29). This leads him to argue that Matthew's account is more suggestive of Moses, since the transformation includes both his face and clothes (cf. Exod 34:30).

79. Nolland, *The Gospel of Matthew*, 34, notes that "the antitheses to follow in 5:21–48 are not to be understood as overturning the Mosaic commandments to which

in comparison with Mark's Gospel, which "only refers to 'the garments of Jesus,' which became glistening, intensely white 'as no fuller on earth could bleach them' (9:3), whereas Matthew adds: 'and his face shone like the sun' (17:2)."[80] This, Davies and Allison argue, recalls Exod 34:29–35, "where the Hebrew reads: 'the skin of [Moses'] face shone' because he had been talking to God."[81] If Moses was of such importance, it is somewhat difficult to justify the appearance of both Moses *and* Elijah. Perhaps it would make more sense to have Moses alone if he is intended to be christologically significant. And the evangelist would have inserted some sort of acknowledgement from Jesus in associating himself with Moses in order to make the link between Jesus and Moses.

Peter's spontaneous reaction here deserves a closer look, as he proposes to build three shelters, one each for Moses, Elijah, and Jesus. It is quite probable that Peter views the authority of these great Old Testament figures as being on par with Jesus. Peter's suggestion is immediately interrupted by a voice from the cloud saying, "This is my Son, whom I love; with him I am well pleased. Listen to him!" (Matt 17: 5) The divine voice rebukes Peter for his misperception of Jesus' authority in relation with these great prophets. The disciples' subsequent fear implies that Matthew is portraying Jesus' authority as far above that of Moses and Elijah. This is also pointed out by Davies and Allison, who stress that "if Jesus is thus made out to be a new Moses, he is also clearly greater than Moses, just as he is greater than Elijah."[82] Nolland also notes that "the presence of both Moses and Elijah makes it less likely that in the Moses echoes of Matt. 17:2 Mathew intends to identify Jesus as in any sense a new Moses. Rather, he is one who shares a certain likeness to both Moses and Elijah, destined as he is to carry forward the purpose of God within which both Moses and Elijah have had important roles."[83] If, indeed, any connections were made with either Moses or Elijah in the understanding of Jesus' identity, the transfiguration passage challenges such a perception, as it is Jesus alone whom they should listen to. Therefore, it is unlikely that Moses is here intended to be of christological

---

they make reference, but as providing a more adequate interpretation of their scope and deeper intention."

80. Davies and Allison, *Matthew 8–18*, 685.
81. Ibid.
82. Ibid., 687.
83. Nolland, *The Gospel of Matthew*, 701.

significance. Rather, Matthew's emphasis on the fulfillment theme and the continuity of the redemptive history of Israel is again displayed in the transfiguration scene. In the baptismal scene, it was John the Baptist who represented the Old Testament prophetic tradition, but here it is represented by Moses and Elijah. J. A. Penner argues that "the appearance of Moses and Elijah in this account seems to center on the Law and the Prophets, indicative of the entire Old Testament. Matthew consistently connects the Law and the Prophets as a single entity (5:17; 7:12; 11:13; 22:40). The appearance of Moses and Elijah, particularly in light of God's pronouncement, seems to indicate the issue at stake is the relationship between Jesus and the Old Testament."[84]

The mention of the two great names of the Old Testament, therefore, is not made in relation to Jesus' identity but they serve to delineate the continuity of the redemptive history of Israel. By recapitulating the major events of Israel's history, Moses' leading the nation out of Egypt and Yahweh's promise of the prophet Elijah before the great Day of the Lord (cf. Mal 4:5), Matthew is stating that the New Exodus is finally inaugurated in Christ Jesus.

Matthew is consistent in his Christology, as he continues to assert Jesus as the Davidic Messiah by again quoting Ps 2:7 (this time with the additional phrase "listen to him"). Jesus' authority is clearly emphasized and placed above the Old Testament prophets. Even though a royal psalm quoted in the passage suggests that this narrative may be interpreted in a royal setting, this alone is not sufficient in understanding Matthew's Christology. Because God declares Jesus' authority to be above these great figures, Jesus' royal status is in fact complemented by something much more profound. He is the epitome of the Old Testament redemptive history but is also far superior to anything Israel has ever seen before. He is of Israel but beyond Israel. He is of human origin but supersedes the greatest figures Israel has ever known. Matthew's Christology is heightened in the transfiguration by the use not only of Ps 2:7 but also of an allusion to Ps 97:2, an enthronement psalm: "Clouds and thick darkness surround him; righteousness and justice are the foundation of his throne."[85] In conjunction with this view, Nolland also draws relevant

---

84. Penner, "Revelation and Discipleship in Matthew's Transfiguration Account," 201–10.

85. Riesenfeld, cited in Davies and Allison, *A Critical and Exegetical Commentary*, 688, 689. Riesenfeld's thesis, however, has not gained wide recognition, since he relies heavily upon Tabernacle motifs, which is considered to be a minor theme in Matthew.

comparisons where Yahweh is ascribed analogous traits as Jesus in the transfiguration: "Yahweh will be our everlasting light (Isa. 60:19); the 'ancient of Days' in Dan. 7:9 whose 'clothing was white as snow'; God compared to 'the light when it is bright in the skies' to make the point that 'around God is awesome majesty' in Job 37:21–22."[86] In both the way the heavenly voice addresses Jesus and in the way Jesus' appearance is transfigured, a "divine-royal" Christology is clearly evident.[87]

In summary, when we appreciate the general christological context from which the transfiguration emerges as a decisive revelatory event, that is, Peter's declaration about Jesus in 16:13-20 and the prophecy of Jesus' passion and vindication in 16:21-23, we can see the importance of the use of the Psalms in Matthew's Christology. The transfiguration's crucial place in the Gospel is due to the fact that the evangelist attributes it several times to God, which is marked by a marvelous epiphany. It is used to confirm the earlier statement regarding Jesus which is progressively built up as the story unfolds and then decisively revealed through the royal-enthronement psalms. The transfiguration also points forward to what is yet to take place. Davies and Allison point out that "the transfiguration narrative has a remarkable twin of sorts in the account of Jesus' execution, 24:32-54. In the one, a private epiphany, an exalted Jesus, with garments glistening, stands on a high mountain and is flanked by two religious giants from the past. In the other, a public spectacle, a humiliated Jesus, whose clothes have been torn from him and divided, is lifted upon a cross and flanked by two common convicted criminals."[88] In both instances Jesus is proclaimed to be the Son of God (17:6; 27:54), but with a sense of profound irony in the latter.

---

86. Nolland, *The Gospel of Matthew*, 701.

87. Ibid., 701. "In both Jesus' face and clothing a glory emanating from God becomes visible to the chosen disciples . . . in the fulfillment of all that is anticipated for the Son of Man in Matt. 16:27-28." See also pp. 704-5: "Most traditional approaches to the transfiguration can be assigned to one of two categories: either the emphasis is upon Christ's divinity or it is upon his humanity . . . in the Hesychiasts of Byzantium the two traditions are fused. Gregory Palamas identified the light of Tabor with the ineffable, uncreated light of Christ which bathes the whole cosmos and which can yet be seen in the chambers of the heart by those who say the Jesus prayer and accomplish poverty of spirit, that is, by those in the process of being deified through participation in the divine life. So the light of the transfiguration belongs to Christ as God but at the same time transforms human beings into their divine destiny."

88. Davies and Allison, *Matthew 8-18*, 706.

Authenticity of the Transfiguration Narrative

The three synoptic writers commonly place the narrative of the transfiguration after Peter's confession where Jesus predicts his passion (cf. Mark 9:2–8; Luke 9:28–36). In this precursor to the passion, Jesus demonstrates that the meaning of his ministry and kingship cannot be fully grasped in isolation from suffering and death on the cross. The transfiguration elaborates the themes of the suffering of the Son of Man and the subsequent glory of resurrection.[89]

David Hill suggests that the story of the transfiguration is a product of a postresurrection Christian community that sought to implement a precursory event of resurrection in Jesus' earthly ministry.[90] This raises a question of whether the account is a genuine event that belongs to Jesus' own experience or whether it is a fabrication of the subsequent Christian writers. In other words, did Jesus himself actually undergo such an experience? More broadly put, to what extent is the Gospel a historically reliable account of Jesus' life and his self-consciousness? Although the aim of this volume is to decipher how Matthew sees and interprets Jesus, the evangelist's account nevertheless needs to be authenticated by Jesus' own experience. If Matthew was guilty of fabricating information about Jesus that cannot be supported by Jesus' own understanding, the Gospel could not have exercised authority in the early Christian community. This point is crucially important for Christians, for whom the Gospels are revelations of Jesus' divine identity and the salvation he brings for humanity. If one accepts the thesis that the Gospel account of Jesus is by and large an artificial product of the early Christians, then one is open to the notion that Jesus' self-consciousness may have been different from what the later New Testament writers described him to be. B. L. Mack's presupposition is an example of such skepticism; Mack argues: "The gospels are not history. They are myths claiming to be history. They are products of the christological and sociological shifts which marked out the boundaries by which the early Christian movement defined itself. They presuppose both the ruptures and the mythic solutions to those ruptures which have been refined. We need to read them as accounts, not

---

89. Hill, *The Gospel of Matthew*. After Jesus' disciples witness the epiphany, Jesus instructs them not to tell anyone what they saw until the Son of Man has been raised from the dead (Matt 17:9). This implies that the suffering of the cross was an integral element in his ministry and a precursor to the glory of resurrection.

90. Ibid., 266.

of the time of Jesus, but of the time of the early Christian communities which produced them."[91]

We have already established that the biblical history may differ from how the world today defines history (cf. chapter 4, part 2). However, to state that the gospels are nothing more than myths pretending to be history is failing to understand the mindset of the early Christians and the nature of the Scriptures. Early Christian use of the Old Testament clearly indicates that they had critical historical awareness, as they consolidated their faith in Christ as the decisive culmination of Israel's redemptive history. For the early Christians and for ancient Israel, a concrete historical awareness is what sustained their faith in God and Israel's Messiah.

If history was of prime importance for the early Christians, then why would it be necessary to assume that there is a gulf between Jesus' own self-consciousness and the later New Testament writers' perception of him? If history is what reinforces the early Christian faith, then would it not be in their interest to record the events surrounding Jesus with accuracy? We have established that Israel consolidated her faith in God on the basis of historical events. In this vein, Matthew's community would also have supported their faith in the Messiah on the basis of events that are historically genuine. This historical awareness of Judaism, which Matthew also identified himself with, is what characterizes its belief system. Even if there was a progressive development of Christology, there is no plausible evidence or any warrant to say that the self-consciousness of Jesus was fundamentally incompatible with the later perception of Christian communities.

Geerhardus Vos would also argue that the messianic consciousness is uniformly present and active in Jesus' mind from the beginning. Also, he argues that even if there was inevitably a certain degree of evolution, it is not after all an unmessianic process, but precisely an evolution at the end of which stands the fully mature messianic idea that was the firm possession of Jesus.[92] Moreover, our discussion of Israel's conception of redemptive history and the messianic expectation all point to the

---

91. Mack, "The Innocent Transgressor," 135–65.

92. Vos, *Redemptive History and Biblical Interpretation*, 336. Cf. also von Rad, *Old Testament Theology*, vol. 2, 327. He also supports the thesis that later editing or a progressive development of a certain concept is a common practice even in the Old Testament prophetic tradition. Therefore, the fact that the later New Testament writers handled the materials of Jesus should not arouse skepticism towards the authenticity of the scriptural account.

view that Judaism reinforced its faith in God through historical consciousness. For Matthew's community, who still regarded themselves as Jewish, the self-consciousness of Jesus' messianic identity must have been historically authentic for them to preserve it in their tradition.[93] Otherwise, if the events surrounding Jesus were not historically viable, their faith could not be legitimated.

The genealogy of Jesus, his baptism, and his transfiguration all convey his messianic identity, and the narratives would be emptied of meaning without this fundamental notion. As we shall discover later, the passion narrative is where the Gospel reaches denouement, as the true identity of Jesus is finally disclosed. It is thus somewhat tentative to argue that the defining moments of Jesus' ministry are nothing more than imaginative fabrications of the early Christian community. Rather, the early Christians, whose faith in the Messiah derives from the records that show Jesus' own self-awareness, had no difficulty in seeing the full consciousness of Jesus in an accurate record of the development of Jesus.

The Passion Narratives

Introduction

Despite the revelation of Jesus' messianic identity in the defining christological moments and the significant number of healings, miracles, and teachings in his earthly ministry, Israel failed to recognize Jesus as her Messiah. The religious authorities were in constant opposition to Jesus, which led them to conspire against him so that he was eventually put to death. This brought judgment on those who persecuted Jesus and salvation for the faithful remnants. In fact, the judgment against Jerusalem (Matt 23:37–39) was pronounced immediately after Jesus denounced the scribes and Pharisees (Matt 23:28–36).[94] It is significant that the lament over Jerusalem in Matthew has a parallel in Luke 13:34–35. The position of this passage in these two gospels is significant. While Luke placed it prior to Jesus' triumphal entry into Jerusalem (Luke 19:28–40), Matthew put the lament after Jesus had already made an entrance into

---

93. Cf. also Hengstenberg, *Christology of the Old Testament*, vol. 1.

94. Flender, *St. Luke*, 107. It is noted that Jerusalem is the place against which judgment is pronounced. Likewise, Jesus has to die in Jerusalem (Luke 13:33) as a means of salvation. Therefore, Jerusalem is the scene where redemptive history is fulfilled. This reinforces the thesis that the early Christians sought to consolidate their religious faith not on an abstract, timeless notion but firmly in a definite place in history.

Jerusalem (Matt 21:1–11). Hyukjung Kwon suggested that Luke's lament can be interpreted as a conditional prediction that offers Jerusalem an opportunity to repent and avoid judgment by receiving her Messiah. However, in Matthew, the urgency of judgment is more closely felt, as this alternative is excluded. Jesus has entered Jerusalem and Israel clearly rejected her own Messiah. Therefore, the lament is strongly poignant in Matthew, which indicates that the judgment was more imminent.[95] Regarding the end of the passion narrative (Matt 24:29–31), Klaus Wengst notes the high density of scriptural quotations, something that is ironic, since Jesus had used the Jewish Scripture in his eschatological warning and turned them against the Jewish leaders who were supposed to abide by its guiding principles.[96] The emphasis on the concept of redemptive history in terms of the judgment and salvation through Christ are therefore maintained throughout the Gospel from the beginning.[97] Jesus is the fulfillment of the Jewish messianic expectation, and it is on the basis of the Old Testament models that Jesus brings about judgment and salvation. In conjunction with our understanding of the redemptive historical perspective, the presentation of the judgment, according to Wengst, "does not exceed the dimensions of concrete experience. End-time is presented very realistically."[98]

Passover Motif and the Atonement

The three Synoptic Gospels unanimously record Jesus' Passover meal with the disciples instituted as the Lord's Supper before Jesus embarks upon the journey to the cross. The fact that the last and most memorable thing Jesus does with his disciples is celebrate the Passover meal surely

---

95. Kwon, *The Reception of Psalm 118 in the New Testament*, 171. Wengst, "Aspects of the Last Judgment," 233, draws attention to the structure of the eschatological sayings in Matthew: "After the introduction of 24:1–3, the actual sermon can be divided into 3 main parts: 1. the events before the end-time are described (24:4–28) 2. its immediate unpredictable proximity are emphasized (24:29–41) 3. finally, the paraenetic conclusions are drawn (24:42—25:46)."

96. The motivation for apocalyptic belief may have also been reinforced by the destruction of the Second Temple by the Romans, since it must have been perceived as evil and unjust.

97. Matthew's genealogy compared with Luke's is clearly distinct, as the emphasis is very much on the whole frame of Israel's redemptive history and that the coming of Jesus as the Son of David represents the era of the New Exodus from the exilic plight (cf. Matt 1:1–17; Luke 3:23–38).

98. Wengst, "Aspects of the Last Judgment," 236.

highlights the importance of the Exodus theme in the mind-set of the Gospel writers. The theme, on a wider scale, shows Yahweh's faithfulness and consistency in his redemptive purpose throughout the history of Israel. Alfred Edersheim stresses the significance of the Passover, as the most important events in Jewish history were connected with the Paschal season. He notes:

> It is supposed to have been at Passover time that the patriarch entertained his heavenly guests, that Sodom was destroyed and Lot escaped, and that the walls of Jericho fell before the Lord. . . . Just as at a later period alike the captains of Sennacherib and the king of Assyria, who tarried at Nob, were overtaken by the hand of God at the Passover season. . . . It was at the paschal time also that the mysterious handwriting appeared on the wall to declare Babylon's doom, and again at the Passover that Esther and the Jews fasted, and that wicked Haman perished. And so also in the last days it would be the paschal night when the final judgments should come upon Edom, and the glorious deliverance of Israel take place.[99]

It is no coincidence, then, that Jesus' suffering and death also took place during the paschal season. Since Passover symbolizes God's salvation for Israel in the Exodus, Jesus' Passover meal with the disciples clearly has redemptive significance and the New Exodus motif in view.[100] This is consistent with the messianic expectation of the Old Testament, as the hope of salvation modeled upon the prototype Exodus is prevalent in the Old Testament prophets. G. L. Balentine also notes that "Jeremiah, a contemporary of Josiah, visualized the future redemption as an event that would even surpass the first, the Exodus from Egypt (Jer. 16:14–15) . . . Ezekiel shared the same hope that the future deliverance of the nation would be a New Exodus (Ezek. 20:33–44) . . . In Deutero-Isaiah the

---

99. Edersheim, *The Temple*, 229–30

100. Balentine, "Death of Jesus as a New Exodus," 27–41 He also notes that the coincidence of the passion with the Passover, the paralleling of the old redemption with the new has resulted in the portrayal of Jesus' death as the New Exodus of salvation. It has been argued elsewhere that the Exodus from Egypt forms the foundation of the later messianic redemption. Cf. also Hill, *The Gospel of Matthew*, 332. He points out that the Synoptics all associate the death of Jesus with the Passover, but only Matthew makes Jesus explicitly declare the approach of the festival. This indicates that Matthew is particularly keen to portray Jesus' passion in the overarching framework of Israel's redemptive history.

Exodus likewise supplies the framework in which the future redemption is conceived."[101]

The Passover meal with the disciples therefore provides a parallel between the prototype salvation and the new salvation through Jesus, thereby delineating the trajectory and consistency of God's redemptive purpose for Israel.[102] However, this will be accomplished not through the politico-military power of the Messiah but through his humility, obedience, and, ultimately, sacrificial death on the cross. This is made clear by Jesus' gesture of raising the cup and saying, "Drink from it, all of you; for this is my blood of the covenant, which is poured out for many for the forgiveness of sins" (Matt 26:28; cf. also Mark 14:12–25; Luke 22:7–23).

In the Synoptic Gospels, Matthew is the only one who comments that the Passover meal signifies the "forgiveness of sins." N. T. Wright argues that "Matthew is not suggesting that Jesus' death will accomplish an abstract atonement, but that it will be the means of rescuing Yahweh's people from exilic plight."[103] According to Wright, Jesus' death on the cross, and the salvation which it offers, is not an abstract notion which is conceived in a spiritual realm but it should be interpreted in a tangible sense, as it is intelligible only within the context of the larger history of Yahweh's salvation of Israel.[104] This is in agreement with what we have been arguing thus far. The early Christians regarded the messianic ministry of Jesus as the New Exodus which will deliver them "from exilic plight." Passover was the manifestation of the wrath of Yahweh which ultimately liberated Israel from the bondage of slavery. Although the reason for Yahweh's wrath may have been the injustice and sinfulness of the Egyptian monarchy, which rebelled against Him and enslaved His chosen people, Passover is not directly linked with the forgiveness of sins. Usually, the atonement is not associated with Passover. However, a commonality exists in the representative roles of the protagonists involved in both religious acts. In the Passover, it is the death of the firstborn that satisfies the wrath of Yahweh and consequently frees Israel from the bondage of slavery in Egypt. In the atonement, the sin offerings by the High Priest as a representative of Israel also satisfy the wrath of

---

101. Balentine, "Death of Jesus as a New Exodus," 28.

102. Cf. Jeremias, *The Eucharistic Words of Jesus*. See also Marshall, *The Last Supper and Lord's Supper*.

103. Wright, *Jesus and the Victory of God*, vol. 2, 561.

104. Ibid.

God from the bondage of sin (cf. Lev 1:4; 4:20, 26, 31, 35; 5:6, 10, 13, 16, 18).[105] The passion narratives of Jesus and his death on the cross took place during the Passover (Matt 26:2, 18; Mark 14:1). Jesus' ministry is characteristically defined as the forgiveness of sins, but this is made especially clear in the scene of the Lord's Supper, which is effectively the Passover meal with the disciples (Matt 26:28). Here, the evangelist seems to draw together both Passover and atonement in the final scenes of the Gospel. It may be surmised then that what Jesus' death on the cross accomplishes is that it satisfies the wrath of God against the sinfulness of people. This, in turn, results in the forgiveness of sins, thereby inaugurating the new eschatological era of salvation.

Trial Scene (Matthew 26:57–68)

All three Synoptic Gospels portray the Jewish authorities in constant opposition to Jesus, and the trial scene in the Gospel account clearly makes them responsible for the execution of Jesus. It is evident that the trial is an artificial gathering of the people determined to level an unjust charge against Jesus to secure the death penalty for him (26:59). The investigation was informal and subjective rather than a proper interrogation according to the regulations of Jewish law. David Hill notes that the account of the procedure of the Sanhedrin does not concur with the Mishnaic regulations regarding trials for capital charges. Rather than the trial being carried out in the court of law, the proceeding took place in the High Priest's house. Rather than the trial being conducted during the day, it was carried out at night, and instead of interrogating the suspect on two consecutive days, the council reached the verdict on the night of Jesus' arrest. Moreover, it is evident that the witnesses were randomly involved in falsely testifying against Jesus, which greatly undermines the credentials of witnesses for the trial.[106]

It is ironic that during the trial of Jesus, his true messianic identity was revealed for the first time to the public. Therefore, the trial scene was

---

105. Cf. Dumbrell, *The New Covenant*, 26. Cf. also Holland, *Contours of Pauline Theology*.

106. Hill, *The Gospel of Matthew*, 344. Hill suggests that the Marcan and Matthean accounts of the trial may be theological rather than historical in essence. This may reflect the social setting of the early Christians in the first century, when they were experiencing painful rupture from the parent Jewish religion, which is possibly one of the reasons for the Gospel's anti-Semitic character. However, the undeniable fact that Jesus was executed on the cross shows that the formal penalty was essentially Roman.

one of the key moments of Christology which is to be seen as a unified narrative sequence with the other key christological passages, that is, Jesus' genealogy, baptism, and transfiguration.

During the interrogation, Jesus' identity was ironically uttered by Caiaphas, who asked Jesus, "Tell us if you are the Messiah, the Son of God." The high priest's question, according to D. A. Hagner, "is made even weightier in Matthew than it is in Mark by the addition of the solemn words, 'I adjure you by the living God.'"[107] It is unlikely that the High Priest is asking if Jesus considered himself to be God; the designation "Son of God" does not identify Jesus as a divine being. It is more probable that his question is addressing whether Jesus regarded himself as the Messiah, referred to as "son of God" in Psalm 2 and 2 Samuel 7.[108] Jesus' initial response, σὺ εἶπας (You have said), is to be interpreted as an affirmative answer. After all, Jesus did not evade or offer a negative answer to the question.[109] However, his response was more than Caiaphas bargained for. Jesus' statement "But I tell you, from now on you will see the Son of Man seated at the right hand of power and coming on the clouds of heaven" (26:64) invokes a royal psalm (Ps 110) and Daniel 7, which are two crucial messianic texts for the early Christians.[110] It is important to note that the High Priest's charge of blasphemy was not directly linked with the testimony of two witnesses that Jesus claimed to destroy the temple and rebuild it in three days (26:61). If this was the basis upon which Jesus was convicted, the High Priest's question would have been something like "Are you able to destroy the temple and rebuild it in three days?" However, the question of Caiaphas is precisely pointing to the *identity of Jesus*. His statement directly addresses the messianic identity of Jesus and whether he regarded himself as the long-awaited Messiah of Israel. The reason for Jesus' execution was not that he claimed that he could destroy the temple and rebuild it in three days, although that implies that Jesus' authority was higher than that of ordinary prophetic figures. More explicitly, the charge of blasphemy was precisely due to his claim of the title "Son of Man" and the portrayal of his authority on par with God Himself. There was no case for arguing that Jesus was referring to someone else other than himself in the

---

107. Hagner, *Matthew 1–13*, 799.
108. Wright, *Jesus and the Victory of God*, 523.
109. Hagner, *Matthew 1–13*, 799.
110. Wright, *Jesus and the Victory of God*, 524.

use of the title Son of Man. The three Synoptic Gospels unanimously present Jesus' answer to Caiaphas as the Son of Man being seated at the right hand of the power of God, thereby claiming divine authority for Jesus himself. This statement is based on Psalm 110 and Daniel 7 and enrages the council, which puts Jesus to death on the charge of blasphemy. However, D. A. Hagner points out that, according to the Mishna, "the blasphemer is not culpable unless he pronounces the Name itself (cf. in the OT Lev. 24:10–23)."[111] It seems, then, that Jesus is not guilty of the charge, since he does not use the word *God* but instead uses the circumlocution δυνάμεως (the power) in verse 64. Therefore, the charge of blasphemy cannot be based on this category but on the fact that Jesus claimed authority for himself which was exclusively reserved for Israel's deity. Hagner also notes that "the cause of the high priest's reaction lay elsewhere, i.e., in the personal claims of Jesus (cf. 9:3 in connection with forgiving sins, which is characterized as blasphemy)."[112]

In Psalm 110, "my lord" refers to the future messianic King who will be seated at the right hand of the Lord, that is, Yahweh. This is carried over to the trial scene, where Jesus is explicitly identified with the messianic King, whom David addresses as his lord, enthroned and seated at the right hand of God.[113] By evoking this Old Testament text, Jesus claimed for himself something which no man could claim. He has disclosed his identity as the Messiah who shares the very authority of God. The royal psalm in this text therefore continues to support the view that Jesus is the Davidic Messiah, but he also transcends the title. This is in conjunction with our thesis that Matthew's use of the royal psalms in the christological context was not entirely sufficient, since Jesus was deemed to be far more authoritative. Therefore, we proposed the thesis that the early Christians viewed the royal psalms and the enthronement psalms as one ideological entity. Although only the royal psalm (Psalm 110) is alluded to in this passage, limiting the category exclusively to the Davidic monarchy does not fully reveal the understanding of the use of the Psalms by the early Jewish Christians. The royal psalms were considered to be messianic and combined with the major themes of the enthronement psalms, which advances the view that the Messiah from the line of David is not confined within the history of Israelite monarchy.

111. Hagner, *Matthew 1–13*, 801.
112. Ibid.
113. Wright, *Jesus and the Victory of God*, 642.

The Messiah's authority is described in lofty terms which are reminiscent of the divine qualities that are exclusively attributed to Yahweh. Especially in Matthew's Gospel with its high Christology, an allusion to a royal psalm in a christological passage also underlines the importance of the motifs that are inherently characteristic of the enthronement psalms.

Therefore, Jesus' Davidic kingship is once again complemented with the qualities that are commonly attributed to God. N. T. Wright notes that "Jesus had claimed that, as the true king, he not only had authority over the Temple, but would share the very throne of Israel's god; and he had done so by evoking texts which resonated with multiple and subversive meaning in the world of his day."[114]

It appears evident that the divine-royal motif is present in the trial scene where Jesus not only admits that he is Israel's Messiah, the Son of God (Ps 2), but also goes beyond Davidic legacy and reveals himself as the one like the Son of Man in Dan 7:13 and the Lord addressed in Ps 110:1. On the basis of these allusions to the Old Testament texts, one can only come to the conclusion that if Jesus was "not precisely claiming deity (cf. John 5:18; 10:33), he was at least ranking himself with God in a unique status."[115]

Crucifixion of Jesus (Matthew 27:32–55)

The paradoxical nature of Jesus' kingship is made progressively clearer as he embarks on his public ministry. After the transfiguration, Jesus commands the disciples not to tell anybody about the epiphany that they have witnessed until after the Son of Man has been raised from the dead. This also indicates that the glory of resurrection foretold at the transfiguration is not to be understood in isolation from the pathway of the cross. The implication is clear: the glory of Jesus' resurrection and his heavenly splendor can only be grasped in the context of his suffering and death on the cross. This is consistently presented in the crucifixion of Jesus as the story reaches its climax. It is commonly accepted that the crucifixion of Jesus alludes to Psalm 22, in which one finds the vivid imagery of the righteous under extreme persecution by his enemies and crying

---

114. Ibid., 643–44. Cf. also Hengel, *Studies in Early Christology*, 186: "The affinity between Ps. 110 and the figure of the son of man which is alluded to for the first time in Dan. 7:13 and broadly developed in the Similitudes, is also present in the answer of Jesus to the question of the high priest about the Messiah in Mark 14:62."

115. Hagner, *Matthew 1–13*, 801.

for much-needed rescue from God, which is nowhere to be found.[116] However, it should be mentioned that Psalm 22 is not categorized as either a royal or enthronement psalm and therefore is not strictly within the scope of our discussion. However, the ultimate thrust of the fulfillment theme which is prevalent throughout the Gospel is also achieved by Psalm 22, as the evangelist seeks to show how even details such as Jesus' garments being divided by casting lots (Ps 22:18; Matt 27:35) are in accordance with God's redemptive will.[117]

In the crucifixion scene, the Davidic theme is as prevalent as it is in other christological passages we have considered. Jesus is designated as the "King of the Jews," which is ironically used to mock Jesus rather than to acknowledge him as the Messiah. It seems that the evangelist wants to convey Jesus' messianic identity at the last moment of his earthly life as well as Israel's failure in recognizing her Messiah. The crucifixion scene should be considered a christological passage where Jesus' identity is revealed in conjunction with passages we have considered which support Jesus' Davidic claims by incorporating royal psalms. However, the crucifixion passage also seems to concur with other christological narratives in that Davidic connotation is not sufficient in the portrayal of Jesus' identity in Matthew. The taunts from the passerby—"You who are going to destroy the temple and build it in three days, save yourself! Come down from the cross, if you are the Son of God!" (Matt 27:40)—seem to point not at Jesus' Davidic claims but at his supernatural power to save himself from the agony. If Matthew wanted to emphasize Jesus as the Son of David in the taunting words of others, he would have explicitly said so. However, the title Son of God in this particular context seems to point at his supernatural abilities. As do the other key christological passages in the Gospel, the crucifixion narrative uses Jesus' Davidic kingship with his divine attributes which transcend Davidic claims. The centurion who kept watch over Jesus on the cross and who had presumably witnessed all the supernatural events that took place following the death of Jesus (27:51–54) declares him to be the Son of God. D. A. Hagner also notes that the confession of the centurion (27:54) is not necessarily related with the actual death of Jesus (cf. Mark 15:39) but to the subsequent extraordinary events in verses 51b–52. He suggests that "by altering the word order of the statement, putting θεοῦ υἱός, lit. 'of

---

116. Nolland, *The Gospel of Matthew*, 36. Cf. also Hagner, *Matthew 1–13*, 835.
117. Hagner, *Matthew 1–13*, 836.

God the Son' (emphatic word order), immediately after ἀληθῶς 'truly,' and putting οὗτος 'this,' at the end of the sentence, Matthew has heightened the impact of the statement in comparison with its form in Mk. 15:39."[118] A series of extraordinary events following Jesus' death serves to highlight Matthew's high Christology. Hagner comments that "the splitting of the curtain 'from top to bottom,' together with the passive verb evsci,sqhsan 'was split,' implying divine action, points to the event as an act of God."[119] This may be interpreted as God's wrath and judgment upon Jewish authorities for the death of Jesus. On a brighter note, this could be seen as a sign that through Jesus' death, access to God's presence is made available to anyone who seeks Him, since the sin has now been dealt with on the cross.[120] Other spectacular events that followed Jesus' death, such as the earthquake (27:51b–53) which is only recorded by Matthew, certainly have apocalyptic connotations (cf. Matt 24:7; 28:2; see also Isa 24:19; 29:6; Jer 10:10; Amos 8:8). Moreover, the awakening of many holy people who had died (27:52) highlights the awesome power of Jesus' death.[121] This confirms the view that the Son of God title (27:54) is referring to Jesus as far more than a mere Davidic Messiah. Hagner concurs with this view, as he notes that "it is virtually impossible that Matthew means us to understand the confession to be that he was merely a son of God."[122] Rather, the confession of the centurion confirms our view of the divine-royal motif in Matthew's Christology. This is consistent with what we have seen from the passages of Jesus' baptism, transfiguration, trial, and death, which form a literary unit in progressively disclosing Matthew's Christology.

It is ironical that in this setting of Jesus' death, some of the major christological titles are expressed in public: "the King of the Jews," "Son of God," and "King of Israel."[123] In this context, these titles are used by the crowd to mock Jesus rather than as a sincere acknowledgement of

---

118. Ibid., 848, also notes that "a final alteration, the omission of Mark's ὁ ἄνθρωπος 'man,' is consonant with the stronger form of the Matthean statement."

119. Ibid., 849.

120. Ibid. Hagner notes that "the curtains of the temple restricted access to the presence of God. The Holy of Holies was entered only once a year, on the Day of Atonement, by the high priest alone to make atonement for the sins of the people (cf. Heb. 9:7)."

121. Ibid., 850.

122. Ibid., 852.

123. France, *Matthew*, 395, 396.

Jesus' identity. The only exception is the centurion's confession after Jesus' death, when he declares him to be the Son of God (Matt 27:55; cf. Mark 15:39; Luke 23:47).[124] The underlining principle of Jesus' kingship, though it may seem paradoxical, is consistently revealed through his obedience, suffering, and death on the cross. This is shown in the baptism, where Jesus approached John even though it is clear that John is not in a position to baptize Jesus. He approached John to be baptized not because he needed his approval before he began his public ministry or because he was in need of repentance, which is what the ritual symbolized (Matt 3:2). In his humility, Jesus approached the Baptist so that all righteousness would be fulfilled. In other words, he demonstrated his kingship through obedience to the Father's will. When this was displayed at the baptism, the heavens were opened and the Spirit of God descended like a dove, and a voice from heaven declared Jesus to be the beloved Son of God.

What is perplexing, however, especially in the context of the evangelist's portrayal of Jesus' messianic status, is the cry on the cross: "My God, my God, why have you forsaken me?" (Matt 27:46). This raises difficulties in the context of how Matthew presented Jesus with a divine-royal motif in his christological passages.[125] The cry of Jesus on the cross conveys his total devastation and abandonment by God, which is an all too human response for someone who claimed the power to destroy the temple and rebuild it in three days (26:61; 27:40; cf. 12:6). This seemingly paradoxical representation of Matthew's Christology is more sharply felt when we consider some of the Son of Man sayings in the Gospel (cf. chapter 6). Jesus is attributed some of the qualities that are characteristic of Yahweh in the Old Testament. Bearing this in mind, the last words of Jesus are a devastating denial of what should have been the high Christology of Matthew. When we consider Matthew's use of the royal-enthronement psalm and how Jesus is attributed Davidic status along with the traits that belong to Yahweh, this pain-filled cry is totally unexpected. However, in Matthew's Gospel, even if it is granted that there are some elements that describe Jesus in divine terms, it is primarily the

---

124. In the Synoptic Gospels, both Matthew and Mark portray the centurion's confession as the acknowledgement of Jesus as the Son of God, whereas Luke's centurion only declares him to be innocent.

125. Cf. also So, *Jesus' Revelation of His Father*, 141. He also raises the question of the appropriateness of this ending in the context of Jesus' divinity.

human heritage expressed in terms of Davidic legacy that is indubitably put forward by the evangelist. Therefore, it may be surmised that Jesus is identified both in human and divine terms. Bearing this in mind, his anguished cry reveals the paradox of Jesus' identity as he experiences the utter cessation of the Father's loving communion.[126]

In his obedience to the Father, Jesus willingly takes the cross for the salvation of his people and experiences excruciating pain and rejection in death. Jesus' divine-royal authority is revealed in a paradoxical way—in obedience, suffering, and death on the cross—so that all righteousness may be fulfilled.[127] This is consistently revealed in all the passages we have examined thus far. In the baptism, Jesus' messianic kingship supported by a royal psalm is complemented by his humility and obedience, as he willingly subjects himself to John's ritual. This pleases God, and He responds to Jesus' obedience by declaring him his beloved son. In the transfiguration scene, the revelation of Jesus' authority in the presence of the great Old Testament figures and God's intervention is again complemented by his command to keep silent until the Son of Man has been raised from the dead. In the trial scene, Jesus' confirmation of his messianic identity in response to the High Priest's question is rejected, which causes him to be executed. In an entirely consistent manner, Jesus' divine-royal identity, which is presupposed by the use of

---

126. Ibid., 156. So describes the moment of Jesus' death: "Even the knowledge of his Father's love cannot contain the immense excruciating pains he suffers on the cross, which in his genuine humanity burst through and are expressed in the words of dereliction. The cross is the singular point where the communion between the Father and the Son through the Spirit, is cut off even though the Father does love his Son and the Son knows his Father's love even there."

127. Fuller, "The Conception/Birth of Jesus," 37–52. On a similar note, Fuller writes that "the cross is the act of God's initiative, as in Romans 8:32, 'He gave him up for us all'; and on the other hand it is the act of the Son's self-surrender, 'the Son of God, who gave himself for me' (Gal. 2:20). Similarly, the resurrection is presented in the New Testament both as an act of God, e.g., 'God raised him' (Acts 2:24), and elsewhere as an act of the Redeemer himself, e.g., 'I have power to take it (my life) again (John 10:18)." Although Matthew is not as explicit as other New Testament writers in relation to Jesus' divinity, the divine-royal motif which forms the crux of his Christology is consistent with the rest of the New Testament authors. It may thus be argued that Matthew provides a platform for the subsequent writers to elaborate upon Jesus' divinity. Dumbrell, *The New Covenant*, 45, notes that "the term 'Son of Man' in Matt. 8:20, is its first mention in Matthew. The term denoted humanity in all its frailty in the Old Testament and Matthew's understanding of it is reflected in his use of the term to denote Jesus' humiliation." On the other hand, however, the Son of Man saying often carries connotations of divine power and judgment later in the narrative (cf. ch. 6).

the royal-enthronement psalms in the Gospel, is revealed in the most humiliating death penalty known to people at the time. It is this paradoxical nature of Jesus' kingship and divine authority disclosed in the most unexpected way which Israel failed to grasp.

The Great Commission (Matthew 28:16–20)

In the prologue of Matthew's Gospel, the genealogy reached all the way back to Abraham, whereas the commission issued by Jesus after his resurrection stretches as far as "the end of the age."[128] It is thus apparent that Matthew has a time frame of redemptive history which begins with the Old Testament era, reaches its decisive culmination in Christ Jesus, and is extended to the end of the age.

Matthew 28:18 presents Jesus as the universal sovereign king by stating that all authority in heaven and on earth has been given to Jesus. In the genealogy and birth narratives, he is presented as the rightful heir to the Davidic throne, which threatens King Herod. However, as the story progresses, we soon discover that Jesus' kingship is far greater than a mere worldly kingship. This is now made abundantly clear in the finale, as all authority not only on earth but also in heaven has been given to him.[129] The image of ruling over the earth and the exaltation after the enthronement are reminiscent of the passages in the royal psalms (Pss 2:6–9; 89:19, 27; 110:1–3). However, we have also established that Jesus is attributed traits that are characteristic of Yahweh in the enthronement psalms. This will become clearer as we examine christological titles in the subsequent chapter, especially the Son of Man.

We can appreciate the literary and theological connection between the selected christological passages in this volume as Matthew consistently highlights the divine-royal motif of Jesus' messianic kingship throughout the Gospel.[130] D. W. K. So notes that "it must be remembered that Jesus' Lordship must not be viewed on its own for Matthew (Mark and Luke) presents his Lordship via his identification or equivalence with Yahweh."[131]

---

128. Cf. Bauer, "The Literary and Theological Function of the Genealogy," 157.
129. France, *Matthew*, 411.
130. Cf. So, *Jesus' Revelation of His Father*, 35.
131. Ibid., 36.

Jesus' messianic kingship—or, as So points out, his equality with God—is made abundantly clear in verse 19 where he commands the disciples to baptize in the name of the Father and of the Son and of the Holy Spirit. This supports our thesis that where a royal psalm is quoted or alluded to in a christological passage, Matthew not only wishes to portray Jesus in royal dignity in the line of David but he also highlights the Son's divinity. One should be cautious not to read this conclusion back into the earlier parts of the Gospel and argue that Jesus is presented as a divine being at his baptism or any other earlier christological event but in the literary dimension, the earlier parts must be congruent with the subsequent narrative development to obviate any irregularities or inconsistencies in the entire literary structure.[132] More simply put, it is highly improbable that Matthew would suddenly suggest something at the conclusion of his story which is incompatible with the rest of the narratives. The Trinitarian concept implied in the Great Commission supports the essence of our thesis that Jesus is clearly described to be someone far more significant and authoritative than a mere Davidic monarch. While Jesus is primarily described as the Son of David in Matthew, the title does not exhaust the true identity of Jesus.

One might raise the question of why Matthew's is not as explicit as John's Gospel in affirming Jesus' divinity. The answer probably lies in the targeted audience of Matthew's Gospel (cf. chapter 3). We have seen earlier that the Gospel is addressed primarily to the Jewish counterparts, as the early Jewish Christians were going through a transitional stage of rupture from their parent body. Therefore, Matthew could not be as explicit as John in ascribing divinity to Jesus because of the stringent monotheistic belief of his Jewish audience. The evangelist nonetheless leads one to the same conclusion in a much more subtle way than one might reach by reading John.[133]

Furthermore, it is hard to imagine that the final statement "I am with you always, to the end of the age" (v. 20) with its loftiness can be made by a mere human being. Here, Jesus is claiming eternal authority

---

132. So also points out that "Matthew, apart from highlighting the Son's equality with the Father in this verse, also brings the reader's attention to their unity through his deliberate use of the singular for name ὄνομα." This also further confirms the view that the distinction made between the royal and the enthronement psalms is meaningless in the early Christian context, as when one is used the other is also in the mind of the evangelist.

133. Cf. also So, 37.

Christology in the Gospel of Matthew   177

over his people, which only a deity is entitled to.[134] What is interesting in this final verse is that the redemptive history which supposedly reaches its decisive culmination in Jesus is somehow still ongoing. There are still many things left to do. These include making disciples of all nations, baptizing them, and teaching them to obey everything that Jesus has commanded. H. N. Ridderbos, in his study of redemptive history and the New Testament Scriptures, argues that in terms of the history of redemption, the canon cannot be open but rather it must be closed. The motive behind his emphasis on the closed nature of the canon and the "once-and-for-all" significance of the New Testament history of redemption is the unique and exclusive nature of the apostolic power. Since this is by nature unrepeatable and exclusive, all the events in Scripture are self-containing and confined.[135] Indeed the canon in redemptive historical perspective is closed, but the ongoing character of redemptive history, particularly in the final section of Matthew, ensures that the salvation still operates within the lives of those who believe in Christ and submit to him as their messianic Savior. Redemptive history from the time of the Old Testament reaches its climax in Christ, but the final consummation, that is, the full establishment of Parousia, is clearly indicated to be something in the future. The redemptive significance of the Christ event is thus an ongoing reality which stretches beyond the historical time of Jesus. In support of this view, Y. S. Chae writes, "In Matthew's closing scene, Jesus is still at work with his disciples; he is not yet in his final glory. While the Danielic Son of Man (Dan. 7:13–14) is about to receive the Kingdom, Jesus on the Mount in Galilee launches the movement to the nations, yet has no intention of leaving them alone in their mission. Jesus at the last scene of Matthew's Gospel is not on the clouds yet, but on the way toward it."[136]

Therefore, the biblical concept of time indicated in the final scene of Matthew, as we have seen, shows that the full exaltation of the resurrected Jesus, in other words, the decisive climax of the redemptive history of

---

134. Molnar, "What Does It Mean to Say that Jesus Christ Is Indispensable," 96–106, notes that "for Karl Barth and for T. F. Torrance there is no accurate knowledge of the creator/creature relationship if such knowledge does not begin and end in faith in Jesus Christ, that is, with a genuine recognition of his deity in its authentic, definitive and essential sense." Cf. Rahner *Foundations of Christian Faith*.

135. Ridderbos, *Redemptive History and the New Testament Scriptures*, 25.

136. Chae, *Jesus as the Eschatological Davidic Shepherd*, 342.

Israel, has not yet been fully revealed.[137] In the meantime, Jesus gives the disciples clear instructions and promises that his everlasting presence will be with them until the end of the age when the kingdom of heaven will be fully established.

It is evident that the use of the royal-enthronement psalms that relate to the Christology of Matthew reveals the fulfillment of Yahweh's divine redemptive purpose. While it may be possible that a Sinai motif or a Moses typology is alluded to in Matt 28:16–20 because of its setting on the mount, the loftiness of Jesus' authority portrayed in the closing scene makes the analogy somewhat tentative. Y. S. Chae argues that Matt 28:16–20 functions as the conclusion of the passion narrative, which is replete with Davidic shepherd images from Zechariah 9–14. He goes on to say that "finally, the section takes the reader back to the beginning of the narrative, to Micah's promises of the Davidic shepherd who will shepherd the restored Israel in Mt. 2:6 (Mic. 5:1–2)."[138]

While we would certainly agree with his emphasis on the Davidic motif, the title is somewhat insufficient in explaining the Christology in the closing scene. For instance, the passage in Zechariah 9–14 mentions the authority of the Davidic shepherd only as a representative of Yahweh, whereas the authority of Jesus in the Great Commission is clearly equated with that of God. Moreover, the Great Commission extends beyond Israel, whereas the Davidic connotation, which is exclusively nationalistic, fails to embrace the universal character of the passage. In other words, Son of David is not effective in the context where Jesus promises to be with his disciples until the end of the age. Therefore, Micah's quotation, although partially relevant, fails to capture the essence of the passage which reveals the divine nature of Jesus and the fulfillment of redemptive history in himself. Rather, it is more likely that a common theme of the royal psalms (Pss 2:6–9; 89:19, 27; 110:1–3), namely, the investiture of the Davidic Messiah with the divine power as the nations become his heritage and the earth his possession, is in view, which best explains the closing scene of Matthew. However, it is not just a Davidic Messianic motif that is intended here, as the command of Jesus in Matt

137. Ibid., 343.

138. Ibid., 347. Chae argues that Ezekiel 34 is also behind the setting laid out in Matthew 28:16–20. This may be possible, but even in Ezekiel 34 the appointee and the appointer are clearly distinguished; i.e., the subordinate status of the agent is clearly implied. The final scene of the Gospel, however, portrays the authority of Jesus and of God as indistinguishable, thereby equating the authority of Jesus with that of God.

28:19 makes little sense if he is only identified as the Son of David. It is also the divine authority of Christ manifested through the judgment of the Son of Man and the subsequent exaltation which Matthew wishes to convey at the closing scene of his Gospel. The royal psalms, although they play a crucial role in identifying Jesus as Israel's messianic king, lack the capacity within themselves to portray Jesus in the way Matthew wishes to at the scene of the Great Commission. We will see in the next chapter how the evangelist applied the major themes of the enthronement psalms of Yahweh to the Son of Man sayings of his Gospel. This supports the view that the combination of the royal and enthronement psalms as one entity helps define the Christology of Matthew's Gospel both in terms of the Davidic Messiah as well as the constituents of the Trinitarian godhead.[139] We now aim to put this thesis under closer scrutiny by examining the major christological titles of the Gospel.

---

139. Ibid., 349. See also So, *Jesus' Revelation of His Father*, 173, 295. The selected key christological passages are the climactic points where the narratives reveal Jesus' divine-messianic status. This is not to say that other narratives are not of any significance in the argument. In fact, Jesus' authority is consistently displayed and developed throughout his ministry. Jesus preaches with great authority, as we read in the Sermon on the Mount, and he heals when implored to do so. He even breaks the traditional religious norm, as he freely dines and befriends sinners such as lepers, Gentiles, and tax collectors. However, Matthew never quite reveals Jesus' divine-messianic status in the teaching and healing narratives. D. W. K. So also notes: "The notion that the genuinely human Jesus exercises divine sovereign power can be found in numerous passages in the gospel narratives, e.g., passages on healings including healings from a distance (e.g., Mt. 8:5–13), exorcisms, his miracles in nature (e.g., rebuking and thereby calming the storm and waves at Galilee), raising people from the dead (e.g., Lazarus) and supernatural knowledge (e.g., Jesus speaking to the Samaritan woman in John 4:16–18). But one may object that the fact that Jesus performs these mighty acts in the power of the Spirit does not necessarily mean that he is *sovereign* and *divine* in these acts" (italics mine). Therefore, while all these passages are of great importance in the entirety of Matthew's Christology, they do not function in the ways the selected passages do to reveal Jesus' divine-messianic identity. In sum, it is not what Jesus does or says that defines his identity but who he already is.

6

Analysis of Christological Titles

THE DIVINE-ROYAL MOTIF AND MAJOR CHRISTOLOGICAL TITLES

Introduction

THE AIM OF THIS volume has been to explore how the Psalms in particular have been used in relation to the Christology of Matthew. A classification of the different types of psalms based on the content, genre, and setting has suggested that these psalms need to be examined in isolation and appreciated in their own right.[1] While it is not our primary intention to get too involved in the debate over what constitutes a certain group of psalms, we have raised doubts as to whether such distinctions are of any value in the early Jewish-Christian context. On the one hand, the royal psalms, which are written to celebrate Davidic kingship in royal ceremonies such as weddings and coronations, have the king of Judah as the subject.[2] On the other hand, the enthronement psalms portray the exaltation of Yahweh as the King and the subsequent judgment by the god of Israel through his servant David, which are the major themes of these particular psalms.[3] For instance, Psalm 110 may be

---

1. Cf. Gunkel, *Introduction to Psalms*.

2. The definition of royal psalms differs among scholars. In this volume, based on Gunkel's classification, we have identified them to be Pss 2; 18; 20; 21; 45; 72; 101; 110; 132; 144:1–11; cf. 89:47–52.

3. Cf. Croft, *The Identity of the Individual in the Psalms*, 84. We have identified the enthronement psalms to be Pss 96:10, 13; 97:2, 8, 10f.; 98:9; 99:4ff.

viewed as a dialogue, as the king takes pride in the promise of Yahweh's glorious salvation from his enemies. The distinction between the maker of the promise and the recipient is clearly drawn, as the Davidic king as the subject in this psalm is subordinate to Yahweh. Having considered how the writer of Matthew intended to develop his "high" Christology, it is doubtful that the royal psalms on their own would have sufficed in conveying Jesus' divine-royal status. While maintaining the religious-national identity of Israel, Jesus was far more than a mere heir to the Davidic throne (cf. Matt 5:17–19 and 22:43–45). In other words, even though Jesus is primarily presented as the Son of David in Matthew's Gospel, he cannot be confined within the legacy of David, for he is far more authoritative in his essence and in his redemptive significance. This also affects the way the Psalms are used by the evangelist. Since Jesus is portrayed as a Davidic descendent, one might be inclined to think that the royal psalms figure prominently in the quotations. We consider that the distinctions between the royal and enthronement psalms are irrelevant for Matthew, but the categorization of these types of psalms help us understand the intention behind Matthew's Christology as he incorporated them into his text. We hope to demonstrate more fully in this chapter through the study of the major christological titles that the theme of divine judgment and the exaltation of Yahweh in relation to the enthronement psalms, together with the Davidic connotations of the royal psalms, are of great importance for the Christology of Matthew. What we seek to demonstrate is how the major christological titles, such as Son of Man, Son of God, and Son of David, interact in the Gospel of Matthew to convey Christ Jesus as the Davidic Messiah whose divine authority of judgment and exalted kingly status after the resurrection bear striking resemblance to the description of Yahweh in the enthronement psalms and who has finally come to draw the redemptive history of Israel to a decisive consummation.[4]

---

4. However, the significance of the titles in the study of Christology is not without its challenges and criticisms. I. H. Marshall, for instance, points out the limitation of christological titles, stating that "although contemporary study of Christology has concentrated its attention on the various titles given to Jesus in the New Testament, many scholars are reluctant to admit that Jesus himself used any of these titles to describe his own person and functions"; *The Origins of New Testament Christology*, 43.

Son of Man

Son of Man in the Old Testament

R. H. Fuller traces the early fragments of apocalyptic material in Isaiah 24–27; Zechariah 9–14, and in the book of Joel, but the most vivid apocalyptic imageries are found in the book of Daniel, which many believe to have been inspired by the Maccabean revolt. The apocalyptic imageries in the book of Daniel influenced other works such as the book of Enoch, the Jewish Sibylline oracles, the Assumption of Moses, the Apocalypse of Ezra (4 Ezra/2 Esdras), and the Apocalypse of Baruch.[5] Apocalyptic emerged out of a context which fervently believed that the end time was imminent, a period which also coincides with the time when the Messiah was eagerly longed for. Therefore, the roots of the Son of Man are likely to have messianic connotations, especially in that Dan 7:13, cited by Jesus, forms the crux of his trial before the High Priest (Matt 26:64). In other words, during the time when Israel longed for divine redemption in the period of the Babylonian exile, the Messiah who would liberate Israel from foreign oppression and restore the nation would be the Son of Man.[6]

Fuller draws attention to the Ethiopic Enoch 46:4; 48:2f.; 62:7–11; 62:14; and 69:27–29, in which the Son of Man is portrayed as a preexistent divine being in the eschatological setting (48:2f.; 62:7).[7] Here, the judgment theme is prevalent, as the Son of Man triumphs over the kings and rulers of the earth who have persecuted the chosen ones of Israel (46:4; 62:11; 69:27).[8]

---

5. Fuller, *The Foundations of New Testament Christology*, 35, 36. Fuller writes, "The History of Religions school has sought its origin in an oriental Gnostic myth of the Heavenly Man. Alternatively, the Uppsala School has sought to derive it from the same root as the messiah concept, namely from the oriental myth and ritual pattern of sacral kingship."

6. Ibid., 38. Fuller also notes that the figure of the Son of Man was established in pre-Christian Jewish apocalyptic as the eschatological agent of redemption.

7. Ibid., 39.

8. Cf. also Lindars, *Jesus Son of Man*. It is also noted that "for the Son of Man concept in Judaism, the most important source was the Similitudes of Enoch. In it the patriarch Enoch sees in a series of visions the eschatological judgment and the vindication of the righteous Jews. For this purpose God has prepared the Messiah as his agent in performing the judgment and as the leader of the righteous in the everlasting kingdom. The description of the Messiah is directly modeled on the setting of Dan. 7:9–14, and the Messiah is identified with the 'one like a Son of Man' of Dan. 7:13 (1 Enoch 46:1–3)."

We can reasonably assume that Enoch relies on Daniel in his eschatological vision, as the Son of Man is portrayed in a similar manner. In Dan 7:13–14, the Son of Man comes with the clouds of heaven to the Ancient of Days. The four beasts, which represent four powerful nations, are destroyed at the judgment, after which the Son of Man is given sovereign power and receives worship from the people of all nations.[9] Here, according to I. H. Marshall, the Son of Man points to an individual figure which remained dominant in subsequent Jewish writings rather than denoting a corporate entity.[10] However, it is not clear whether the figure is to be identified as a human figure or a heavenly being with human characteristics.[11] It seems unlikely that the Son of Man in the Similitudes of Enoch and the vision of Daniel 7 is believed to be divine in nature by the authors but is rather referring to a man who is representative of the elect and who wields the divine power of Yahweh.[12] This idea may be reinforced when we look at certain psalms, such as Pss 8:4, 80:17, and 144:3, where the avnqrw,pou in the context of a prayer for Israel's restoration is most likely to refer to a king who acts as a representative of the nation. This indicates that the title has a messianic connotation and refers to the one who will establish salvation for Israel.[13]

---

9. Cf. also Marshall, *The Origins of New Testament Christology*.

10. Ibid., 67. He further notes, "The Similitudes of Enoch shows a developed concept of the Son of Man in which he has become a glorious figure, invested with power to rule and to judge, and attracting to himself some of the traits of the Messiah in the Old Testament."

11. Lindars, *Jesus Son of Man*, 10. He points out that the Son of Man is most likely to be a "symbolic representative figure for the loyal Jews, or an angel, in which case he might be the guardian angel of their interests, i.e., Michael."

12. Ibid., 14. It is noted that "the idea of a heavenly agent for the judgment is attested independently in the fragmentary Melchizedek document from Qumran."

13. Cf. Fuller, *The Foundations of New Testament Christology*, 42. He would argue that while references to these texts may shed some light on the origin of the Son of Man within Judaism, it is irrelevant to the New Testament usage of the term since this particular psalm is never quoted in the New Testament. However, we have argued in this volume that the act of quotation is not merely confined within the literal dimension. On the basis of Matthew's attachment to the Old Testament and the way he freely used Psalms without proper referencing, it is highly probable that the evangelist had possessed full knowledge of the text and expected his audience to recognize them without the need to spell them out. Therefore, the use of the Psalms in the New Testament should not be defined solely in terms of explicit literal quotation. Allusions to prevalent themes of the Old Testament text are also of importance in the New Testament. Cf. Wright, *Jesus and the Victory of God*; Holland, *Contours of Pauline Theology*.

On the contrary, however, Maurice Casey has raised doubts as to whether the Son of Man is an apocalyptic title. He argues that "the Aramaic term *bar nash(a)*, 'son of man,' was a normal term for 'man.'"[14] Since its use was simple and rather mundane, the term would have been an unlikely candidate to qualify as a major messianic title. Its function is when "a speaker might use a general statement, in which the general term was *bar nash(a)*, 'son of man,' in order to say something about himself or a group of people including himself."[15] However, in order to avoid being unduly direct or arrogant, a speaker would in fact refer to himself or a group in third person so that any explicit identification is blurred. According to this view, when Jesus says in Luke 12:8–9, "whoever acknowledges me before men, the Son of Man will also acknowledge him before the angels of God" (cf. also Mark 8:38), Matthew simply replaces it with "I" in reference to Jesus (Matt 10:32–33).[16] Casey's suggestion that it is simply a way of indirectly referring to Jesus without the Son of Man being in any sense a messianic title is somewhat unconvincing. Without fail, the synoptic tradition uses the Son of Man in apocalyptic passages where Jesus will return as heavenly Judge with great power and glory (cf. Mark 13:26; Matt 24:30; Mark 14:62; Matt 26:64).[17] If the early Christians had given no special status to the son of man, it is difficult to explain its prevalence in the apocalyptic passages where Jesus predicts the Parousia. Casey's argument seems to be derived from the fact that Son of Man is used interchangeably with "I" in reference to Jesus, but this is no ground for arguing that the term had no apocalyptic or christological significance. Rather, it serves to demonstrate that when Jesus uses the Son of Man title in the apocalyptic sayings, he is in fact referring to himself as the divine-messianic judge who, after vindication, will return for the ultimate judgment upon the nations. Therefore, there should be no confusion in thinking that Jesus is pointing to yet another figure when the Son of Man is used.

Jesus the Son of Man

The discussion of Son of Man in relation to Jesus has been one of the most controversial areas of New Testament Christology. We seek to at-

---

14. Casey, *From Jewish Prophet to Gentile God*, 47.
15. Ibid., 48.
16. Ibid., 50.
17. Ibid., 53.

tempt a general survey of scholarly opinion regarding the Son of Man which will demonstrate the diversity of opinion in this particular area of discussion.

The title is particularly important because the study of the Gospels through the historical-critical method suggests that the title goes back to Jesus himself.[18] The advocates of the historical-critical method attempt to find criteria for isolating the primitive strata from the later editorial workings of the early Church. Rudolf Bultmann is perhaps one of the pioneering figures who employed this method in isolating the primitive tradition which is directly attributed to Jesus himself from the later additions of the early Christians, who obviously had ideological agenda against opposing groups. He argues that the Son of Man sayings originally come from the Gnostic redeemer myth and that later writers edited the original material in order to link Jesus with the Son of Man. According to Bultmann, the authentic sayings of Jesus regarding the Son of Man were those where Jesus seems to be referring to someone else other than himself (unless he was referring to himself as the third person singular), which means that he was not conscious of himself as the Son of Man.[19] Therefore, the most primitive Son of Man sayings do not support the view that Jesus regarded himself as the Son of Man but he was pointing to another figure in the future. He was referring to a future judgment which will be wrought by the Son of Man.[20] In fact much of the discussion regarding the Son of Man in a standard "liberal" view of Jesus is that the christological claims in the Gospels reflect the thinking of the early Church rather than Jesus' claim about himself. However, this presupposition is highly debatable, since tracing the original Aramaic language in the Gospel writings has revealed that Jesus frequently used the Son of Man title to refer to himself (cf. Mark 13:26), in which case discovering what the title meant for Jesus and the early Christians becomes crucially

---

18. Hooker, "Christology and Methodology," 480–87, expresses concerns with regard to the limitations of the form-critical and traditio-critical methods and the assumptions they make in reaching conclusions that are often unwarranted by the biblical texts under discussion.

19. Nebe, "The Son of Man and the Angels," 119, notes in relation to Mark 8:38 and Luke 12:8–9 that "Jesus has conceived of the Son of Man as a person of dignity who is coming as an eschatological figure in the future; that Jesus has clearly distinguished between himself and this Son of Man; that he nevertheless saw a soteriological relation between himself and the Son of Man."

20. Bultmann, *Theology of the New Testament*.

important in the study of early Christology.[21] Both Ferdinand Hahn and R. H. Fuller corroborate this conclusion by suggesting that in the early Christian context, the title "Messiah" was not applied to Jesus, but for the first Palestinian Christians he was designated as the "Son of Man."[22] It is then highly probable that the Son of Man title reached all the way back to the primitive stage of the life of Jesus, and the early Christians use of it in christological context suggests that the title was considered to be messianic in essence.

Tom Holland in his PhD dissertation deals with this issue as he focuses on the priestly aspects of the Son of Man.[23] On the basis of ἀνθρώπων in 1 Timothy 2:5, which describes Jesus' role as the mediator between God and man, he points out that the role of a mediator is usually ascribed to the priests in the Old Testament. He also notes that the authority of judgment which is delegated to the Son of Man in the synoptic tradition is due to the sin which is defined as the defilement of the temple. He argues that the Son of Man's judgment is the response of the great high priest whose role is to defend the temple against desecration and preserve its purity. Fundamentally, the role of the Son of Man as the high priest goes back to the Exodus tradition, where the firstborn in the Passover tradition functioned as a mediator that saved the people of God from the destruction of the divine wrath that fell upon Egypt. Subsequently, the Levites were selected as the priestly family who would replace the function of the firstborn and fulfill the role of the mediator between Yahweh and Israel so that the covenantal relationship would be maintained through the atonement of sin. The Son of Man thus reaches all the way back to the Exodus-Paschal tradition.

More recently, Robert Snow has examined Daniel's Son of Man in Mark's Gospel in the temple context, which leads him to a conclusion similar to that of Holland.[24] He relies largely on M. D. Hooker's study of the title, as she argues that all the elements of the Son of Man in Mark's

---

21. Lindars, *Jesus Son of Man*, 1. It is also noted that there are those who deny that any of the Son of Man sayings are authentic. All of them are attributed to development at a later stage when Hellenistic influence exercised dominant influence upon the foundations of Christology.

22. Cf. Fuller, *The Foundations of New Testament Christology*. See also Hahn, *The Titles of Jesus in Christology*.

23. Holland, *The Paschal-New Exodus Motif*. Cf. also Ellingworth, "Priesthood"; Robinson, "The Priesthood of Paul in the Gospel of Hope."

24. Snow, "Daniel's Son of Man in Mark."

Gospel, that is, the necessity of suffering and confidence in final vindication and the endowment of heavenly authority, can be traced to Daniel 7.[25] In the first section of Mark's Gospel where the Son of Man appears (Mark 1:14—8:21), he represents the divine presence. The Son of Man has the authority to forgive sins, and he is even lord over Sabbath, which is a prerogative exclusively reserved for Yahweh. In conjunction with Holland, Snow also defines sin as the defilement of the temple, and the authority of judgment which has been invested in the Son of Man should be understood as God's wrath upon the unrepentant Israel. The threatening note of judgment is therefore the response of the great high priest who will punish the ones who have desecrated the holy temple and those who have violated Yahweh's holy sanctuary. Mark's Son of Man redefines the sacred temple around himself. However, in Mark's second section (Mark 8:27—10:45), the necessity of suffering and death is emphasized, which is a crucial part of Markan Jesus' ministry. It is no surprise that the ones who cause the death of the Son of Man are the corrupt temple leaders who constantly threaten the Son of Man throughout the Gospel story. In the final section where the Son of Man appears (Mark 11:1—16:8), he is finally vindicated and is portrayed with the heavenly language as the priestly Son of Man in the celestial temple.[26]

The title is certainly an unusual way of simply referring to oneself, and the way the title has been used by Jesus indicates that the designation is more than a circumlocution (cf. Dan 7:13). At a superficial level, it seems that υἱὸς τοῦ ἀνθρώπου in correspondence with the Aramaic expression simply means "a man."[27] Barnabas Lindars notes that the context in which it appears in Jewish tradition refers to mankind in a collective sense. Moreover, in Ezekiel, the title is used in referring to the prophet as the representative of the people whom he was sent to serve.[28] In the synoptic tradition, Matthew agrees with Mark that the

---

25. Nebe, "The Son of Man and the Angels," 123, concurs, and he also argues that "it seems evident that the conception of the Son of Man as a special, individual, endtime-eschatological person of dignity, as we find it also in the New Testament has somehow been developed out of Daniel 7; the book of Ezekiel can be important for the development only indirectly."

26. Snow, "Daniel's Son of Man in Mark," 306, 307.

27. The term may also have associations with the firstborn of creation, Adam, in which case the Son of Man may also suggest a figure who comes from God and was ideally fitted to be His agent.

28. Lindars, *Jesus Son of Man*, 3.

Son of Man is an authoritative figure who has power over the Sabbath and has the authority on earth to forgive sins (Matt 9:6; 12:8; cf. Mark 2:28). On the other hand, however, the Son of Man is subject to suffering and the humiliation of death by crucifixion (cf. Matt 17:9, 12, 22; 20:18, 28; 26:2, 45). In addition, it is perplexing to read Jesus' statement in Matt 12:32, where blasphemy against the Son of Man has somewhat lighter consequences in comparison with blaspheming the Holy Spirit. This particular statement may suggest that Matthew's Jesus does not utilize the title as an expression of royal or heavenly authority but simply as a replacement for the first singular expression "I," provided that we agree on the general principle that Jesus was referring to himself when the Son of Man title was used. In other words, he is referring to himself in the third person singular. However, this suggestion becomes tentative in the context of other Son of Man sayings which are clearly imbued with characteristics of divine authority for judgment and the heavenly exaltation as he is vindicated by God (cf. Matt 19:28; 24:30; 25:31; 26:64).

R. H. Fuller raises doubts as to whether Jesus could have been so inconsistent in employing the term, as he sometimes seems to distinguish between himself and the Son of Man and sometimes to equate himself with the messianic figure. He notes: "It is on the grounds of this inconsistency that Bultmann concludes that only the passages in which the distinction is drawn, or identification not asserted, are authentic. Those in which Jesus identifies himself with the Son of Man are creations of the Church, which after the resurrection identified Jesus with the Son of Man."[29]

Perhaps not as radical as Bultmann's position, Fuller argues more or less for an understanding of the text along similar lines of thought. He writes that "while Jesus distinguished himself from the future Son of Man who was to come in glory he nevertheless regarded himself as proleptically performing the functions of the coming Son of Man."[30] Jesus was merely fulfilling the task of preparing the way for the one who is to come, which in essence is what John the Baptist was portrayed as doing in the synoptic tradition.

Fuller's thesis, that the Son of Man and Jesus are not necessarily the same entity, derives from the observation that the author of the Gospel

---

29. Fuller, *The Foundations of New Testament Christology*, 122. Cf. also Bultmann, *Theology of the New Testament*.

30. Ibid., 122.

indicates that the kingdom is breaking through in Jesus but its final consummation is still in the future.[31] Because of this chronological distinction, Jesus is seen to take the initiative of inaugurating the heavenly kingdom, but the final consummation is to be carried out by the future Son of Man.[32]

The "most primitive Christology of all," according to Fuller, revolves around two poles: "The earthly work of Jesus as proleptic Son of Man and his future coming in glory as the transcendent Son of Man."[33] This argument can only be sustained if it is conceded that Jesus' self-consciousness was different from that of the future messianic Son of Man. Secondly, the early Church had an ideological agenda possibly against Jewish opponents, which led them to add the sayings of Jesus that do not necessarily reflect Jesus' own understanding of his identity and ministry.

However, this argument has several fundamental flaws. Firstly, there is no convincing evidence within the Gospel that Jesus was merely performing the role of a "forerunner" for the Son of Man to come. This task was in fact ascribed to John the Baptist, who was sent to prepare the way for the coming Lord (Matt 3:3). The reaction of John (Matt 3:14) clearly implies the Baptist's recognition of Jesus as the Lord whom he is not worthy to baptize. In the transfiguration shortly before the passion narratives, Jesus affirms that Elijah has already come, but, just like the Son of Man, whose fate was soon to be revealed, he had suffered at the hands of those who did not recognize him (cf. Matt 17:12). It is evident that the forerunner had come prior to the coming of the Messiah and had fulfilled his duty according to the prophecy in Scripture. The notion that Jesus is pointing to yet another figure in the future is entirely inconsistent with the plot and the development of the story.[34]

---

31. Ibid., 123.

32. Ibid., 144, 145. In arguing that the future Son of Man sayings differ from the authentic sayings in Jesus' own self-consciousness, Fuller points out that the later editors of the early Church elaborated the apocalyptic imagery. He notes that "Jesus' intention was not to give apocalyptic instruction about the future, but simply to invoke an ultimate sanction for his own word and work." Secondly, the early Church inserted Old Testament phraseology into the Son of Man sayings, which was not the original intention of Jesus' own Son of Man sayings. The reason was christological, as the early Jewish Christians needed to defend the legitimacy of Christ on the basis of the Old Testament Scripture against Jewish opponents.

33. Ibid., 151.

34. Cf. also Hooker, *The Son of Man in Mark*, 188. She affirms that "there is nothing in the Marcan sayings to suggest that Jesus believed that he was destined to 'become'

Secondly, Fuller's distinction between Jesus and the Son of Man based on the observation that the kingdom is to be finally consummated with the coming of the future Son of Man is based on a misperception of the redemptive history of Israel as depicted in the New Testament. Although the promised salvation has been achieved through Christ, the final consummation or Parousia is still expected in the future (28:16–20). It should be emphasized, however, that the future is no longer, as in Judaism, the τέλος or "end" which defines the meaning as a whole (cf. chapter 4, section 2). In the Great Commission, Matthew makes it clear that the assurance of salvation has already been demonstrated through the resurrection of Jesus. There is a sense of assurance and triumph but also a sense of incompleteness in that the final consummation is still a future event. In the meantime, the followers of Christ are to live by faith and carry out the task of the Great Commission until the Lord returns for the final judgment.

In this volume, we are seeking to determine how Matthew saw and interpreted Jesus, but this can only be validated if the evangelist's account of Jesus is consistent with that of Jesus' own understanding of himself. An attempt to understand how the evangelist saw and interpreted Jesus naturally inclines us to consider whether Jesus himself would agree with what Matthew thought of him. Otherwise, what is the point of relying on the Gospel for the knowledge of Jesus? We have rejected the view that the early Christians may have formulated their own understanding of Jesus due to ideological interest which is essentially incompatible with Jesus' own experience. There is a lack of evidence between Jesus' life and the early Christian setting which substantiates the views of the likes of Bultmann. This tension is manifested in the diversity of opinions among scholars concerning whether or not Jesus viewed himself as the coming Son of Man. Perhaps one of the main reasons for skepticism concerning Jesus' self-consciousness as the Son of Man is, as M. D. Hooker calls it, "psychological." Some scholars find it difficult to accept that a sane man would identify himself with an eschatological supernatural figure traveling on the clouds, and thus they feel it is more likely that the Son of Man sayings are artificial products of the early Church.[35] However,

---

Son of Man; the future sayings all refer to 'coming,' not 'becoming,' and none of the other sayings contains a hint that Jesus regards himself as acting only as the Son of Man designates."

35. Hooker, *The Son of Man in Mark*, 183. Hooker says that it is the form-critical approach that places the majority of Son of Man sayings in the faith of the early Church.

this is certainly not an easier option for explaining the Son of Man title. Why would the early Church put on the lips of a man something that is so far-fetched which Jesus would never have dreamt of? Even if the early Church was responsible in handling the text at a later stage, this does not necessarily mean that it could have no place in the life of Jesus. Moreover, the fact that Jesus designated himself in such lofty terms need not mean that he may have been insane and that therefore the Son of Man sayings must be the product of later editors who had ideological interests. In response to this, Hooker points out that there is evidence that the visions surrounding the Son of Man figure were interpreted literally and were thus regarded as palpable reality rather than mere metaphorical images, in which case Jesus meant it literally when he prophesied that the Son of Man will be seated at the right hand of power and will come on the clouds of heaven. In her study of 1 Enoch and 2 Esdras, Hooker writes, "We should note that 2 Esdras interprets the details of Daniel's vision in a more crude and literal sense than 1 Enoch, a fact which suggests that this kind of literal interpretation was still developing after the time of Jesus."[36]

Accordingly, Hooker asserts that the Danielic imagery of "one like a Son of Man" was not simply apocalyptic imagery, but was "intended to express a very real and fundamental truth about the righteous nucleus of Israel."[37] The vindication of the Son of Man by God and the judgment are thus firmly rooted in the reality of eschatological judgment. This is in tune with our understanding of the redemptive history of Israel, which portrays the relationship between Yahweh and His people in a concrete historical manner. The Son of Man is therefore not simply one who will appear in the distant future and a figure described in metaphorical language. For Jewish Christians, his judgment is very real, and the verdict

---

The advocates of this methodology seek to unravel the historical process by which these sayings came to be attributed to Jesus. However, Hooker notes that "the argument that these sayings originated in the early Church can be convincingly maintained only if it can be shown that the early Church possessed a living 'son of man' theology which might create such sayings, and if it is impossible to set the sayings within the life of Jesus himself. There is no sign of a creative 'son of man' theology in the Church; and the pattern which we have discovered in the Marcan sayings suggests that they are more coherent, and therefore less likely to be the accidental products of the community, than is often supposed."

36. Ibid., 184, 185.
37. Ibid., 189.

will be pronounced on the basis of how they have responded to the Son of Man in this present time (Mark 8:38; Matt 10:32–33; Luke 12:8). The title is directly related to the fundamental nature of Jesus' person and ministry. Hooker aptly remarks, "It is because he is the Son of Man that Jesus claims authority; it is his obedience as Son of Man that involves him in suffering; it is the fact that he is Son of Man that is the ground of his faith in his ultimate vindication."[38]

The image of Jesus as the Son of Man is indeed dynamic and multifaceted. It is because he is the obedient Son of Man that he willingly undergoes suffering, crucifixion, and death. However, his true messianic identity and divine power are paradoxically revealed through the Son of Man's suffering and death on the cross.[39]

Son of Man: Divine-Royal Messiah?

It has often been pointed out by scholars that the Son of Man in Matthew stands out from other major christological titles such as "christos" ("messiah"), "King of Jews," "Son of David," and "Son of God." J. D. Kingsbury notes that the title differs from others, for it does not function confessionally with regard to Jesus' identity, that is, "who Jesus is."[40] The passages which reveal Jesus' identity include some of the christological narratives we have already looked at (3:17; 16:16; cf. 14:33; 17:5; 27:54). In the majority of these passages, Jesus is designated as the Son of God.[41] In none of these texts is Jesus identified as the Son of Man, and only Jesus used the title to refer to himself.[42] In conjunction with this, Ulrich Luz points out that the title Son of Man does not receive the same level of christological focus as does the title Son of God. He notes, "Unlike the title 'Son of God,' one cannot say that Matthew places his Son of the Man logia at crucial points in his narrative. Neither the beginning nor the end

---

38. Ibid., 190.

39. Cf. Marshall, "The Synoptic Son of Man Sayings," 327–51. See also Maddox, "The Function of the Son of Man," 45–74; Moule, "Neglected Features in the Problem of 'the Son of Man,'" 419–22.

40. Kingsbury, "The Figure of Jesus in Matthew's Story," 3–36.

41. Cf. Ibid., 25.

42. Ibid., 26. Kingsbury notes that Son of Man is absent from the first part of Matthew's story (1:1—4:16), which functions as a "frame" to present Jesus to the reader and largely determines who he is throughout the rest of the story.

of the Gospel, nor texts opening or closing a main section of the Gospel, are normally 'marked' by the title 'Son of the Man.'"[43]

Luz is in agreement with Kingsbury in saying that syntactically Son of Man never appears as a confessional title in addressing who Jesus is. Rather, the title is functional in that it tells the reader what Jesus the Son of Man does or suffers.[44] Kingsbury would also concur that Son of Man is associated with Jesus' earthly activity in terms of his suffering, death, and resurrection.

However, the distinction between how the title is to be regarded in terms of making the confessional statement of who Jesus is and what he does is not axiomatic in terms of Christology. Even though Jesus is not confessed to be the Son of Man by the disciples or, indeed, addressed in such a way by God, the passages where Son of Man is found disclose Jesus' heavenly authority, namely in the context of final judgment (Matt 9:6; 12:8; 13:41; 16:27; 19:28; 24:30; 25:31; 26:64).[45] In the majority of the Son of Man sayings in Matthew's Gospel, the dominant theme is the authority of Son of Man as he is exalted in the heavenly realm and is given the power to execute judgment.[46] It is also interesting to note that Matthew is the only one in the synoptic tradition who narrates how the judgment will take place in language which is reminiscent of the exaltation and judgment themes found in the enthronement psalms. For instance, Matthew 19:28, which portrays the Son of Man's royal

---

43. Luz, "The Son of Man in Matthew," 3–21.

44. Ibid., 5, 6.

45. Nebe, "The Son of Man and the Angels," 115, argues that in the pronouncement of Jesus and in the Christology of the early Church in the New Testament, the Son of Man is not conceived as an angelic figure, but he is in certain cases the figure of a judge.

46. Cf. Marshall, *The Origins of New Testament Christology*, 77. "Throughout the sayings there runs the general thought of the authority of Jesus. The Son of Man is a figure of authority on earth and will one day appear endowed with heavenly authority when he participates in the last judgment; yet his authority is spurned by men and it is only by the action of God that his authority is finally vindicated." See also Hooker, *The Son of Man in Mark*, 180, 198. In her study of the Marcan Son of Man sayings, she also detects the theme of authority. It is an authority which is exercised by Jesus in his earthly ministry but is soon rejected and so leads to suffering and ultimately death. However, the Son of Man will be vindicated and exalted at the end of the age. Hooker quotes Philippians 2 as an example where this pattern is also common: "Christ, in the form of God, and therefore entitled to authority, was nevertheless humble and obedient, accepting even the consequence of that obedience, which was crucifixion. As a result God has exalted him and given him lordship and dominion over everything in heaven and on earth and under the earth."

authority at the "renewal of all things" when the judgment will be established, is reminiscent of the prominent themes in the psalms that were written to celebrate Yahweh's kingship (Pss 96:10, 13; 97:2, 8, 10f.; 98:9; 99:4ff.). Psalm 96:10 reads, "Say among the nations, 'The LORD reigns.' The world is firmly established, it cannot be moved; he will judge the peoples with equity." Here, the Lord is declared king, and he will judge the people with authority and justice. In the same manner, the major themes of heavenly exaltation and divine judgment are prominent in the enthronement psalms: "they will sing before the LORD, for he comes, he comes to judge the world in righteousness and the peoples in his truth" (Ps 96:13); "Zion hears and rejoices and the villages of Judah are glad because of your judgments, O LORD" (Ps 97:8); "Let them sing before the LORD, for he comes to judge the earth. He will judge the world in righteousness and the people with equity." (Ps 98:9)

Likewise, the Son of Man in Matthew's Gospel at the last judgment (25:31–46) in his exalted status is king and judge (cf. Dan 7:13ff.; 1 Enoch 40ff.).[47] Moreover, the Son of Man will be sitting at the right hand of the Might One and will return on the clouds of heaven, which is reminiscent of Psalm 97:2. The heavenly authority of the Son of Man is consistently attested in Matthew's Gospel. His authority surpasses any mere earthly king in that he has the authority to forgive sins, which results in miraculous healing (9:6), and he is above all religious regulations to the extent that he is "lord of the Sabbath" (12:8). He is in command of heavenly angels who will assist him in judgment by removing and purging from his kingdom everything that causes sin and all evildoers (13:41; 16:27; cf. 25:31). In this respect D. A. Hagner's view that the Son of Man is to be regarded as the second major title after the most exalted confession, Son of God, is somewhat dubious.[48] Also, it is doubtful whether Holland's and Snow's linking the Son of Man with the high priest would be of any value in the manner which Matthew wants to portray Jesus. Although they both argue that the Son of Man's role as the mediator between mankind and God is what establishes the connection with the role of the high priest, the comparison does not adequately draw the parallel in terms of the essence of the Son of Man's authority, which is certainly greater than what the high priest could claim of his own.

---

47. Hill, *The Gospel of Matthew*, 330.
48. Hagner, *Matthew 1–13*, lxi.

Perhaps one of the most decisive moments in which Jesus revealed himself as the authoritative Son of Man was in his trial before the Sanhedrin (26:64). Being seated at the right hand echoes a royal psalm (Ps 110:1) which supports the case that Jesus is identified as Israel's long-awaited Davidic Messiah, but the theme of exaltation and his authority to judge in these Son of Man sayings clearly brings the enthronement psalms into focus. He is not only the Davidic Messiah who will liberate Israel from tyranny but he shares the divine authority of Yahweh in that his judgment extends beyond Israel. The prerogative of judgment, as we have seen in the Psalms, is something that is uniquely Yahweh's. On the basis of the study on the Enochic Son of Man, A. H. I Lee notes that in Psalm 110:1, the one who sits at the right hand of God participates directly in God's reign. He further notes: "The sitting at the right hand of God means the transference of divine authority and judgment. Similarly, in LXX Dan. 7:9–11 the dominion of God and of the 'one like a Son of Man' becomes one in its execution. The 'one like a Son of Man' almost takes the place of God and his authority becomes identical to the authority of God and his dominion identical to God's dominion."[49]

In support of this view, R. T. France notes that "Jesus' answer to the High Priest's charge lifts the whole idea of Messiahship out of the sphere of Jewish earthly politics into that of heavenly authority."[50] Just as in the enthronement psalms where Yahweh is described in royal terms, the Son of Man is likewise addressed as the King (cf. 25:34) who in essence is not a mere human royal. Matthew, in comparison with other synoptic writers, is certainly not reticent in speaking of the kingdom of the Son of Man.[51] He sits ἐπὶ θρόνου δόξης αὐτου (19:28; 25:31), acting as God's vice-regent regarding salvation, and he also shares God's authority.

In Mark's Gospel, the emphasis of the Son of Man sayings is on the suffering of Jesus (Mark 8:31; 9:12, 31; 10:33, 45). However, in Matthew's Gospel, the emphasis has shifted from the necessity of the suffering and humiliation of the Son of Man to his vindication, and the subsequent enthronement as the King. France, in his study of the Son of Man title in Matthew's Gospel, notes, "It is undoubtedly for Matthew primarily a title of majesty, not of humiliation. The later patristic use of this title to focus

---

49. Lee, *From Messiah to Preexistent Son*, 208.

50. France, *Matthew*, 381.

51. Ibid., 291. He notes that "it is Matthew alone who includes sayings about the parousia of the son of man (24:27, 37, 39) which is a term for the king's visitation."

on Jesus' humanity and humiliation in contrast to his divinity and glory would have had no appeal for Matthew."[52]

The ideas of the throne of the Son of Man in the context of judgment recalls the unique kingship of Yahweh vividly described in the enthronement psalms (cf. Pss 96:10, 13; 97:2, 8, 10f.; 98:9; 99:4ff.), and it is this divine kingship which is also echoed in the kingship of the Son of Man in Matthew's Gospel.[53] This becomes more evident in Matthew 16:28: "Truly I tell you, there are some standing here who will not taste death before they see the Son of Man coming in his kingdom." When we read this verse in the light of its parallel in Mark 9:1, which omits the Son of Man and instead simply has the "kingdom of God," it seems reasonable to suggest that Matthew intends to ascribe to the Son of Man divine attributes. On the basis of the assumption that Mark's Gospel was the original source Matthew had at his disposal, we suggest that Matthew's view of the Son of Man may have been unique in the synoptic tradition. Lindars notes, "Thus the tradition which Matthew received was, 'You will not have gone through the towns of Israel, before the kingdom of God comes.' As before, Matthew has understood the kingdom of God to be a periphrasis for God himself. In agreement with the christological interpretation of eschatological sayings, he has identified the coming of God with the Parousia of Jesus. It is normal and natural for him to express this by means of the titular Son of Man."[54]

This is an important point for the Christology of Matthew even if the evangelist does not explicitly identify the Son of Man with God *per se*. Matthew's tendency to use the Son of Man title in this manner draws attention to how John's Gospel uses these motifs attached to the messianic figure. Johannine theology is somewhat different from the Synoptic Gospels in that the text reflects a later stage of christological development based on earlier sources. One of the chief characteristics which distinguishes John is the way he presents Jesus as the preexistent being and in so doing identifies the Messiah with God Himself. This statement would be premature in the context of the synoptic tradition. Although the Son of Man title is not the central feature of Johannine Christology, it nonetheless forms the part of the material presenting Jesus as the messianic agent of divine salvation (cf. John 1:51 and also Mark 1: 10). In

---

52. Ibid., 292.

53. Ibid., 309. Cf. also Nebe, "The Son of Man and the Angels."

54. Lindars, *Jesus Son of Man*, 123.

John 3:11–13, it becomes evident that the bringer of divine salvation must also come from above. In other words, the Son of Man must be preexisting in order to qualify as the Messiah. Lindars puts it succinctly: "John does believe that Jesus is pre-existent, in the sense that he has divine origination, and therefore the Son of Man is pre-existent, because the Son of Man is none other than Jesus."[55] Matthew does not go as far as John in that Jesus must be of divine origin in order to accomplish his messianic task, but the traits that are attributed to the Son of Man, albeit with more subtlety, do point to the divine qualities of the representative who has come to establish God's salvation.

This leads us to enquire further about the origin of the title. The Son of Man is not an arbitrary creation of the early Church but is in fact rooted within the Jewish tradition. This view is advanced by Lee in his recent attempt to rediscover Jesus' self-consciousness by examining how early Christians interpreted and used messianic psalms in their Christology. It is noted that there are very few intermediary figures that are described as sharing God's throne in Second Temple Jewish literature. These figures are, namely, personified Wisdom, Moses, and the Son of Man.[56] Lee notes that of all these figures, it is the Son of Man in the Parables of Enoch who is of significance here. This highly exalted human/angelic figure is uniquely portrayed, as "he sits on the divine throne (62:2, 5; 69:27, 29; cf. 51:3)" and "he receives worship (46:5; 48:5; 62:6, 9)."[57] This is strikingly similar to the exaltation and judgment themes prevalent in the enthronement psalms. It seems evident that early Christian use of the messianic title Son of Man results from Jewish influence rather than Hellenistic influence.[58]

In addressing his audience, which was predominantly Jewish, Matthew would naturally have resorted to the concepts that were familiar to them. As he believed Jesus to be the fulfillment of the redemptive history of Israel, he sought to convey to his Jewish readers that the Davidic Messiah has indeed come as was promised. We have seen how Matthew has achieved this by using royal psalms in the decisive

---

55. Ibid., 150.
56. Lee, *From Messiah to Preexistent Son*, 23.
57. Ibid., 24.
58. Ibid., 25. Lee emphasizes that "first-century Jewish monotheism was not broken or compromised by growing speculations about intermediary figures but firmly maintained with a strong commitment to the one God of Israel."

christological moments. However, it is clear that Jesus was no ordinary king, that is, merely the rightful heir to the Davidic throne. Matthew reveals Jesus to be someone far greater. The Son of Man sayings clearly reflect Jesus' divine authority in the context of judgment which echoes Yahweh's Kingship and His righteousness as the judge in the enthronement psalms. Therefore, if this is true, then the major themes of both royal and enthronement psalms were consciously employed by Matthew as he formulated his divine-royal Christology. However, this must be differentiated from John's preexistent Christology, which identifies Jesus with God and states that he must be of divine origin in order to have accomplished what he was appointed to fulfill. Formulating his Christology in the way John felt convicted to do would no doubt have been very sensitive and indeed threatening for his Jewish counterparts. For this reason, Matthew, who would have regarded himself as part of the true remnant of Israel with its piety in Jewish religion demonstrated by his adherence to the Law, employs literary and theological subtlety in conveying the divine-royal Christology to Jewish unbelievers. This is masterfully done in a way that is not as explicit as John's Gospel, which is not timid in disclosing Jesus' preexistent divine nature, which would have been immediately dismissed by Matthew's Jewish audience at this early stage, but the fundamental essence of Matthew's message concerning Christ cannot be regarded as contradictory to John's Gospel (cf. Matt 5:17, 18; 7:12; see also the evangelist's initial emphasis on Israel in Matt 2:6; 10:6; 15:24).

Son of David

Introduction

We have attempted to trace the Jewish expectation of the Messiah and have found that Matthew's Son of David fulfilled the messianic role of securing Israel's salvation (cf. 22:42). Matthew believed that Jesus fulfilled the Old Testament promise and that he inaugurated the messianic era. The promised salvation was already at hand. Matthew, above all the other synoptic writers, was particularly keen to emphasize that Jesus was the Son of David and used the title more frequently than any other gospel writer (Matt 1:1; 9:27; 12:23; 15:22; 20:30, 31; 21:9, 15; 22:42; cf. Mark 10:47, 48; 12:35; Luke 1:32; 3:31; 18:38, 39). Jesus' identity as the Son of David was explicitly spelled out (Matt 1:1; 15:22; 21:9, 15) and less explicitly affirmed by quoting from the royal psalms in christological passages of the Gospel (see chapter 5).[59] What is puzzling, however, is the context in which the title Son of David occurs in the narratives of Matthew's Gospel. This has posed major difficulties for commentators who have sought to explain the redemptive function of Jesus as the Son of David. J. D. Kingsbury, in his study of the christological titles, noted that "one of the most striking features of the activity of Jesus as the Son of David is its restricted significance apart from his entrance into Jerusalem (21:5, 9)." Kingsbury points out that the "public activity of Jesus Son of David is set forth by Matthew within the confines of a double restriction: it extends exclusively to healing (21:14–15), only to particular individuals (cf. 9:27; 12:22; 15:22; 20:30)."[60] The title occurs elsewhere, such as in the triumphal entry into Jerusalem (21:9, 15) and in Jesus' debates with the scribes concerning the Messiah (22:42), but these are addressing the matters of the Messiah's identity rather than his redemptive function (cf. also 2:2; 27:11, 37). It is the messianic *function* of Jesus as the Son of David rather than issues concerning his identity that will be discussed in this section.

Son of David in the Healing Narratives

In Matthew's Gospel, the function of the Son of David is associated with healing (9:27; 15:22; 20:30, 31).[61] In the healing narratives of Matthew (cf. 8:2—9:35), Jesus' Messiahship is demonstrated. This has puzzled many who sought to interpret the Son of David's messianic activities in the context of the messianic expectations of the Old Testament. Y. S. Chae has recently attempted to provide an interpretation for the healing activities of the Son of David on the basis of the Davidic shepherd tradition (especially Mic 2–5; Zech 9–14; Ezek 34–37).[62] He clearly ac-

---

59. We also need to note that basileu,j is synonymous with Son of David (cf. Matt 2:2; 21:5; 27:11, 37).

60. Kingsbury, *Matthew: Structure, Christology, Kingdom*, 100.

61. Dumbrell, *The New Covenant*, 43, 45, notes that the three healing miracles of Jesus affirm that the messianic era, the age of the kingdom of God, had arrived (Matt 8:2–17). It is interesting to note that the healing is extended to the Gentiles as a reward of their faith. This is put in sharp contrast with the unbelieving Israel, against whom a severe warning is pronounced by Jesus. He also highlights that the miracles in Matthew 8:18—9:35 signify "the newness of Jesus' ministry and its relation to the forgiveness of sins." See also Kingsbury, "The Title 'Son of David' in Matthew's Gospel," 591–602.

62. Chae, *Jesus as the Eschatological Davidic Shepherd*, 4, 5.

knowledges the centrality of the title in Matthew's Gospel, as the text systematically discloses how Jesus is the Son of David beginning with the prologue (1:1). Chae further argues that the evangelist expounds on the Davidic expectation in terms of "the return of the eschatological shepherd and his Davidic-Appointee" in these prophetic writings and applies it to Jesus in the context of healing where he is addressed as the Son of David.[63] Although Chae identifies the narrative strategy of the Gospel and the Davidic shepherd tradition to be largely within the framework of *Heilsgeschichte*, he fails to explain how the Messiah's healing is associated with salvation in the context of Israel's redemptive history. Can it be argued that the healing of the Son of David has its foundation within the Old Testament understanding of Yahweh's redemptive activity? If so, in which biblical theme is it best explained and understood?

It is our contention that the healing activity of Jesus as the Son of David should be interpreted through the New Exodus motif in the context of Israel's redemptive history. We have explained elsewhere that the most representative redemptive event that Israel as a state has experienced is the Exodus from Egypt. As significant as this event was for the faith of Israel in Yahweh as her redeemer, the Exodus under the leadership of Moses was never seen as deliverance from sin. It was no doubt an extremely important event for the subsequent generations of Israel in terms of their history and theology, but it was never more than political liberation from a foreign oppressor. In other words, it liberated Israel from the bondage of slavery, but it did not free her from sin. Even though the Mosaic covenant secures Israel's ongoing relationship with Yahweh, it does not deal with the fundamental matters of the fall and sin.[64]

Although it is not the intention of this volume to compare Matthew's theology with that of other New Testament writers such as Paul—and to impose Paul's theology on Matthew—we may reasonably assume that the communities these New Testament writers were addressing shared the same mind-set, especially regarding the Old Testament and its fulfillment in Jesus as the Davidic Messiah. Tom Holland argues that in Romans 7, "Paul is showing that the Exodus Israel experienced under Moses never brought her into the freedom from sin that she professed to have received." He notes that "the covenant people still share in the

---

63. Ibid., 299.
64. Cf. Caird, *New Testament Theology*.

existence of sin and death, as do all other people."[65] This meant that the greater Exodus was needed in order to bring about true salvation from sin. The original sin of Adam, which has permeated the relationship between God and His people, has not been resolved by the Exodus event.[66]

For the people of the Old Testament, it is important to note that sin is equated with death (cf. 1 Kgs 17:18; also Isa 53:12). The early Christians were no exception in this sense, as they regarded death as the ultimate consequence of sin. Holland argues that in Romans 8, Israel has made a covenant with death, that is, the covenant with sin as she ran from the claims of Yahweh (cf. Isa 28:15).[67] Therefore, death is equated with sin, and both are personified as the enemy, namely, Satan.[68] One might refer to 1 Corinthians 15:45–55 and Revelation 20:14, where death is portrayed as the last enemy standing and is finally destroyed by Christ.[69]

On the basis of this insight, one may suggest that the forgiveness of sin indicates that a man is delivered from death unto life. In fact, this is what seems to be at the heart of the evangelist, as Matthew places the Son of David in the healing narratives. The act of healing, in other words delivering man from the pathway of death, may also be seen as the forgiveness of sin. Jesus' healing, therefore, symbolizes the forgiveness of sin which the prototype Exodus could not bring. Indeed, Jesus explicitly said this when he healed a paralytic in Matthew 9:2, as the cause of physical restoration was the forgiveness of sins. Jesus' exorcism and curing of the sick are complemented by a formula quotation from Isa 53:3–4 which signifies the sacrificial death of the messianic servant in the event of the New Exodus. It is highly significant that Matthew should have had this passage from Isaiah in mind in the healing narratives of Jesus. The prophet Isaiah goes on to say, "But he was pierced for our transgressions, he was crushed for our iniquities; the punishment

---

65. Holland, *Contours of Pauline Theology*, 97.

66. Cf. Ibid., 98, 99. In his reading of Romans 8, Holland notes that "the deliverance is not according to the flesh, but according to the Spirit. This freedom is not through the keeping of the law, but is based on a perfect sacrifice for sin."

67. Ibid., 100, 101.

68. Ibid., 102. He also notes that the Targum equates death and sin, which are personified as Satan. For instance, in Exodus 12, the angel of death in the Passover is identified with Satan.

69. Ibid., 103. Holland argues that these are New Exodus passages. See also p. 110, where Holland notes that the nature of Paul's doctrine of sin is that Christ delivers man and nature from alienation and death.

that brought us peace was upon him, and by his wounds we are healed. We all, like sheep, have gone astray, each of us has turned to his own way; and the LORD has laid on him the iniquity of us all" (Isa 53:5-6).

It is only the greater New Exodus inaugurated by Jesus that will establish true messianic redemption from the bondage of sin, and the healing of the Son of David suggests that this New Exodus is already at hand. R. E. Watts has connected Jesus' healing activities with the theme of the New Exodus which Isaiah prophesized. He argues that the restoration of sight and hearing in Isaiah (cf. Isa 6:8-9) has huge significance in the context of the exilic setting.[70] He writes,

> In [Isa.] 29:18f. the restoration of sight and hearing is one of the characteristics of Israel's redemption, while 32:1 speaks of the righteous king in whose reign the judgments of blinding and deafening will no longer occur and the tongue of stammer will speak clearly. It is in chapter 35 that this restorational healing of Israel is set most firmly in the context of a New Exodus. In terms of "heal," Isaiah 30:26, in keeping with the reversal of judgment in 6:10, describes the day of redemption as a time when YHWH will heal the bruise of his people and bind up the fracture he inflicted (cf. 1:6).[71]

In Deutero-Isaiah (chapters 40–66), the New Exodus is brought about by the messianic Servant figure, who, by healing the nation, establishes Yahweh's restoration (cf. 57:18f.). Matthew, in addressing his Jewish audience, must have had in mind this idea of redemptive healing which Isaiah predicted would happen in the time of the New Exodus through the Messiah, who is from the line of David. On the basis of the Old Testament promise, which Matthew's Jewish counterparts must have been familiar with, Jesus is addressed as the Son of David in the healing narratives. It is thus in the context of Israel's redemptive history that Jesus' healing as the Son of David becomes intelligible. R. T. France notes, "In the light of the widespread ancient conviction that sickness is the result of sin, it is possible that the modern distinction between physical healing and spiritual salvation is inappropriate to the thought of

---

70. Watts, *Isaiah's New Exodus in Mark*, 170.

71. Ibid., 171. He notes that "in non-biblical literature, although there are general references to healing or the banishing of illness in association with eschatological salvation (e.g., Jub 23:29f.; T. Zeb 9:8; 2 Bar 73:2; 4 Ezra 13:50), there is little evidence to suggest that a messianic figure was specifically connected with the healing of the blind, deaf and lame during the New Testament period."

Isaiah or of Matthew, so that a reference to physical healing would not be out of place in the account of the Servant's redemptive work."[72]

There is further evidence within the synoptic tradition that Jesus' healing signified more than mere physical restoration. In Mark 2:1–12, the healing of a paralytic is achieved through the forgiveness of sin, which causes indignation among the scribes concerning Jesus' authority. This, Watts argues, is strikingly consistent with Yahweh's declaration to Israel in Isa 43:25, where He forgives her sins as the restoration of the nation is promised at the New Exodus. These attributes of Yahweh and his authority to forgive sins are applied to Jesus as the inauguration of the New Exodus takes place through the Messiah's ministry.[73] The New Exodus under the kingship of both Yahweh and His messianic agent mean that the problem of sin is now dealt with, whereas the prototype Exodus had not been able to purge Israel of sin. The evidence suggests that there exists a link between the forgiveness of sin and the healing of diseases (cf. also Ps 103:3). This further implies that Jesus is in fact offering salvation from the bondage of sin when he heals.[74] As we have argued, this testifies to the establishment of the New Exodus in the redemptive history of Israel.

What is of importance here is the authority of the Son of David in his forgiveness of sins for the people whom he heals. The authority to forgive someone of sin seems to be reserved only for Yahweh in the Old Testament (cf. Num 14:20; 30:12; Josh 24:19; 1 Kgs 8:30; 2 Chr 6:21; Neh 9:17; Pss 25:18; 65:3; 79:9; Jer 31:34; Ezek 16:63; cf. also Matt 9:6; Mark 2:7). This has also been pointed out by Watts, who notes that "although there is evidence of a general expectation of an eschatological removal of sin, there are no clear grounds to suggest that forgiveness of sin is pronounced by any other than Yahweh."[75] It is interesting to note that out of all of the healing narratives in Matthew's Gospel where Jesus is addressed as the Son of David (Matt 9:27; 15:22; 20:30, 31), in Matthew 9:6, it is the Son of Man who heals a paralytic by forgiving his sin. It may be suggested that the Son of Man and Son of David both function as messianic christological titles that are interchangeable. This is also consistent with our argument earlier concerning the Son of Man and the divine

72. France, *Matthew*, 301.
73. Cf. Watts, *Isaiah's New Exodus in Mark*, 173.
74. Ibid., 174.
75. Ibid., 175.

authority which originally belong to Yahweh. The Son of Man's authority in the context of the divine judgment is ultimately connected with the forgiveness of sins which is brought about through the healing of the Son of David. Therefore, two contrasting aspects of the New Exodus can be seen. The Son of David brings about salvation through healing for those who call upon Jesus and accept him as their Messiah. By contrast, the Son of Man promises divine judgment and the wrath of God upon the unbelievers who reject and persecute Jesus. Furthermore, this implies that although Jesus fulfills the messianic promise as the Son of David, he exceeds David in his authority to forgive sins. This is possibly the reason that the evangelist uses Son of Man instead of Son of David in 9:6. It seems that Son of David on its own does not sufficiently portray Jesus' identity and his role as the Messiah. In other words, although Jesus is primarily identified as the Son of David, the title does not exhaust the identity of Jesus. It is evident that Matthew intends to develop his Christology beyond a mere Davidic kingship into something that closely resembles Yahweh by attributing to Jesus such authority as was exclusively ascribed to Israel's deity.[76]

Son of God

Introduction

The title Son of God in the Christian setting denotes Jesus as the divine figure who was preexistent before time began. It is certainly the key confessional title for Christians, whose faith in Christ reveals Jesus as the second person of the Trinitarian Godhead. All christological titles carry significance to varying degrees as different titles interact with each other to form a dynamic understanding of Jesus, but it is Son of God which is by far the most prominent of all for Christian communities. The core

---

76. Cf. Fuller, *The Foundations of New Testament Christology*, 159. It is noted that the title "Messiah," i.e., Son of David, undergoes development after Jesus' ascension into heaven, and in the context of judgment the term *Christos* becomes an equivalent for the apocalyptic title Son of Man. He also notes that "there was already a tendency within Jewish apocalyptic for the Son of Man to take over elements from the Davidic messianology, particularly in the Book of Enoch"; *The Foundations of New Testament Christology*, 161. It also seems that the two titles were interchangeable. Fuller points out that "since 'son of man' is not a confessional title and therefore could not be used kerygmatically, an alternative title was needed as soon as the Church began to reflect on Jesus' death. So it settled for 'messiah' which had already been adopted as a substitute for 'son of man' in the Parousia context."

of orthodox Christian faith is to confess Jesus as the Son of God who, although he shares the very nature of God, nevertheless came to save mankind from sin in the form of a servant (cf. Rom 15:8; Acts 3:13). We have thus far endeavored to argue that the divine authority of Christ is one of the major concerns for Matthew's Christology, but one needs to continually examine whether one is claiming more than is warranted by the text. This is one of the key critical factors we need to be aware of in the field of biblical exegesis.[77] The pressing question which is going to be dealt with in this section is whether in Matthew' Gospel the Son of God title denotes what later Christians commonly understand by the term, namely, the preexistent divine being. Nevertheless, we need to decipher what first-century Christians at their particular stage of christological development understood by the title. This does not mean that we are negating or contradicting the thesis of this volume but that there is a need for a critical examination of the title in the context of the early Jewish-Christian setting. The same concern has been expressed by J. D. G. Dunn, who notes that "it is generally taken for granted, axiomatic, part of the basic definition of what Christianity is, that to confess Jesus as the 'Son of God' is to confess his deity, and very easily assumed that to say 'Jesus is the Son of God' means and always has meant that Jesus is the pre-existent, second person of the Trinity, who 'for us men and our salvation became incarnate.'"[78]

What Dunn is urging is that one needs to assume an unbiased position in an attempt to discover what the first readers of the text understood by the term. It is a critical question of whether the Son of God in the original setting of Matthew's Gospel carried the same connotation as that of the later Christian understanding of the title.

The Origin of the Son of God Title

The issue here is whether the Old Testament can be shown to be the background for using the Son of God title in the New Testament as referring to Jesus as the preexistent divine being. This is a crucial question for Christians, who profess that their Messiah is the second person of Trinity, in other words, the divine Son of God on the basis of the Old Testament. More simply put, if the divine sonship of Jesus and his preexistence only become intelligible in the light of the Old Testament, then

---

77. Cf. Dunn, *Christology in the Making*.
78. Ibid., 12–13.

the critical question arises as to whether the Old Testament actually uses the title in that manner.

In the Old Testament period, it seems that kings and judges were described on several occasions with language which would seem to attribute a certain degree of divinity to them (Ps 45:6; 82:6; cf. Exod 21:6; 22:8; Isa 9:6f.).[79] However, these are constructed in a way that does not compromise Jewish monotheistic belief. There are several examples of figures who are portrayed as transcending a mere human existence and are later revered as great figures in terms approaching deity status. For instance, Moses' death (cf. Deut 34:6) is described with obscurity, which in effect projects Moses to a status above ordinary human counterparts. In a similar manner, Elijah's end is described as a translation into heaven by Yahweh (2 Kings 2:1f.). However, there is no implication whatsoever that the prophets were in any way thought to have been deified. There are other great figures such as Jeremiah, Enoch, and Melchizedek whose status is clearly elevated to something that resembles deity, but the Jewish authors are careful not to present them in a way that compromised their fundamental belief system (cf. Gen 5:24).[80]

Therefore, when "Son of God" is used to refer to Jesus on the basis of the Old Testament, it would be stretching the evidence to argue that Jesus is here described as a deity. Rather, when the term Son of God is applied, it indicates primarily that Jesus is a royal king of Israel in the line of David. R. H. Fuller notes that "the adoption of the empirical king as the Son of God was a firmly embedded feature of the royal ideology of Israel."[81] God's promise to His anointed Davidic king addresses him as His son, and although the expression "begetting" does not quite convey the king's divinity, it certainly displays an intimate relationship

---

79. Ibid., 17. (The Scripture references are quoted from Dunn.)

80. Ibid., 19; see also pp. 15, 16. There are some interesting finds in the Dead Sea Scrolls regarding the son of God: "one speaks of the time when God will have begotten the Messiah among them (1Q Sa 2:11f.); the hoped for Davidic Messiah is described specifically in the language of divine sonship using 2 Sam. 7:11–14 ('he shall be my son') and possibly associating it with Ps. 2:7 (4QFlor. 1:10-fin); the other says of one who apparently is to be a mighty king (Messiah?): 'He shall be hailed as the Son of God and they shall call him Son of the most High' (4Qps Dan Aa; cf. Test. Levi. 4:2)." The above evidence points in the direction that the title seems to have a clear association with the messianic king. He is also begotten by God, which either indicates that he is of divine nature or that he is simply adopted as God's representative. Cf. also Vermes, *The Dead Sea Scrolls in English.*

81. Fuller, *The Foundations of New Testament Christology*, 31.

that the royal king shares with Yahweh (Ps 2:7). Seeing that Ps 2:7 is used in key christological passages (cf. Matt 3:17; 17:5), it is plausible to say that Jesus is primarily identified as the Davidic king of Israel. Therefore, Son of God and Son of David share a common heritage in terms of the origin of their meaning. These titles are used as messianic titles by the early Jewish Christians in interpreting Jesus' identity and ministry.[82] In the Jewish mind-set of Matthew and his readers, the Son of God title is applicable to Jesus only in the context of Israel and her redemptive history. Matthew's clear attachment to his Jewish heritage naturally points the reader to look for clues in the Old Testament. Ferdinand Hahn has pointed out that "it is from this [royal messianism] that the use of the title Son of God in the primitive Christian tradition has to be explained."[83] This coheres with the suggestion above that Son of God is in alignment with Son of David in terms of its background. In other words, as Hahn writes, "The motif of the divine sonship in its distinctive form, in the sense of appointment to office and assignment of dominion, practically belongs to royal messianism within the sphere of Palestinian late Judaism."[84] Therefore, at this stage, the Son of God remains embedded in the political realm of Israel rather than denoting the supernatural status of the Messiah.

If our interpretation of the Son of Man is correct, it seems, then, that it is not so much that the Son of God functions to convey the divinity of Christ; rather, the former would come closer in its portrayal of Jesus' divine authority in the Gospel. Usually, the Son of Man has been

---

82. Ibid., 32; see also pp. 69, 71, 72. Scholars who treat the New Testament texts as a product of Hellenistic influence argue that the Hellenistic concept of the 'divine man' has permeated the Christology. For instance, the concept of the divine man appears in the *Letter of Aristeas*, Josephus' *The Jewish War*, and Philo's *Life of Moses*. Fuller notes that "the author of the *Letter of Aristeas* claims for the heroes of the Jewish Old Testament the Hellenistic term ἄνθρωπος θεοῦ divine man. Philo elaborates his picture of Abraham, the Old Testament prophets and above all Moses with traits drawn from the Hellenistic concept of the divine man." Fuller also argues that the title Son of God was influenced by the divine man concept of Hellenistic religiosity which contributed to the composite picture of the Son of God. However, such an argument is beyond the textual evidence in Matthew's Gospel, as there is no sufficient proof to support the thesis that Matthew's Christology was in any way influenced by Hellenistic thinking. Matthew with his formula quotations and fulfillment themes makes it clear from the text that his mind-set is thoroughly rooted in the Jewish tradition. His Christology should also be interpreted through the understanding of the Old Testament.

83. Hahn, *The Titles of Jesus in Christology*, 281.

84. Ibid., 284.

understood to convey the human nature of Jesus. The Son of God, on the other hand, was seen to point to his divinity. However, such assumptions are very doubtful in the context of Matthew, where the Son of Man clearly has the most exalted status, speaking as one who is bestowed with the divine power of judgment which is reminiscent of the powerful images of Yahweh as depicted in the enthronement psalms. If Son of Man merely referred to Jesus' human existence then we are immediately faced with serious difficulties in explaining Matthew 9:6–8, where Jesus declares that "the Son of Man has authority on earth to forgive sins" (cf. also Mark 2:10).[85] Moreover, Matthew 12:8 states that "the Son of Man is lord even of the Sabbath" (cf. Mark 2:28; Luke 6:5). If the evangelist's use of the title was merely to point to a man, then a more obvious choice of an ordinary Greek word ἄνθρωπος would have sufficed.[86] This challenges the common Hellenistic titular understanding of the christological titles, as the Son of God on the basis of the Old Testament tradition is to be seen within the ideological framework of the royal dynasty of Israel (2 Sam 7:14; Ps 2:7).[87] Furthermore, Hahn points out that in Mark 14:62, the eschatological function of Jesus which is envisaged according to an apocalyptic mode of thinking is explicitly connected with the messianic Son of God title. Indeed, the high priest's question was to confirm whether Jesus considered himself as the "Son of the Blessed One." However, in response to the question, Jesus does not refer to himself as the Son of God but as the Son of Man. This possibly suggests that the Son of God title had not yet been fully developed in Matthew as a title of divinity, as it would be in John's Gospel. It is likely that the Son of Man tradition and its supernatural traits in the context of an eschatological

---

85. On the basis of Holland and Snow's thesis, it could be argued that priests forgave sins in the Old Testament. The Son of Man thus speaks as the supreme priest. However, the role of priest was that of a mediator whose representative function redeemed Israel from Yahweh's wrath as a consequence of sin. This is not the same as having the authority to forgive sins. In Matthew, the Son of Man is described as having the authority to forgive sins, which is uniquely reserved for Yahweh in the Old Testament.

86. Cf. Jay, *Son of Man, Son of God*, 33. Jay notes that "it is difficult to suppose that Mark, whose Greek, if not elegant, was adequate, should have 'perpetrated the howler' of rendering *bar nasha* (if he understood it to mean simply man) by the cumbrous υἱοῦ τοῦ ἀνθρώπου when a perfectly ordinary Greek word ἄνθρωπος would have been the obvious choice."

87. Elsewhere it is used to designate God's representatives, such as angelic beings (Gen 6:2; Job 1:6; 2:1; 38:7) and Israel as a nation (Exod 4:22; Hos 11:1).

setting have later influenced the Son of God title (cf. 1 Thess 1:10).[88] All we can say from the text of Matthew is that when the Son of God title is applied to Jesus, he is clearly aware of his intimate relationship with God as His messianic agent. He is also aware that the divine sonship entails a deep sense of vocation to fulfill God's redemptive purpose for Israel and to establish a New Covenant with the people of God. This would be achieved through the sacrificial death of the Son of God on the cross and as a result of his exaltation and vindication. In the Great Commission, the resurrected Jesus appeared to the disciples and instructed them to baptize in the name of the Father and of the Son and of the Holy Spirit, as all authority in heaven and earth has been given to the Son. It this respect, there is a close connection between the Son of God who is finally glorified at the resurrection and the Son of Man who after suffering was nevertheless promised to return as the heavenly Judge.[89] When Jesus speaks in Matthew 11:27 (cf. also Luke 10:22), he is certainly aware of his authoritative status, as the true revelation of God is made available only through the Son. However, this cannot be seen as denoting Jesus' divinity in the way the later apostles construct preexistent Christology (cf. Col 1:15ff.; Heb 1:3; John 1:1–3).

Does Matthew's Jesus *Become* Son of God?

This prompts us to look further into how Jesus regarded himself in relation to the Son of God title and whether it can be authentically attributed to him. As we have pointed out earlier, in a study which deals with how Matthew saw and interpreted Jesus, we cannot totally ignore the aspect of the historical Jesus. All scholarly endeavors in the study of Christology are concerned with how Jesus thought of himself in relation to how later writers portrayed him. Did Jesus regard himself as the Son of God in a way that coheres with the later Christian belief concerning the preexistent Christ? Scholars have expressed their skepticism concerning Jesus' self-consciousness that the notion of Christ's divinity must indubitably be attributed to subsequent Christian writers. The advocates of such a view maintain that a sane man could not present himself as a deity, and

---

88. Hahn, *The Titles of Jesus in Christology*, 286. Cf. Dunn, *Christology in the Making*. Luz, *The Theology of the Gospel of Matthew*, 112, notes that "Jesus' references to himself as the Son of Man appear with increasing frequency in the second half of the Gospel. There are 7 references in the main section from 12:1 to 16:20, 8 from 16:21 to 20:34, 7 again in the Apocalyptic Discourse of chapters 24 and 25 and 6 in chapter 26."

89. Cf. Luz, *The Theology of the Gospel of Matthew*, 104.

therefore, later editors with ideological interests must have put on the lips of Jesus words which he would not necessarily have used in reference to himself.[90] In discussion of Jesus' self-consciousness of sonship, Dunn cites Mark 13:32 as an example: "If indeed Mark 13:32 does go back in its entirety to Jesus himself, yet it would go beyond the evidence to conclude that it implies a consciousness of 'superhuman existence' on the part of Jesus; it is more likely that Jesus was looking forward with apocalyptic assurance to his future glory in the presence of God."[91] From this it may be surmised that although Jesus was certainly aware of the special eschatological task for which he was appointed, he did not necessarily regard himself as a divine messianic being. This would be the work of later Christian writers. For this reason, John's Gospel cannot be used as a reliable historical source of Jesus' self-consciousness, as the original tradition is believed to have been considerably worked over and developed. It is commonly agreed that "the Johannine Christology of conscious pre-existent sonship, of self-conscious divinity, belongs most clearly to the developed tradition and not the original."[92] Consequently, scholars turn to the synoptic tradition in looking for the origin of a Christology of sonship and Jesus' self-awareness of his identity and ministry. Bearing this in mind, we have argued against historical scholars who proposed the view that the early Christian conception of Jesus was essentially incompatible with that of Jesus' own self-understanding (see chapter 3). Such skepticism is unwarranted since Judaism consolidated its faith on the basis of concrete historical events. This fundamental aspect is most likely to have been the major characteristic of Matthew, who is evidently Jewish in his mind-set. He would therefore have been keenly interested in the historical events surrounding Jesus. A distinction between Matthew's view and Jesus' own self-consciousness stems from the presupposition commonly held by historical scholars, but we have rejected such an understanding, as it cannot be substantiated with

---

90. Cf. Lee, *From Messiah to Preexistent Son*. Lee suggests that "although it is beyond question that the christological title was given to Jesus in the early Church, the discussion concerning Jesus' divine sonship would be much more profitable if we approach the problem with the questions whether and in what sense Jesus conceived himself to be the Son of God and how such self-consciousness of his sonship to God made an impact to the understanding of him in the early Church, and not the other way around."

91. Dunn, *Christology in the Making*, 28–29.

92. Ibid., 31, 32.

evidence or logic. We propose, then, that Matthew's view closely reflect Jesus' own self-consciousness.

The question is, in what way did Jesus regard himself as the Son of God? This, we propose, is consistent with the enquiry as to in what way Matthew regarded Jesus as the Son of God. This is an important question which has attracted historical critics into debates concerning the earliest Christian writings. Dunn contends that "the resurrection of Jesus was regarded as of central significance in determining his divine sonship, either as his installation to a status and prerogative not enjoyed before, or as a major enhancement of a sonship already enjoyed."[93] This proposition is likely to lead us to the conclusion that Jesus *becomes* the Son of God through his sacrifice on the cross and through his resurrection from death. In other words, Jesus attains his status as the Son of God from the resurrection. This implies that Jesus earns his status through what he *does*. For instance, the earliest Christian use of Ps 2:7 in reference to Jesus' resurrection in Acts 13:33 had led some to deduce that the resurrection is to be seen as a fulfillment of the divine promise to Israel as expressed in Ps 2:7. According to Dunn, this uniquely important passage uses the language of "begetting" and specifies a particular day of royal coronation on which the king becomes God's son. Likewise, on the day of resurrection, Jesus is enthroned as the Son of God. If this argument is accepted as a correct interpretation of the title, it means that, as Dunn notes, Jesus was introduced into a relationship with God at his resurrection which is decisively new, eschatologically distinct, and even qualitatively different from what he had enjoyed before.[94] This view is called "adoptionist." According to this view, the resurrection effects a decisive change in Jesus' status. This may also be described as a "two-stage" Christology in which Jesus undergoes a change of status from the Son of David to the Son of God, which the Church later came to regard as an ontological title. Historical scholars such as Bultmann and Fuller would argue that this title was gradually pushed back from the point of resurrection to the earlier part of Jesus' ministry, all the way back to his conception and birth.[95]

---

93. Ibid., 35.

94. Ibid., 36.

95. Marshall, *The Origins of New Testament Christology*, 119. John's Gospel would push it further to the beginning of the creation.

However, can we assume that this is how Jesus viewed himself? Or is this how Matthew understood Jesus? First of all, there is no textual evidence to support the view that Jesus somehow becomes deified at the resurrection, although it is evident that he triumphed over death as someone clearly above the status of an ordinary human being. Moreover, to argue that the resurrection is the point when Jesus becomes the Son is inconsistent and, indeed, contradictory to what Matthew wishes to convey (cf. Matt 1:18). It is not what Jesus does that is of prime importance in Matthew's Christology but rather who Jesus *is* in an existential sense that defines his Christology (see chapter 5). In Matthew's major christological passages, Jesus' identity is revealed and reaffirmed not through what he does or achieves but simply as a statement of who Jesus already is, which is then confirmed by God.

When one considers the entire narrative structure and the progressive disclosure of Jesus' identity, the resurrection is merely a climax of something that is ubiquitous throughout Jesus' life. This is completely different from saying that Jesus experiences a change of his status. To appreciate what is intended, we need to consider the Gospel in its entirety rather than focusing on the fragmented parts of the story. Our task is to attempt to discover what Matthew wanted his readers to see in the Gospel concerning Jesus which is fundamentally consistent with Jesus' own self-consciousness. For instance, in the Great Commission, there is a clear understanding of Jesus as being a part of the triune Godhead, and he is described as someone worthy of worship (28:16–20). This climactic statement concerning the identity of Jesus could not stand on its own if the earlier part of the story were not in support of the claim. It would be illogical to suggest that Matthew only wishes to portray Jesus as the divine Son of God at the end of the Gospel and that in the earlier part he refrained from such a view. Rather, when one considers the entire narrative structure of the text, one discovers that Matthew skillfully brings the reader's attention to the development of the major character of the story, which is decisively brought to a conclusion at the end. Matthew begins his Gospel with reference to Jesus' extraordinary conception by the Holy Spirit (Matt 1:18), and the epiphany at his baptism serves as a confirmation of Jesus' awareness of his divine sonship (3:15, 17). In the context of his earthly ministry, he demonstrates numerous signs and wonders, which implicitly points to his divine appointment. For instance, when he heals, he does so by forgiving the sins of the afflicted, which again leads to the question of Jesus' identity; he is clearly professing himself to be more than what others in Jewish circles can claim about themselves (9:2–3). This is reinforced by his claim that the Son of Man is lord even of the Sabbath (12:8). At the transfiguration, as the story progresses toward his passion, Jesus' identity as the Son of God is once again confirmed. One of the most decisive and climactic scenes in which Jesus discloses his identity is the trial scene, where Jesus as the Son of Man asserted his divine authority of judgment (26:57–64). After the resurrection, just before Jesus ascended to heaven, he revealed that all authority in heaven and on earth had been given to him, and he promised the disciples that he would be with them to the end of the age (28:16–20). On the basis of these passages, the question must be raised as to whether Matthew's Jesus would have been content to be known simply as the Son of David, which is essentially concerned with Israel.

Jesus is surely confirmed as the Son of God at the resurrection, but the preceding part must be in support of the claim. Matthew would not abruptly introduce something which he has not been prepared for, and certainly not for such a momentous declaration. When we consider the Gospel as a whole literary unit, it is more likely that Jesus' identity as the Son of God reaches its full disclosure at the resurrection, but this is different from saying that Jesus becomes someone distinctly new and qualitatively different than what he was before.

Matthew's Conception of Son of God and Its Development

The context of narratives where the title Son of God appears in Matthew's Gospel supports the view that the title is an appropriate confessional response for the disciples of Jesus (cf. 4:3, 6; 8:29; 14:33; 16:16; 26:63; 27:40).[96] However, we need first to note that the title is primarily identified with Jesus as Israel's royal representative. Dunn points out that "one of the most striking features of Matthew's Son of God Christology is his clear identification of Jesus with Israel (2:15; 4:3, 6)." However, it must be remembered that the identification is made with a figure rather than with Israel in a corporate sense. In other words, the title is linked with an individual who is representative of Israel and who, we have suggested,

---

96. Cf. Dunn, *Christology in the Making*, 48. Synoptic writers place emphasis on different aspects of Jesus' sonship. For instance, it is noted that "Mark's chief concern in his Son of God Christology seems to be to emphasize the link between Jesus' sonship and his death. This is clearly so in the climax of 15:39."

is the Davidic king. Therefore, Son of God is almost synonymous with Son of David in Matthew's Gospel. When Jesus is addressed as the Son of God, he is primarily identified as the royal representative of Israel who will fulfill the redemptive role and inaugurate the messianic era.

The Son of God title, however, is double-edged in terms of Matthew's Christology in that it not only denotes Jesus' identity as Israel's royal Davidic Messiah but it also points to his divine messianic status.[97] This is not to say that it portrays Jesus as the preexistent divine being who was at the beginning of creation, as is described in John's Gospel (John 1:1), but the context in which the title is used does portray Jesus as someone with supernatural qualities. For instance, in Matthew 14:33, Jesus' identity is revealed in a manner that is worthy of worship and inclines the disciples to confess him as the Son of God. Here, one could argue that the Old Testament figures, such as Moses in the Exodus tradition, also perform miracles, but nowhere do we find evidence in the Old Testament of a venerated figure being worshipped. When the disciples saw Jesus walking on the water, they *worshipped* him, and used the title Son of God in their subsequent confession. In the Old Testament, the act of worship is exclusively made to Yahweh alone as Israel's divine King (cf. Zech 14:16, 17). In fact, the regulations concerning worship are very stringent; for Israel, to worship any other being apart from Yahweh is to forsake their loyalty to God altogether (cf. Isa 2:20; Jer 25:6; Ezek 20:32; Dan 3:18, 28; Jonah 2:8).[98]

Of particular interest in conjunction with the observation above is Matthew's account of the trial, where the high priest asks whether the charges put against Jesus are true or not. Here, again, the connection is made with the Messiah and the Son of God. The latter is certainly derived from messianic tradition, in other words, the Son of David according to the Jewish understanding of the term. However, it is doubtful whether the high priest could lawfully sentence someone to death solely on the basis of his claiming to be the Messiah, Son of David. It does raise suspicion as to whether claiming to be a Son of David, that is, the Messiah, constitutes blasphemy, which was worthy of the death penalty

---

97. The connection between the two christological traits may be supported by Peter's confession (cf. Matt 16:16). Both titles are messianic, as Simon Peter answers by using both χριστὸς and ὁ υἱὸς τοῦ θεοῦ.

98. προσκυνέω used in Genesis 42:6; 48:12; 2 Kings 2:15 can also mean "kneel, bow low, fall at another's feet," but is not used in the same manner as in Matthew 14:33.

in Judaism.⁹⁹ Even if it is argued that the Jewish authorities sought to condemn Jesus under Roman law, Pilate shows reluctance to putting Jesus to death, and Matthew clearly places the blame upon Israel (cf. 27:25). All in all, Jesus' response, his saying that he is the Son of Man, is clearly more than the high priest bargained for, as it immediately solicits a charge of blasphemy (26:63–65). Again, it is not abundantly clear whether Jesus is claiming divinity or merely claiming for himself something only God can give, which, in the eyes of the Jewish religious authorities, would constitute blasphemy. It would be arguing beyond the evidence to suggest that Jesus is here identifying himself with Yahweh or as a preexistent divine being, but such a uniquely intimate relationship with God certainly provides a ground for the later understanding of Jesus as a divine Son of God. This is subsequently picked up and clarified at the climax of the Gospel as Jesus gives the final commission to his disciples (28:19). Here, the title Son is elevated to a status which is almost equivalent to God's. Dunn notes that "the title Son is used with Father and Holy Spirit in a triadic formulation which foreshadows the later Trinitarian understanding of God."¹⁰⁰ This is not to say that Jesus is in any way declared to be the preexistent Son of God, but what Matthew wants to say concerning Jesus seems evident from the beginning to the end of his Gospel: Matthew has portrayed Jesus' divine sonship from his conception, for which the "creative power" of the Spirit is responsible. Jesus' sonship is primarily depicted in terms of his messianic mission for Israel's salvation as the Son of David, but we soon discover that the title falls short of conveying who Jesus really is (cf. 22:42–45). While he is primarily identified with Israel's royal heritage, Jesus is portrayed to be someone far greater than a Davidic Messiah. In other words, while the Davidic heritage of Jesus helps to illumine the pinnacle of Israel's redemptive history and gives a fuller understanding of God's sovereignty, it does not exhaust the Christology of Matthew. How emphatically this is spelled out in comparison with John's Gospel is a different matter of discussion. Dunn notes that "it is less easy to see how Matthew's and Luke's accounts of Son of God can be harmonized with John's idea of

---

99. Cf. Hecht et al., eds., *An Introduction to the History and Sources of Jewish Law*. The legal proceeding in Jewish and Roman jurisdiction makes the debate difficult, and the fact that crucifixion was a Roman death penalty further complicates the discussion. From a Roman perspective, Jesus could easily be seen as an insurrectionist and thus a threat to the Emperor who must be eliminated.

100. Dunn, *Christology in the Making*, 49.

the incarnation of a divine being who always was Son of God from before the foundation of the world."[101] We are not denying the fact that there has been a considerable development of belief and understanding of Jesus as the Son of God, and Matthew is certainly not as explicit as John in stressing Jesus' divinity. However, it would be unfounded to state that there is no evidence at all in the earliest Christian tradition which supports Jesus' consciousness of divinity and sonship rooted in a preexistent relationship with God.[102] This implies that Matthew's Christology is deemed to be inconsistent in comparison with that of John. Of course, Matthew does not explicitly make such a claim concerning Jesus, most probably because he was conscious of his Jewish audience. Being the most Jewish writer in the synoptic tradition in that he wrote specifically for the Jews, Matthew would not want to be seen as compromising or diluting his monotheistic belief. As we have seen, however, there are indications that point toward Jesus' divinity, which is achieved in the most skilful manner possible in the way that Matthew presents his Gospel within the broad spectrum of Judaism. If our reading is correct, then the whole debate concerning the distinction between Matthew's and John's Son of God Christology becomes somewhat sterile. We need to at least consider the possibility that John and Matthew are fundamentally saying the same thing but from a different perspective, with different styles of language, addressing different audiences in their own unique context. R. T. France aptly summarizes that in three of the "Son" passages, Matthew goes far beyond simply redefining the nature of Jesus' Messiahship. Matthew 11:27 and 28:18 undoubtedly go far beyond the concept of one who merely obeys the Father's will. In 28:19 the Son is actually placed on a level with the Father and the Holy Spirit.[103]

101. Ibid., 60. Dunn cites the Nicene Creed as an example to illustrate the development of Christology.

102. Cf. Ibid., 62–63. He does not in fact take such an extreme position of denying any evidence of Jesus' divine sonship in the earlier Jesus tradition. He argues that such a concept at this stage of christological development is premature so is neither affirmed nor denied.

103. France, *Matthew*, 297–98. Cf. also Nolland, "No Son of God Christology," 3–12. It is acknowledged that "the Jesus of Matthew's Gospel is a more God-like figure in the responses that he elicits than is the case in the other Synoptic Gospels. The nature of the presence of Jesus contemplated in 18:20 and 28:20 is of a spiritual kind." However, to equate Jesus with God is "too powerful a christological statement to be carried in an account which is otherwise clearly concerned with the irregular incorporation of Jesus into the Davidic line." Nolland concludes that "the christological focus of the pericope

Summary

It is the thesis of this volume that the royal-enthronement psalms in the key christological passages of Matthew's Gospel portray Jesus primarily as the Davidic Messiah who has come to establish the New Exodus in the redemptive history of Israel. However, it is patent that Matthew is not content with conveying Jesus' identity solely in terms of Israel's royal dynasty. We have seen that Jesus is attributed traits that are exclusively reserved for Yahweh in the Old Testament. The royal psalms that celebrate the kingship of David are thus deemed to be somewhat insufficient in Matthew's Christology. For this reason, the evangelist also utilizes the themes of the enthronement psalms, such as Yahweh's authority to judge and his heavenly exaltation as Israel's true King who is worthy of worship. It is this divine-royal motif which forms the backbone of Matthew's Christology.

The major christological titles also repeatedly reveal Jesus' identity in terms of the divine-royal motif. In Matthew's Son of Man sayings, the dominant theme is the heavenly authority of Jesus as he is vindicated and exalted by God. He is given the power to execute judgment. This is closely reminiscent of the exaltation and judgment themes of Yahweh prevalent in the enthronement psalms. In Mark's Gospel, the emphasis of the Son of Man sayings is on the necessity of obedient suffering that Jesus endures (Mark 8:31; 9:12, 31; 10:33, 45). In Matthew, however, the emphasis has shifted from suffering and humiliation to the Son of Man's vindication and subsequent enthronement as the King.

The Son of David title posed some difficulties regarding the redemptive function of Jesus as the Messiah. In Matthew, the function of the Son of David is associated with healing (9:27; 15:22; 20:30, 31). We have argued that the healing activity of Jesus as the Son of David should be interpreted within the New Exodus motif. Unlike what was achieved through the prototype Exodus, the New Exodus is believed to establish salvation from sin. There is evidence in the Old Testament that sin is equated with death, which is identified with Satan (cf. Isa 28:15). Therefore, the forgiveness of sin indicates that a man is delivered from death into life. Healing, which is an act of delivering man from the pathway of death, may also be perceived as the forgiveness of sin. The prototype Exodus event did not liberate Israel from the bondage of sin

(Mt. 1:18-25) is upon the initiative of God in the incorporation of Jesus into the line of David."

but from the bondage of slavery in Egypt. It is therefore in the context of Israel's redemptive history and the New Exodus motif that Jesus' healing as the Son of David becomes intelligible.

Lastly, when the title Son of God is used to refer to Jesus on the basis of the royal psalms, it would be reading into the text—eisegesis as opposed to exegesis—to suggest that Jesus is described as a deity. Rather, it indicates primarily that Jesus is a royal king of Israel in the line of David. Therefore, there is an interface between Son of David and Son of God, as they share a common origin. In Matthew's Gospel, it seems that Son of God has not yet been fully developed as a title of divinity, in which case, it is likely that the Son of Man tradition in the eschatological setting has subsequently influenced the Son of God title (cf. 1 Thess 1:10). In contrast to the common perception that Son of Man denotes the humanity of Jesus and Son of God points to his divinity, it seems that in Matthew the former has the most exalted meaning, which brings the themes of the enthronement psalms into focus. There is also a commonality between the two titles as they testify to Jesus' self-understanding of his intimate relationship with God and his vocation to fulfill God's redemptive purpose for Israel. At the stage of the writing of Matthew's Gospel, the title Son of God is double-edged in that it not only denotes Jesus' identity as Israel's royal Davidic Messiah but it also points to his divine qualities; this is later developed into the fully fledged, preexistent divine Son of God. In Matthew's Gospel, Jesus is aware that the divine sonship entails a profound sense of vocation to fulfill God's redemptive purpose for Israel and establish a New Covenant with the people of God. (See chapter 5, especially the transfiguration, where Jesus commands his disciples to remains silent until the Son of Man has been raised from the dead. This is one of the crucial christological passages where Jesus' identity as the Son of God is disclosed). This can only be attained through the sacrificial death of the Son of God and his vindication at the resurrection. In the Great Commission, the resurrected Jesus appears to the disciples and commissions them to baptize in the name of the Father and of the Son and of the Holy Spirit, as all authority in heaven and earth has been given to the Son. In this regard, there is a close connection between the Son of God, who is finally glorified at the resurrection, and the Son of Man, whose suffering was nevertheless predicted and who is to return as the heavenly King/Judge, which mutually reinforces the divine-royal motif of Matthew's Christology.[104]

---

104. Cf. Luz, *The Theology of the Gospel of Matthew*, 104.

To conclude, these major christological titles interact with each other and in so doing formulate a dynamic portrait of Jesus. These titles do not contradict but reinforce and complement each other in Matthew's Christology (cf. Matt 16:13–16). The Son of Man's vindication and his authority of judgment; the Son of David's forgiveness of sin in his healing; the Son of God who ruled on Yahweh's behalf, according to the royal psalms, who is worthy of worship (14:33), and with whose everlasting authority the disciples are to make disciples of all nations, baptizing them in his name and in the name of the Father and the Holy Spirit (28:18–20)—all point to possibly the most crucial aspect of Matthew's Christology: Jesus is the royal Davidic Messiah who is ascribed certain traits that are characteristic of Yahweh, and it is through Christ Jesus that the New Exodus is finally established in the redemptive history of Israel.

7

Conclusion

IT SEEMS EVIDENT THAT the fundamental principles of early Christianity in terms of its Christology had not an accidental link with Judaism but a profound historical and theological connection. Even though Matthew's community was located within a Hellenistic environment, which was the dominant culture at the time, the Jewish mindset of the evangelist was neither compromised nor diluted. There is a growing recognition that the Old Testament religion of Israel forms the bedrock of the early Christian message concerning Christ.[1] This has led scholars to shift their attention from Hellenistic texts to Jewish texts for comparative analysis in order to reinforce New Testament exegesis. We have embarked upon the quest of christological studies of Matthew's Gospel on the basis of this basic presupposition. While we would promote the view that the New Testament in general is thoroughly Jewish in its message of salvation, we have rejected the use of intertestamental Jewish literature as the intellectual bridge between the Old and New Testaments.[2] The major reason for this is that nowhere in the Gospel of Matthew does Matthew quote or draw parallels from these extracanonical texts. Quite simply, there is no textual evidence whatsoever that encourages the reader to look elsewhere other than the Old Testament for understanding Matthew's text. For this reason, we have not attempted to survey these texts for Matthean studies, since it was deemed to be

---

1. Clements, "The Messianic Hope in the Old Testament," 3–19.
2. Ibid., 9. Clements notes that Ernst Troeltsch, Hermann Gunkel, and Wilhelm Bousset played a large role in emphasizing the importance of intertestamental Judaism.

counterproductive. What other Jewish groups thought about the Son of David has no bearing on what the Christian community thought, for the essence of their understanding was about the crucified Son of God. Through various measures such as the formula quotations, Matthew makes it very clear that the real seedbed of messianic doctrine was derived exclusively from the Old Testament tradition.

Once we have established that it was ultimately the Old Testament which Matthew consulted for the construction of his Christology, the issue of consistency becomes a major concern. In other words, if the Old Testament is the source and the evangelist repeatedly used typological exegesis, then the type must to a certain measure be congruent with the antitype. Otherwise, if they are contradictory with one another and there is a gulf between the fundamental principles of salvation, then Matthew's Christology would be based on shaky grounds. We may assume that this also must have been a crucial issue for the early Christians, who were constantly debating against their Jewish opponents with regard to the legitimacy of their christological understanding on the basis of the Jewish Scriptures. From the early Christian point of view, being able to prove that Jesus is the Messiah of Israel who fits into the Jewish messianic expectation was of paramount importance. Therefore, the question of whether the two testaments are in essence consistent—or perhaps *compatible* is a better word—was the major methodological challenge. This issue is also acknowledged by R. E. Clements, who notes that "a great gap needed to be filled in demonstrating how Jewish messianic expectation of the New Testament period had emerged out of older hopes and affirmations which are demonstrably present in the Old Testament literature."[3] The importance of the Old Testament for the Christology of Matthew is undisputed, since it is readily accepted that regardless of the precise environment in which a New Testament text was fostered, whether it be Paul or Matthew, the life, ministry, death, and resurrection of Jesus and his impact upon the status of Law, the concept of redemption, theology and eschatological views are made intelligible only in the light of the Old Testament.[4] In fact, the theme in which the

---

3. Ibid., 8.

4. Beaton, *Isaiah's Christ in Matthew's Gospel*, 4, 17, 175, begins with the presupposition that "the image of the servant presented through Matthew's text is central to his overall portrayal of Jesus and to his profound Christology." However, he arrives at the conclusion that the designation "servant" lacks christological capacity. Rather, he concludes that "the two explicit servant texts (Isa. 42:1–4; 53:4) attend to a more

Old Testament promise is fulfilled by the New Testament message of Christ is a dominant characteristic that lies at the heart of Matthew's Christology, since this distinct feature stands out as a unique literary feature among contemporary Jewish sources. This fulfillment theme which is inherent in the Gospel was a major overarching concept upon which the methodology of this volume was largely based.[5] A discussion of typology as biblical hermeneutics, the use of various theological themes and imageries of the Old Testament in the New, and, more specifically, the use of the royal-enthronement psalms in Matthew's Christology and how this generates a unique understanding of the redemptive history of Israel are all based on this fundamental concept of fulfillment. In view of the "Jewishness" of the early Christian community, the major distinct feature in terms of the consistency or the compatibility of the two testaments is no doubt the nature of the salvation established by Jesus. It is the Christocentric element of the New Testament which has a paradoxical function in binding the two testaments together but at the same time makes the New Testament message distinct from the Old Testament. This, in our opinion, is a crucial methodological gap that needs to be explicated in discussions regarding the typological use of the Old Testament by the New Testament writers, which is seldom tackled by the contemporary scholarship. W. J. C. Weren took on this challenge when he examined the continuity and discontinuity between Matthew's concept of salvation and that of Isaiah. He clearly sees a significant continuity between the two texts, since the Davidic monarchy takes a prominent position in Isaiah's message (Isa 7:2, 13), which is also the primary concern of Matthew, as he begins with the designation that Jesus is the Son of David (Matt 1:1, 20).[6] He reckons that the most decisive difference that shifts the balance to discontinuity is that Matthew's concept of salvation manifested in Christ is essentially "theological and soteriological," which indicates that the salvation is somehow translated in a spiritual dimension. We have discussed in the earlier parts of this

---

descriptive task." In other words, the title reveals the nature and the character of the messianic ministry of the enigmatic individual. Lindars, *New Testament Apologetic*, argues that Isaiah 41:1–4 was associated with the baptism and transfiguration narratives in the synoptic tradition (cf. Mark 1:11; 9:7; Luke 9:35).

5. Ibid., 23, its uniqueness is highlighted in that "its translational equivalent never occurs in the Mishnah and no real parallel can be found in the Qumran literature either."

6. Weren, "Quotations from Isaiah and Matthew's Christology," 447–65.

dissertation that the doctrine of sin figures prominently in Jesus' message of salvation, whereas the concerns of the Old Testament prophets such as Isaiah were predominantly nationalistic and geopolitical in nature. The Old Testament message does have a more political connotation, since it is dealing with the history of Israel and how the nation came to be blessed or cursed through the political leadership of kings. For instance, the threat to the house of David is none other than a military/political overthrow of Ahaz by the newly established political alliance (Isa 7:5–6) rather than the spiritual matters of sin, which seems more suited for the New Testament message of salvation. Weren suggests here that a process of "semantic transformation" lies at the heart of the discontinuity in terms of the definitions of redemption in the Old and New Testaments. In other words, liberation from political atrocity is transformed by Matthew as he redefines salvation which deals with the fundamental matters of sin through the death and resurrection of Jesus Christ. However, the division of political and spiritual conceptions with regard to the definition of redemption in the Old and New Testaments may not have been relevant in antiquity. In the mind-set of modern society, especially in Western civilization, the dimension of politics does not easily mix with religious beliefs and views. Indeed such a fusion would be discouraged today. However, we should not neglect the strong possibility that the demarcation between the political reality and religious beliefs in ancient Israel would neither have been consciously delineated nor promulgated. Weren concedes that Jesus does not threaten to overthrow the established Roman order in the manner in which the Old Testament prophets would have liked their kings to defeat the foreign oppressor and restore Israel's political stability. However, he notes that Matthew does portray Jesus as the leader of the people who provokes various responses from religious and political elites of the time (Matt 1:21; 2:3). Jesus' kingship is primarily for the people of Israel (Matt 2:6), and his compassion for the crowd as described in Matthew 9:36 acts as a reminder of what true leadership should be, which entails fulfilling the role of shepherd for the sheep that are helpless on their own. In principle, therefore, this is not necessarily deviant from what the Old Testament writers eagerly expected their leadership to accomplish.

This is comprehensively explicated by N. T. Wright, who points out that the vital feature of the Jesus and Judaism discussion is that eschatological beliefs were deeply embedded within the political/historical realms of Israel. He argues that to draw a distinction between politics and theology, between national and eschatological views, is to fail to appreciate the unique nature of the Jewish religion and early Christianity. He states that "we cannot either insist a priori on a non-political Jesus in order to reject a revolutionary reading, or to expose the weakness in the revolutionary case and imagine that we have thereby argued for a non-political Jesus."[7]

Perhaps the prevalent perception of Jesus' identity and ministry even in the modern Christian community is that it is strictly spiritual in nature and that there is a tendency to regard the message of the New Testament to be "otherworldly." However, it is a grave mistake to separate its political character from the biblical principles, since in the world of the biblical writers, "to be non-political is to be irrelevant."[8] When the message of judgment and salvation was preached, in the early Christian world it was perceived not in a metaphorical way but in a very "this-worldly" manner. Therefore, the message of Christ would have had both functions in that it was a spiritual awakening and sought to revive the hearts of God's people to repentance, but it would have also had a sociopolitical impact upon the astutely minded elites to whom Jesus was a marvel. This is continually demonstrated in the way King Herod reacted—he was immediately stricken with fear at the news of Jesus' birth—and in the Jewish religious leadership, who felt threatened by Jesus' critical teaching. In the minds of the ancient Jewish community—for instance, in the prophetic tradition—apocalyptic language was utilized to bring out the fuller significance of the sociopolitical reality of the contemporary world. This mind-set which views the religious and political dimensions as one entity characterized the nature of the early Christian message.[9] It was a common phenomenon in Jewish circles that highly charged apocalyptic language was used in order to refer to major

---

7. Wright, *Jesus and the Victory of God*, vol. 2, 97–98.

8. Ibid., 98, 325. Wright argues that "the warnings which utilize apocalyptic language are not to be siphoned off as dealing only with some far-off future 'final judgment' in the sense of the end of the space-time universe."

9. Ibid., 515, 516. It is suggested that "the combination of Daniel 7 and 9 provides part of the major theme of Jesus' Temple-discourse, in the middle of which the clear implication is that the Temple's destruction and Jesus' own vindication, *precisely as Messiah*, somehow belong together" (emphasis original). Wright further notes that "it is unwise to rule out a reference to Daniel 7 in the sayings of Jesus on the grounds that such an allusion would designate Jesus simply as a transcendent figure."

political/historical events regarding Israel. This is the reason why we have emphasized the importance of ascertaining the New Testament's use of the Old Testament texts in the light of Israel's redemptive history, which is the central investigation and methodological assumption of this volume. Every quotation from the Old Testament in the apostolic writing is to be seen within the overarching concept of the redemptive history of Israel, as God establishes an intimate relationship with His people and ultimately delivers them from sin through the appointed messianic agent.[10] On the basis of the evidence and the scholarly arguments presented, the concepts of redemption in the Old and New Testaments are in fact neither inconsistent nor incompatible. If the political/historical awareness of Israel determined her religious faith, this basic concept guided early Christian writers.[11] In conjunction with this, Clements states that "the New Testament does not impose a wholly fresh way of understanding the writings of the Old. It is itself the product of the continual work of re-applying and re-vitalizing that which the Old Testament contains."[12]

This brings us to the final and the most important question, with which we would like to conclude this volume. Is the Christology of Matthew in particular consistent or compatible with the Old Testament's definition of the Messiah? Those who argue that it is essentially incongruent mostly emphasize God's Kingship, as opposed to the positive attributes of the messianic ruler in the Old Testament. H. G. M. Williamson notes that "Isaiah 33 contains two striking references to God as King—in v. 17 and in v. 22. Here, the considerable emphasis is on the

---

10. Ibid., 518. Wright argues that "there is no need to suggest, as has been done often enough since Wrede, that Jesus could not have referred to himself as the 'Son of Man,' on the grounds that the phrase carries so many overtones of incarnational or Trinitarian theology." He argues that "the phrase, with its Danielic associations, would have referred first and foremost to the anointed king through whom YHWH would defeat the pagans."

11. Alexander, "The King Messiah in Rabbinic Judaism," 457, 458, begins with the post-Talmudic era with the eighth treatise of Saadia Gaon's *The Book of Beliefs and Opinions*. According to Alexander, "he is the first clearly datable authority to make messianism a dogma of rabbinic Judaism." In conjunction with the argument that historical awareness played a crucial role within the Jewish messianic faith, Alexander also notes that "for Saadia the coming of the Messiah is most decidedly a real historical event. There is not a trace of mysticism in his account."

12. Clements, "The Messianic Hope in the Old Testament," 16. Cf. Childs, *Introduction to the Old Testament as Scripture*.

importance of Zion which is not matched by any allusion whatsoever to the restoration of the Davidic monarchy. It would seem that the stress on God's kingship has completely supplanted that of the human king."[13] The main thesis of this volume was that this was a partial understanding of the redemptive history of Israel and the messianic expectation of the Old Testament. To argue that the biblical account unilaterally presents Yahweh as the sole redeemer of Israel fails to do justice to the prevalent expectation of the Davidic Messiah who will manifest Yahweh's reign on earth. The kingship of Yahweh and that of the messianic agent are mutually complementary in that they collaborate in establishing the deliverance which God intends to bring about for His people. We believe that the fundamental reason that some scholars are reluctant to say that the Old Testament portrays the Davidic dynasty in a positive light is due to the historical fact that the kings did not live up to the idealized standards as prescribed in Scripture. Even the greatest king of Israel, David himself, was not without flaws. The exile was a painful and embarrassing reminder of the fact that human leadership is inevitably vulnerable and thus subject to temptation and failure. In the context of such disappointment, it is extremely doubtful that Israel would have looked for a replica of David. Rather, they looked for someone in the line of David so that the covenant with Yahweh would be sustained, but there are implications that the ultimate messianic deliverer must be someone more than just a Davidic descendent in order to bring about true redemption. This may explain why some scholars are puzzled by the fact that while prophetic writings such as Isaiah show "knowledge of the Davidic origins of the monarchy in Jerusalem and specifically some familiarity with the dynastic promise, this feature has not emerged as a central theme. The stress throughout is on the role rather than the person of the king."[14]

This has interesting implications for the typological nature of Matthew's Christology; Matthew primarily portrays Jesus as the Son of David, yet nevertheless shows that Jesus is more than just the rightful heir of Davidic kingship.[15] The reason we have turned to the Psalms

13. Williamson, "The Messianic Texts in Isaiah 1–39," 241, 253, suggests that "God's commitment to his people overrides a specific concern for any particular historical dynasty."

14. Ibid., 269.

15. Clements, "The Messianic Hope in the Old Testament," 3–19, notes that "at times, as in Isa. 2:2–4, God himself was to be the messianic ruler, but in general W. O. E. Oesterley accepted the fundamental conviction that either a purely human ruler, as

in particular lies in the fact that the ideas that appear in the messianic expectation are found in certain of the royal psalms (Pss 2, 72, 110). However, we soon discovered that this particular type of psalm, which was originally designed to celebrate Davidic kingship, was insufficient for portraying the nature of Jesus' messianic ministry. The author of Matthew, who is very keen to legitimize his christological statements by drawing from the Psalms, must have felt that the royal psalms could not fully explain the identity of Jesus.[16] This has led us to believe that the enthronement psalms, which were originally designed to celebrate the divine kingship of Yahweh, were also used by the evangelist. The major themes of the enthronement psalms, namely, divine judgment and exaltation, form the crux of the Son of Man sayings of the Gospel. The use of both royal and enthronement psalms has crucial implications, as it presupposes the use of the divine-royal formula in the construction of Matthew's Christology. Matthew is certainly more reserved in disclosing Jesus' divinity in comparison with John's Gospel. However, the Son represents the Father and shares the very authority of God Himself. This is not quite the same thing as saying that Jesus is the preexistent divine person, as he is depicted in John's Gospel, but in essence we have found that Matthew, although more implicitly, is in fact presenting Jesus' authority on a par with God through the use of the royal-enthronement psalms.[17] This was particularly well documented in the Son of Man sayings, where

---

in Isa. 11:1–5, or a divine-human figure, as in Isa. 9:5–6, was expected to come." Cf. Oosterley, *The Evolution of the Messianic Idea.*

16. The prophetic texts such as the royal Psalms originally refer to the kings of Judah, but these texts were continually reinterpreted in the newly emerging circumstances. R. E. Clements notes that "the entire sequence of prophecies from Isa. 6:1–11:16 has been evidently subjected to a series of expansions and interpretive notes which demonstrate how a continuing effort at updating was taking place as the literary form of the prophetic corpus of the canon was in process of formation." Cf. Engnell, *Studies in Divine Kingship in the Ancient Near East.*

17. Hengel, *Studies in Early Christology*, 183, notes that the Son of Man sayings in Matthew 19:28; Luke 22:30; 1 Corinthians 6:2f.; and Revelation 20:4ff. portray the Messiah who is given the authority to judge, which is a divine prerogative exclusively reserved for Yahweh. Hengel notes that "this is documented in the Similitudes of 1 Enoch and in particular in the teaching of Jesus and in earliest Christianity including Matt. 25:31ff." He also draws similar traits of the Messiah from the LXX version of Dan 7:13, which contains the mysterious "one like a human" who is connected very closely to the Ancient of Days and judge. It is pointed out that the "LXX gives the impression that the one like a human is given God's authority as judge and is appropriately waited upon."

Jesus' authority was equated with that of God. We have noted that the themes of divine judgment and exaltation which characterize the content of these apocalyptic sayings of the Gospel were prominent motifs of the enthronement psalms. Also, bearing in mind that the Son of Man is frequently traced back to the Danielic vision, Martin Hengel makes an important observation that supports the thesis that the Messiah of Israel inherently possesses divine attributes which far exceed those possessed by any ordinary human king. He notes that "the 'one like a human' in the LXX version of the judgment scene almost takes the place of God and his dominion identical to God's dominion." Moreover, he advances this view by arguing that "the sitting at the right hand in Ps. 110:1 means similarly the transference of divine authority and judgment; at the same time it is the most intimate relation of one who is chosen by God with God Himself."[18] This enigmatic figure who sits at the right hand of God is not necessarily subordinate but participates directly in the divine authority of judgment and heavenly exaltation.[19] The thesis of our argument is that through the use of the royal-enthronement psalms, Matthew's Christology portrayed the kingdom of God and the kingdom of the Messiah in a mutually complementary manner and placed Jesus' authority in the seat of the divine throne.[20] This is not so evident in the beginning of the Gospel, but the narratives progressively build up to a final disclosure of Jesus' identity prior to the ascension to heaven as one of the constituents of what later developed as the Trinitarian concept.[21]

18. Ibid., 185.

19. Ibid., notes that "in Dan. 7:9-11 too, the dominion of God and of the Son of Man becomes one in its execution."

20. Ibid., 220. The reason we have turned to the study of Psalms is the fact that "the psalter was from the beginning—next to or even exceeding Isaiah—the most important collection of texts that was used by the new messianic movement as scriptural proof."

21. Ibid., 188, 189, 221. It is pointed out that "the Son is thereby not 'separated' from the Father. This is the case particularly for the Gospel of Matthew in which there is twice mentioned that the Son of Man 'sits on the throne of his glory' and the twelve disciples as the followers of Jesus become his college of associate judges (Matt. 19:28; cf. 25:31). Christ 'on the throne of his glory' acts as the representative of God with God's authority." The Apostle Paul also shares the same mind-set in this regard. "Paul in 2 Cor. 5:10 can speak of the revelation of all Christians before the 'judgment of Christ' as the throne of the eschatological judge. One must assume here the eschatological unity of action between Father and Son; this makes their functions interchangeable." The heavenly attributes of Jesus should not be perceived in angelic terms. "In Hebrews every tendency in the direction of an angel Christology is strictly rejected." It is noted that "in the New Testament the angels have a position beneath the Son they praise and serve him as God himself."

This is done in a rather subtle manner in comparison with John's Gospel, which is mostly probably due to the fact that Matthew's audience was Jewish; he did not want to be accused of having deviated from the monotheistic belief of his ancestral religion. All in all, Matthew's conviction that Jesus is the Messiah through whom the divine redemptive purpose unfolds in the history of Israel is decisively revealed in the way he utilizes the royal-enthronement psalms.[22]

---

22. Motyer, *Look to the Rock*, 36, argues that Jesus' kingship is more than of this world. While he is David's descendent and is primarily identified with the Davidic royal dynasty, he is also the mighty God (Isa 9:6–7) for the King is God (Ps 45:6) and yet shows humility as he worships God (Ps 45:7). Edersheim, *The Life and Times of Jesus the Messiah*, vol. 1, 171, 174, 175, 178, also points out that the concept of "divine-human" Messiah is not uncommon in the Rabbinic tradition. This Jewish literature contains the idea of a divine personality and of the union of the two natures in the Messiah. The Messiah is portrayed as far above an ordinary human, royal, angelic being. The author points out that "even in strictly Rabbinic documents, the 'pre-mundane,' if not the eternal 'existence of the Messiah' appears as matter of common belief."

Bibliography

Alexander, P. S. "The King Messiah in Rabbinic Judaism." In *King and Messiah in Israel and the Ancient Near East: Proceedings of the Oxford Old Testament Seminar*, edited by John Day. JSOT Supplement Series 270. Sheffield: Sheffield Academic Press, 1998.

Alexander, T. D. "Royal Expectation in Genesis to Kings: The Importance for Biblical Theology." *Tyndale Bulletin* 49, 1998.

Allison, Dale C., Jr. "The Baptism of Jesus and a New Dead Sea Scrolls." *Biblical Archaeological Review* 18:2 (1992).

———. *The New Moses: A Matthean Typology*. Minneapolis: Fortress, 1993.

———. "The Son of God as Israel: A Note on Matthean Christology." *IBS* 9 (1987).

Bacon, B. W. "The Five Books of Matthew against the Jews." *The Expository Times* 15 (1918).

———. "Jesus and the Law: A Study of the First Book of Matthew." *JBL* 47 (1928).

———. "Studies in Matthew." *The Expository Times* 15 (1918).

Baker, D. L. *Two Testaments, One Bible*. Leicester: InterVarsity, 1976.

Balentine, George L. "Death of Jesus as a New Exodus." *Review & Expositor* 59:1 (1962).

Banks, Robert. "Jesus and the Law in the Synoptic Tradition." *Journal of Biblical Literature* 93 (1974) 226–42.

Barth, G. "Matthew's Understanding of the Law." In *Tradition and Interpretation in Matthew*. Translated by Percy Scott. London: SCM, 1963.

Barton, J. "The Messiah in Old Testament Theology." In *King and Messiah in Israel and the Ancient Near East: Proceedings of the Oxford Old Testament Seminar*, edited by John Day. JSOT Supplement Series 270. Sheffield: Sheffield Academic Press, 1998.

Bassler, Jouette M., "A Man for All Seasons: David in Rabbinic and New Testament Literature." *Interpretation* 40:2 (1986).

Bateman, Herbert W. "Psalm 110:1 and the New Testament." *Bibliotheca Sacra* 149:596 (1992).

Bauer, David R. "The Kingship of Jesus in the Matthean Infancy Narrative: A Literary Analysis." *CBQ* 57:2 (1995).

———. "The Literary and Theological Function of the Genealogy in Matthew's Gospel." In *Treasures New and Old: Recent Contributions to Matthean Studies*. Symposium Series 1. Atlanta: Scholars, 1996.

Bauer, David R., and Mark Allan Powell. *Treasures New and Old: Recent Contributions to Matthean Studies*. Symposium Series 1. Atlanta: Scholars, 1996.

Beale, G. K. "The New Testament Use of the Old Testament." In *The Right Doctrine from the Wrong Texts? Essays on the Use of the Old Testament in the New*, edited by G. K. Beale. Grand Rapids: Baker, 1994.

Beasley-Murray, G. R. *Baptism in the New Testament*. Grand Rapids: Eerdmans, 1973.

———. *Jesus and the Kingdom of God*. Grand Rapids: Eerdmans, 1986.

Beaton, Richard. *Isaiah's Christ in Matthew's Gospel*. SNTSMS Monograph Series 123. Cambridge: Cambridge University Press, 2002.

Becker, Joachim. *Messianic Expectation in the Old Testament*. Translated by David E. Green. Philadelphia: Fortress, 1980.

Bentzen, Aage. *King and Messiah*. Edited by G. W. Anderson. Oxford: Blackwell, 1970.

Best, E. "Spirit-Baptism." *Novum Testamentum* 4 (1960).

Blair, H. J. "Kingship in Israel and its Implications for the Lordship of Christ Today." *Evangelical Quarterly* 47 (1975).

Bleeker, C. J. "The Religion of Ancient Egypt." In vol. 1 of *Historia Religionum: Handbook for the History of Religions*, edited by C. J. Bleeker and G. Widengren, 40–124. Leiden: Brill, 1969.

Bornkamm, G. "End-Expectation and Church in Matthew." In *Tradition and Interpretation in Matthew*. Translated by Percy Scott. London: SCM, 1963.

Bornkamm, G., G. Barth, and H. J. Held. *Tradition and Interpretation in Matthew*. Translated by Percy Scott. London: SCM, 1963.

Bowman, R. M., Jr., and J. Ed Komoszewski. *Putting Jesus in His Place: The Case for the Deity of Christ*. Grand Rapids: Kregel, 2007.

Branscomb, B. H. *Jesus and the Law of Moses*. New York: Richard R. Smith, 1930.

Bretscher, Paul G. "Exodus 4:22–23 and the Voice from Heaven." *JBL* 87:3 (1968).

Bright, J. *A History of Israel*. Rev. ed. London: SCM, 1972.

Brooke, G. J. *The Dead Sea Scrolls and the New Testament*. Minneapolis: Fortress, 2005.

———. "Kingship and Messianism in the Dead Sea Scrolls." In *King and Messiah in Israel and the Ancient Near East: Proceedings of the Oxford Old Testament Seminar*, edited by John Day. JSOT Supplement Series 270. Sheffield: Sheffield Academic Press, 1998.

———. "The Psalms in Early Jewish Literature in the Light of the Dead Sea Scrolls." In *The Psalms in the New Testament*, edited by Steve Moyise and Maarten J. J. Menken. London: T. & T. Clark, 2004.

Brooks, O. S. "Matthew 28:16–20 and the Design of the First Gospel." *JSNT* 10 (1981).

Brown, R. E. *The Birth of the Messiah: A Commentary on the Infancy Narratives of Matthew and Luke*. Garden City, NY: Doubleday, 1977.

Brown, S. "The Matthean Apocalypse." *JSNT* 4 (1979).

Bruce, F. F. *Jesus and Christian Origins outside the New Testament*. London: Hodder & Stoughton, 1974.

———. "The Sure Mercies of David: A Study in the Fulfillment of Messianic Prophecy." London: Evangelical Library, 1954.

Brueggemann, Walter. *The Message of the Psalms: A Theological Commentary*. Minneapolis: Augsburg, 1984

Buchanan, G. W. *Typology and the Gospel*. Lanham, MD: University Press of America, 1987.

Bultmann, Rudolf. "Prophecy and Fulfillment." In *Essays on Old Testament Interpretation*, edited by Claus Westermann. Translated by J. L. Mays. London: SCM, 1963.

———. *Theology of the New Testament*. Translated by Kendrick Grobel. London: SCM, 1952.
Caird, G. B. *New Testament Theology*. Completed and edited by L. D. Hurst. Oxford: Clarendon, 1994.
Carmichael, D. Bleicher. "David Daube on the Eucharist and the Passover Seder." *JSNT* 42:1 (1991).
Carter, Warren. "Evoking Isaiah: Matthean Soteriology and an Inter-Textual Reading of Isaiah 7–9 and Matthew 1:23 and 4:15–16." *JBL* 119:3 (2000).
———. "Resisting and Imitating the Empire: Imperial Paradigms in Two Matthean Parables." *Interpretation* 56:3 (2002).
Casey, M. *From Jewish Prophet to Gentile God: The Origin and Development of New Testament Christology*. Louisville: Westminster, 1991.
Chae, Y. S. *Jesus as the Eschatological Davidic Shepherd: Studies in Old Testament Second Temple Judaism and in the Gospel of Matthew*. Wissenschaftliche Untersuchungen Zum Neuen Testament 2. Reihe 216. Tubingen: Mohr Siebeck, 2006.
Charles, J. Daryl. "The 'Coming One' / 'Stronger One' and His Baptism: Matt. 3:11–12, Mk. 1:8, Lk. 3:16–17." *Pneuma* 11:1 (1989).
Childs, B. S. *The Book of Exodus*. Philadelphia: Westminster, 1974.
———. *Introduction to the Old Testament as Scripture*. London: SCM, 1979.
———. "The Messianic Hope in the Old Testament." *JSOT* 43 (1989).
———. "Psalms Titles and Midrashic Exegesis." *Journal of Semitic Studies* 16:2 (1971).
Ciampa, Roy E. "The History of Redemption." In *Central Themes in Biblical Theology: Mapping Unity in Diversity*, edited by Scott J. Hafemann and Paul R. House. Leicester: InterVarsity, 2007.
Clements, Ronald E. "The Messianic Hope in the Old Testament." *JSOT* 43 (1989).
Combrink, H. J. B. "The Macrostructure of the Gospel of Matthew." *Neotestamentica* 16 (1982).
———. "The Structure of the Gospel of Matthew as Narrative." *Tyndale Bulletin* 34 (1982) 61–90.
Cooke, G. "The Israelite King as Son of God." *ZAW* 73 (1961).
Croft, Steven J. L. *The Identity of the Individual in the Psalms*. JSOT Supplement Series 44. Sheffield: JSOT, 1987.
Cullmann, O. *Baptism in the New Testament*. London: SCM, 1950.
———. *Christ and Time: The Primitive Christian Conception of Time and History*. London: SCM, 1951.
———. *The Christology of the New Testament*. Translated by S. C. Guthrie & C. A. M. Hall. Philadelphia: Westminster, 1959.
Daniélou, Jean. *Theology of Jewish Christianity*. London: Darton, Longman, & Todd, 1964.
Daube, D. *The Exodus Pattern in the Bible*. London: Faber & Faber, 1963.
Davidson, Richard M. *Typology in Scripture*. Berrien Springs, MI: Andrews University Press, 1981.
Davies, W. D., and Dale C. Allison Jr. *A Critical and Exegetical Commentary on the Gospel according to St. Matthew: Introduction and Commentary on Matthew 1–7*, vol.1. Edinburgh: T. & T. Clark, 1988.
Day, John, editor. *King and Messiah in Israel and the Ancient Near East: Proceedings of the Oxford Old Testament Seminar*. JSOT Supplement Series 270. Sheffield: Sheffield Academic Press, 1998.

———. *Psalms: Old Testament Guide*. Sheffield: JSOT, 1990.
De Vaux, Roland. *Ancient Israel: Its Life and Institutions*. Translated by John McHugh. London: Darton, Longman & Todd, 1961.
Dewey, A. J. "The Locus for Death: Social Memory and the Passion Narratives." In *Memory, Tradition, and Text: Uses of the Past in Early Christianity*, edited by Alan Kirk and Tom Thatcher. Semeia Studies 52. Atlanta: Society of Biblical Literature, 2005.
Doble, Peter. "The Psalms in Luke-Acts." In *The Psalms in the New Testament*, edited by Steve Moyise and Maarten J. J. Menken. London: T. & T. Clark, 2004.
Dodd, C. H. *According to the Scripture: The Sub-structure of New Testament Theology*. London: Nisbet, 1952.
———. *The Authority of the Bible: A Contribution to the Philosophy of Revelation*. London: Nisbet, 1928.
Dumbrell, William J. *The New Covenant: The Synoptics in Context: Matthew, Mark and Luke*. The Bible Society of Singapore. Singapore: Koorong, 1999.
Dunn, J. D. G. *Christology in the Making: An Inquiry into the Origins of the Doctrine of the Incarnation*. 2nd ed. London: SCM, 1989.
Durham, J. I. "The King as 'Messiah' in the Psalms." *Review & Expositor* 81:3 (1984).
Eaton, J. H. *Kingship and the Psalms*. 2nd ed. Sheffield: JSOT, 1986.
Edersheim, Alfred. *The Life and Times of Jesus the Messiah*, vol. 1. London: Longmans, Green, 1886.
———. *The Temple: Its Ministry and Services as They Were at the Time of Jesus Christ*. London: Religious Tract Society, 1908.
Eichrodt, W. "Is Typological Exegesis an Appropriate Method?" In *Essays on Old Testament Hermeneutics*, edited by Claus Westermann. Translated by J. L. Mays. London: SCM, 1963.
Ellingworth, P. "Priesthood." *New Dictionary of Biblical Theology*. Leicester: InterVarsity, 2000.
Elliott, John H. *A Home for the Homeless: Social-Scientific Criticism of 1 Peter, Its Situation and Strategy*. Philadelphia: Fortress, 1981.
Ellis, E. E. *The Old Testament in Early Christianity: Canon and Interpretation in the Light of Modern Research*. Grand Rapids: Baker, 1992.
Ellison, H. L. "Typology." *Evangelical Quarterly* 25 (1953).
Engnell, I. *Studies in Divine Kingship in the Ancient Near East*. Uppsala: Almquist & Wiksells, 1943.
Evans, Craig A., and James A. Sanders. *Early Christian Interpretation of the Scriptures of Israel: Investigations and Proposals*. JSNT Supplement Series 148; SSEJC 5. Sheffield: Sheffield Academic Press, 1997.
———. *Paul and the Scriptures of Israel*. JSNT Supplemet Series 83; SSEJC 1. Sheffield: JSOT, 1993.
Fairman, H. W. "Worship and Festivals in an Egyptian Temple." *BJRL* 37 (1954–55).
Ferguson, Everett. *Backgrounds of Early Christianity*. 2nd ed. Grand Rapids: Eerdmans, 1993.
Feuillet, A. *The Background of the New Testament and Its Eschatology*. Edited by W. D. Davies and D. Daube. Cambridge: Cambridge University Press, 1956.
Filson, F. V. "How Much of the New Testament Is Poetry?" *JBL* 67:2 (1948).
Fishbane, M., *Biblical Interpretation in Ancient Israel*. Oxford: Clarendon, 1985.

Flender, Helmut. *St. Luke: Theologian of Redemptive History*. Translated by Reginald H. and Ilse Fuller. London: SPCK, 1967.

France, R. T. *Matthew: Evangelist and Teacher*. Carlisle, Cumbria: Paternoster Press, 1989.

———. *The Gospel according to Matthew: An Introduction and Commentary*. Tyndale New Testament Commentaries. Leicester: InterVarsity, 1985.

Frankfort, H. *Kingship and the Gods*. Chicago: Chicago University Press, 1948.

Freeman, C. W. "Matthew 3:13–17." *Interpretation* 47:3 (1993).

Fretheim, T. F. "'Because the Whole Earth Is Mine': Theme and Narrative in Exodus." *Interpretation* 50:3 (1996).

———. "The Reclamation of Creation: Redemption and Law in Exodus." *Interpretation* 45 (1991).

Fruchtenbaum, A. G. "The Quest for a Messianic Theology." *Mishkan* 2 (1985).

Fuller, R. H. "The Conception/Birth of Jesus as a Christological Moment." *JSNT* 1 (1978).

———. *The Foundations of New Testament Christology*. Fontana Library of Theology and Philosophy. London: Collins, 1969.

Gadd, C. J. *Ideas of Divine Rule in the Ancient East*. London: Oxford University Press, 1948.

Gaffin, R. B., Jr., editor. *Redemptive History and Biblical Interpretation: The Shorter Writings of Geerhardus Vos*. Phillipsburg, NJ: Presbyterian & Reformed, 1980.

Gelston, A. "The Royal Priesthood." *Evangelical Quarterly* 31 (1969).

Gibbs, J. A. "Israel Standing with Israel: The Baptism of Jesus in Matthew's Gospel (Mt. 3:13 17)." *CBQ* 64:3 (2002).

Gilfillan-Upton, Bridget. *Hearing Mark's Endings: Listening to Ancient Popular Texts Through Speech Act Theory*. Leiden: Brill, 2006.

Goldingay, J. *Approaches to Old Testament Interpretation*. Leicester: Apollos, 1990.

Goppelt, L. *Typos, the Typological Interpretation of the Old Testament in the New*. Grand Rapids: Eerdmans, 1982.

Gowan, D. *Theology in Exodus: Biblical Theology in the Form of a Commentary*. Louisville: Westminster, 1994.

Grant, Jamie. "The Psalms and the King." In *Interpreting the Psalms: Issues and Approaches*, edited by Philip S. Johnston and David G. Firth. Leicester: Apollos, 2005.

Gray, G. B. *Sacrifice in the Old Testament: Its Theory and Practice*. Oxford: Clarendon, 1925.

Groningen, Gerard van. *Messianic Revelation in the Old Testament*. Grand Rapids: Baker, 1990.

Guelich, Robert A. *The Sermon on the Mount: A Foundation for Understanding*. Waco, TX: Word, 1982

Gundry, R. *The Use of the Old Testament in St. Matthew's Gospel, with Special Reference to the Messianic Hope*. Supplements to Novum Testamentum 18. Leiden: Brill, 1967.

Gunkel, Hermann. *Introduction to Psalms: The Genres of the Religious Lyric of Israel*. Completed by Joachim Begrich. Translated by J. D. Nogalski. Macon, GA: Mercer University Press, 1998.

———. *The Psalms: A Form-Critical Introduction*. Translated by T. M. Horner. Biblical Series 19. Philadelphia: Fortress, 1967.

Hafemann, Scott J., and Paul R. House, editors. *Central Themes in Biblical Theology: Mapping Unity in Diversity*. Leicester: InterVarsity, 2007.

Hagner, D. A. *Matthew 1–13*. Word Biblical Commentary, vol. 33A. Dallas, TX: Word, 1993.

Hahn, F. *The Titles of Jesus in Christology: Their History in Early Christianity*. Translated by H. Knight and G. Ogg. Cambridge: Clarke, 1963.

Hanson, A. T. *Jesus Christ in the Old Testament*. London: SPCK, 1965.

Harmon, Allan M. "Aspects of Paul's Use of the Psalms." *Westminster Theological Journal* 32 (1969–70).

Hays, Richard B. *Echoes of Scripture in the Letters of Paul*. New Haven: Yale University Press, 1989.

Hecht, N. S. et al., editors. *An Introduction to the History and Sources of Jewish Law*. The Institute of Jewish Law, Boston University School of Law 22. Oxford: Clarendon, 1996.

Heim, K. M. "The (God-)forsaken King of Psalm 89: A Historical and Inter-textual Enquiry." In *King and Messiah in Israel and the Ancient Near East: Proceedings of the Oxford Old Testament Seminar*, edited by John Day. JSOT Supplement Series 270. Sheffield: Sheffield Academic Press, 1998.

Hempel, J. "Royal Psalms." In *The Interpreter's Dictionary of the Bible*, edited by George Arthur Buttrick. New York: Abingdon, 1962.

Hengel, Martin. *Studies in Early Christology*. Edinburgh: T. & T. Clark, 1995.

Hengstenberg, E. W. *Christology of the Old Testament*. 2 vols. McLean, VA: MacDonald, n.d.

Hill, David. "Son and Servant: An Essay on Matthean Christology." *JSNT* 6 (1980).

———. "The Figure of Jesus in Matthew's Story: A Response to Professor Kingsbury's Literary-Critical Probe." *JSNT* 21 (1984).

———. *The Gospel of Matthew*. New Century Bible. London: Marshall, Morgan & Scott, 1972.

Holland, Tom. *Contours of Pauline Theology: A Radical New Survey of the Influences on Paul's Biblical Writings*. Fearn: Mentor, 2004.

———. *The Paschal-New Exodus Motif in Paul's Letter to the Romans with Special Reference to its Christological Significance*. PhD Diss., University of Wales, 1996.

Hooke, S. H. *Myth, Ritual, and Kingship: Essays on the Theory and Practice of Kingship in the Ancient Near East and in Israel*. Oxford: Clarendon, 1958.

———., editor. *The Labyrinth: Further Studies in the Relation between Myth and Ritual in the Ancient World*. London: SPCK, 1935.

Hooker, M. D. "Christology and Methodology." *NTS* 17 (1970–71).

———. *The Son of Man in Mark: A Study of the Background of the Term "Son of Man" and Its Use in St. Mark's Gospel*. London: SPCK, 1967.

Horbury, William. "Messianism in the Old Testament Apocrypha and Pseudepigrapha." *JSOT* 270 (1998).

Horrell, David G. *Social-Scientific Interpretation of the New Testament: Retrospect and Prospect*. Edinburgh: T. & T. Clark, 1999.

Howard, J. K. "Christ Our Passover: A Study of the Passover-Exodus Theme in 1 Corinthians." *Evangelical Quarterly* 41 (1969).

Huie-Jolly, Mary R. "Threats Answered by Enthronement: Death/Resurrection and the Divine Warrior Myth in John 5:17–29, Psalm 2 and Daniel 7." In *Early Christian Interpretation of the Scriptures of Israel: Investigations and Proposals*, edited by Craig A. Evans and James A. Sanders. JSNT Supplement Series 148; SSEJC 5. Sheffield: Sheffield Academic Press, 1997.

Jacobson, Delmar L. "The Royal Psalms and Jesus Messiah: Preparing to Preach on a Royal Psalm." *Word & World* 5:2 (1985).
Jay, E. G. *Son of Man, Son of God*. London: SPCK, 1965.
Jeremias, Joachim. *The Eucharistic Words of Jesus*. Translated by Arnold Ehrhardt. Oxford: Blackwell, 1955.
Jobes, K. H., and M. Silva. *Invitation to the Septuagint*. Grand Rapids: Baker Academic, 2000.
Johnson, Aubrey R. "The Role of the King in the Jerusalem Cultus." In *The Labyrinth: Further Studies in the Relation between Myth and Ritual in the Ancient World*, edited by S. H. Hooke. London: SPCK, 1935.
———. *Sacral Kingship in Ancient Israel*. Cardiff: University of Wales Press, 1967.
Johnson, M. D. "Reflections on a Wisdom Approach to Matthew's Christology." *CBQ* 36 (1974).
Johnson, Sherman E. "The Davidic-Royal Motif in the Gospels." *JBL* 87:2 (1968).
Johnston, Philip S., and David. G. Firth, editors. *Interpreting the Psalms: Issues and Approaches*. Leicester: Apollos, 2005.
Kaiser, Walter C. *The Uses of the Old Testament in the New*. Chicago: Moody, 1985.
Keesmaat, Sylvia C. "Paul and His Story: Exodus and Tradition in Galatians." In *Early Christian Interpretation of the Scriptures of Israel: Investigations and Proposals*, edited by Craig A. Evans and James A. Sanders. JSNT Supplement Series 148; SSEJC 5. Sheffield: Sheffield Academic Press, 1997.
Kelber, Werner H. "The Works of Memory: Christian Origin as MnemoHistory—A Response." In *Memory, Tradition, and Text: Uses of the Past in Early Christianity*, edited by Alan Kirk and Tom Thatcher. Semeia Studies 52. Atlanta: Society of Biblical Literature, 2005.
Kilpatrick, G. D. *The Origins of the Gospel according to St. Matthew*. Oxford: Clarendon, 1946.
Kingsbury, Jack Dean. *The Christology of Mark's Gospel*. Philadelphia: Fortress, 1983.
———. "The Figure of Jesus in Matthew's Story: A Literary-Critical Probe." *JSNT* 21 (1984).
———. *Matthew: Structure, Christology, Kingdom*. Philadelphia: Fortress, 1975.
———. "The Title 'Son of David' in Matthew's Gospel." *JBL* 95 (1976).
———. "The Structure of Matthew's Gospel and His Concept of Salvation History." *CBQ* 35:4 (1973).
Kirk, Alan, and Tom Thatcher. *Memory, Tradition, and Text: Uses of the Past in Early Christianity*. Semeia Studies 52. Atlanta: Society of Biblical Literature, 2005.
Kissinger, W. S. *The Sermon on the Mount: A History of Interpretation and Bibliography*. Metuchen, NJ: Scarecrow, 1975.
Kittel, Gerhard, editor. *Theological Dictionary of the New Testament*, vol. 1. Translated by Geoffrey W. Bromiley. Grand Rapids: Eerdmans, 1974.
Knoppers, G. N. "David's Relation to Moses: The Contexts, Content and Conditions of the Davidic Promise." In *King and Messiah in Israel and the Ancient Near East: Proceedings of the Oxford Old Testament Seminar*, edited by John Day. JSOT Supplement Series 270. Sheffield: Sheffield Academic Press, 1998.
Krentz, E. "The Extent of Matthew's Prologue: Toward the Structure of the First Gospel." *JBL* 83:4 (1964).
Kruse, Heinz. "Psalm 132 and the Royal Zion Festival." *Vetus Testamentum* 33:3 (1983).

Kwon, Hyukjung. "The Reception of Psalm 118 in the New Testament: Application of a 'New Exodus Motif?'" PhD Diss., University of Pretoria, 2007.

Lee, A. H. I. *From Messiah to Preexistent Son: Jesus' Self-consciousness and Early Christian Exegesis of Messianic Psalms*. Wissenschaftliche Untersuchungen Zum Neuen Testament 2. Reihe 192. Tubingen: Mohr Siebeck, 2005.

Legarth, P. "Typology and its Theological Basis." *EJT* 5 (1996).

Levine, Amy-Jill. *The Social and Ethnic Dimensions of Matthean Salvation History*. Studies in the Bible and Early Christianity 14. Lewiston, NY: Edwin Mellen, 1988.

Lindars, Barnabas. *Jesus Son of Man: A Fresh Examination of the Son of Man Sayings in the Gospels in the Light of Recent Research*. London: SPCK, 1983.

———. *New Testament Apologetic: The Doctrinal Significance of the Old Testament Quotations*. London: SCM, 1961.

Luz, Ulrich. "The Son of Man in Matthew: Heavenly Judge or Human Christ." *JSNT* 48 (1992).

———. *The Theology of the Gospel of Matthew*. Translated by J. Bradford Robinson. Cambridge: Cambridge University Press, 1995.

Machen, J. G. *The Virgin Birth of Christ*. New York: Harper & Row, 1930.

Mack, B. L. "The Innocent Transgressor: Jesus in Early Christian Myth and History." In *Rene Girard and Biblical Studies*, edited by Andrew J. McKenna. Semeia 33. Decatur, GA: Society of Biblical Literature, 1985.

Maddox, R. "The Function of the Son of Man according to the Synoptic Gospels." *NTS* 15 (1968).

Malina, B. J. "The Literary Structure and Form of Matt. 28." *NTS* 17 (1970–71).

Mann, T. W. "Passover: The Time of Our Lives." *Interpretation* 50:3 (1996).

Marshall, I. H. *Aspects of the Atonement: Cross and Resurrection in the Reconciling of God and Humanity*. London: Paternoster, 2007.

———. *Last Supper and Lord's Supper*. Grand Rapids: Eerdmans, 1980.

———. *The Origins of New Testament Christology*. Issues in Contemporary Theology. Downers Grove, IL: InterVarsity, 1976.

———. "Son of God or Servant of Yahweh?: A Reconsideration of Mark 1:11." *NTS* 15 (1968–69).

———. "The Synoptic Son of Man Sayings in Recent Discussion." *NTS* 12 (1965–66).

Marshall, I. H., D. A. Carson, and H. G. M. Williamson, editors. *It Is Written: Scripture Citing Scripture*. Cambridge: Cambridge University Press, 1988.

Mawhinney, Allen. "Baptism, Servanthood, and Sonship." *WTJ* 49 (1987).

Mays, James L. *The Lord Reigns: A Theological Handbook to the Psalms*. Louisville: Westminster, 1994.

———. "Prayer and Christology: Psalm 22 as Perspective on the Passion." *Theology Today* 42:3 (1985).

McCann, J. Clinton, Jr. *A Theological Introduction to the Book of Psalms: The Psalms as Torah*. Nashville: Abingdon, 1993.

McCasland, S. V. "Matthew Twists the Scriptures." *JBL* 80:2 (1961).

Meier, John P. "Salvation History in Matthew: In Search of a Starting Point." *CBQ* 37 (1975).

———. "John the Baptist in Matthew's Gospel." *JBL* 99:3 (1980).

———. *Law and History in Matthew's Gospel: A Redactional Study of Mt. 5:17–48*. Analecta Biblica 71. Rome: Biblical Institute Press, 1976.

———. *The Vision of Matthew: Christ, Church, and Morality in the First Gospel.* Theological Inquiries. New York: Paulist, 1979.

Menken, Maarten J. J. "The Psalms in Matthew's Gospel." In *The Psalms in the New Testament*, edited by Steve Moyise and Maarten J. J. Menken. London: T. & T. Clark, 2004.

———. "The Sources of the Old Testament Quotation in Matthew 2:23." *JBL* 120:3 (2001).

Mettinger, T. N. D. *In Search of God: The Meaning and Message of the Everlasting Names.* Translated by F. H. Cryer. Philadelphia: Fortress, 1988.

———. *King and Messiah: The Civil and Sacral Legitimation of the Israelite Kings.* Lund: LiberLaromedel/Glerrup, 1976.

Miller, Patrick D., Jr. *Interpreting the Psalms.* Philadelphia: Fortress, 1986.

Molnar, Paul D. "What Does It Mean to Say that Jesus Christ Is Indispensable to a Properly Conceived Doctrine of the Immanent Trinity? A Response to Jeffrey Hensley." *Scottish Journal of Theology* 61:1 (2008).

Moo, Douglas J. "Jesus and the Authority of the Mosaic Law." *JSNT* 20 (1984).

Morgenstern, J. "The Cultic Setting of the Enthronement Psalms." *Hebrew Union College Annual* 35 (1964).

Motyer, J. A. *Look to the Rock: An Old Testament Background to Our Understanding of Christ.* Leicester: InterVarsity, 1996.

Moule, C. F. D. "Neglected Features in the Problem of 'the Son of Man.'" In *Neues Testament und Kirche: für Rudolf Schnackenburg*, edited by Joachim Gnilka. Freiburg: Herder, 1974.

Mowinckel, Sigmund. *The Psalms in Israel's Worship.* Translated by D. R. Ap-Thomas. Oxford: Blackwell, 1962.

Moyise, Steve, and Maarten J. J. Menken, editors. *The Psalms in the New Testament.* London: T. & T. Clark, 2004.

Müller, Ulrich B. *Messias und Menschensohn in Jüdischen Apokalypsen und in der Offenbarung des Johannes.* Studien zum Newen Testament 6. Gütersloh: Gütersloher Verlagshaus Mohn, 1972.

Nebe, G. "The Son of Man and the Angels: Reflections on the Formation of Christology in the Context of Eschatology." In *Eschatology in the Bible and in Jewish and Christian Tradition*, edited by Henning Graf Reventlow. JSOT 243. Sheffield: Sheffield Academic Press, 1997.

Neusner, Jacob, W. S. Green, and E. S. Frerichs. *Judaism and Their Messiahs at the Turn of the Christian Era.* Cambridge: Cambridge University Press, 1987.

Nicholson, Ernest. *God and His People: Covenant and Theology in the Old Testament.* Oxford: Clarendon, 1986.

Nolland, John. "No Son of God Christology in Matthew 1:18–25." *JSNT* 62 (1996).

———. *The Gospel of Matthew: A Commentary on the Greek Text.* The New International Greek Testament Commentary. Bletchley: Paternoster, 2005.

Oesterley, W. O. E. *The Evolution of the Messianic Idea: A Study in Comparative Religion.* London: Pitman, 1908.

Old, Hughes Oliphant. "The Psalms of Praise in the Worship of the New Testament Church." *Interpretation* 39:1 (1985).

Ollenburger, B. C. *Zion, the City of the Great King: A Theological Symbol of the Jerusalem Cult.* Sheffield: JSOT, 1987.

Olson, D. T. "The Jagged Cliffs of Mount Sinai: A Theological Reading of the Book of the Covenant (Exod. 20:22–23:19)." *Interpretation* 50:3 (1996).

Pannenberg, Wolfhart. *Jesus, God and Man*. Translated by L. L. Wilkins and Duane A Priebe. London: SCM, 1968.

———. "Redemptive Event and History." In *Essays on Old Testament Hermeneutics*, edited by Claus Westermann. Translated by J. L. Mays. London: SCM, 1963.

Pate, C. Marvin et al. *The Story of Israel: A Biblical Theology*. Leicester: Apollos, 2004.

Patte, Daniel, and Aline Patte. *Structural Exegesis: From Theory to Practice: Exegesis of Mark 15 and 16, Hermeneutical Implications*. Philadelphia: Fortress, 1978.

Penner, J. A. "Revelation and Discipleship in Matthew's Transfiguration Account." *Bibliotheca Sacra* 152:606 (1995).

Piper, Otto A. "Unchanging Promises: Exodus in the New Testament." *Interpretation* 11:1 (1957).

Porter, Stanley E. "The Use of the Old Testament in the New Testament." In *Early Christian Interpretation of the Scriptures of Israel: Investigations and Proposals*, edited by Craig Evans and James Sanders. JSNT Supplemet Series 148; SSEJC 5. Sheffield: Sheffield Academic Press, 1997.

Purves, G. T. "St. Paul and Inspiration." *Presbyterian and Reformed Review* 13 (1893).

Rabbinowitz, Noel S. "Matthew 23:2–4: Does Jesus Recognize the Authority of the Pharisees and Does He Endorse Their Halakah?" *Journal of the Evangelical Theological Society* 46:3 (2003).

Rad, Gerhard von. "Typological Interpretation of the Old Testament." In *Essays on Old Testament Hermeneutics*, edited by Claus Westermann. Translated by J. L. Mays. London: SCM, 1963.

———. *Old Testament Theology*. Translated by D. M. G. Stalker. 2 vols. Edinburgh: Oliver & Boyd, 1962.

Rahner, Karl. *Foundations of Christian Faith: An Introduction to the Idea of Christianity*. New York: Seabury, 1978.

Reimer, D. J. "Old Testament Christology." In *King and Messiah in Israel and the Ancient Near East: Proceedings of the Oxford Old Testament Seminar*, edited by John Day. JSOT Supplement Series 270. Sheffield: Sheffield Academic Press, 1998.

Rengstorf, K. H. "Old and New Testament Traces of the Formula of the Judean Royal Ritual." *Novum Testamentum* 5:4 (1962).

Reventlow, Henning Graf, editor. *Eschatology in the Bible and in Jewish and Christian Tradition*. JSOT 243. Sheffield: Sheffield Academic Press, 1997.

Ridderbos, Herman. *Redemptive History and the New Testament Scriptures*. Translated by H. De Jongste. Phillipsburg, NJ: Presbyterian & Reformed, 1988.

Ringgren, H. "The Messiah in the Old Testament." *Studies in Biblical Theology* 18 (1956).

Robinson, D. W. B. "The Priesthood of Paul in the Gospel of Hope." In *Reconciliation and Hope*, edited by J. R. Banks. Exeter: Paternoster, 1974.

Robinson, J. A. T. *The Human Face of God*. London: SCM, 1973.

Rooke, D. W. "Kingship as Priesthood: The Relationship between the High Priesthood and the Monarchy." In *King and Messiah in Israel and the Ancient Near East: Proceedings of the Oxford Old Testament Seminar*, edited by John Day. JSOT Supplement Series 270. Sheffield: Sheffield Academic Press, 1998.

Root, Michael. "Dying He Lives: Biblical Image, Biblical Narrative and the Redemptive Jesus." In *Christology and Exegesis: New Approaches*. Semeia 30. Decatur, GA: 1984.

Rowland, C. C. *The Open Heaven: A Study of Apocalyptic in Judaism and Early Christianity.* New York: Crossroad, 1982.

———. "Christ in the New Testament." In *King and Messiah in Israel and the Ancient Near East: Proceedings of the Oxford Old Testament Seminar,* edited by John Day. JSOT Supplement Series 270. Sheffield: Sheffield Academic Press, 1998.

Sanders, J. A. *The Psalms Scroll of Qumran Cave 11.* Oxford: Clarendon, 1965.

Schwartz, B. "Christian Origins: Historical Truth and Social Memory." In *Memory, Tradition, and Text: Uses of the Past in Early Christianity,* edited by Alan Kirk and Tom Thatcher. Semeia Studies 52. Atlanta: Society of Biblical Literature, 2005.

Segal, J. B. *The Hebrew Passover, from Earliest Times to A.D. 70.* Oxford: Oxford University Press, 1963.

Selvanayagam, Israel. "Interpreting a Riddle: Jesus' Subversion of the Davidic Legacy." *Black Theology* 6:2 (2008) 262–68.

Senior, Donald. *What Are They Saying about Matthew?* New York: Paulist, 1996.

Snow, R. "Daniel's Son of Man in Mark: A Redefinition of the Earthly Temple and the Formation of a New Temple Community." *Tyndale Bulletin* 60:2 (2009).

So, Damon W. K. *Jesus' Revelation of His Father: A Narrative-Conceptual Study of the Trinity with Special Reference to Karl Barth.* Paternoster Theological Monographs. Milton Keynes: Paternoster, 2006.

Soares-Prabhu, G. M. "The Formulary Quotations in the Infancy Narrative of Matthew." Analecta Biblica 63. Rome: Biblical Institute Press, 1976

Stanley, Christopher D. "The Rhetoric of Quotations: An Essay on Method." In *Early Christian Interpretation of the Scriptures of Israel: Investigations and Proposals,* edited by Craig Evans and James Sanders. JSNT Supplemet Series 148; SSEJC 5. Sheffield: Sheffield Academic Press, 1997.

———. "The Social Environment of 'Free' Biblical Quotations in the New Testament." In *Early Christian Interpretation of the Scriptures of Israel: Investigations and Proposals,* edited by Craig Evans and James Sanders. JSNT Supplemet Series 148; SSEJC 5. Sheffield: Sheffield Academic Press, 1997.

Stanton, Graham N. *A Gospel for a New People: Studies in Matthew.* Edinburgh: T. & T. Clark, 1992.

Stegemann, E. W., and Wolfgang Stegemann. *The Jesus Movement: A Social History of Its First Century.* Translated by O. C. Dean Jr. Edinburgh: T. & T. Clark, 1999.

Stegner, "The Use of Scripture in Two Narratives of Early Jewish Christianity (Matthew 4:1–11; Mark 9:2–8)." In *Early Christian Interpretation of the Scriptures of Israel: Investigations and Proposals,* edited by Craig A. Evans and James A. Sanders. JSNT Supplement Series 148; SSEJC 5. Sheffield: Sheffield Academic Press, 1997.

Stendahl, Krister. *The School of St. Matthew, and Its Use of the Old Testament.* Philadelphia: Fortress, 1968.

Stewart, R. A. "The Jewish Festivals." *Evangelical Quarterly* 43 (1971).

Strauss, Mark L. *The Davidic Messiah in Luke-Acts: The Promise and Its Fulfillment in Lukan Christology.* JSNT Supplement Series 110. Sheffield: Sheffield Academic Press, 1995.

Strecker, G. "The Concept of History in Matthew." *JAAR* 35 (1967).

Suggs, M. J. *Wisdom, Christology, and Law in Matthew's Gospel.* Cambridge, MA: Harvard University Press, 1970.

Swete, H. B. *An Introduction to the Old Testament in Greek.* 2nd ed. Cambridge: Cambridge University Press, 1914.

Synge, F. C. "The Transfiguration Story." *The Expository Times* 82 (1970).
Tasker, R. V. G. *The Gospel according to Matthew: An Introduction and Commentary*. Tyndale New Testament Commentaries. London: Tyndale Press, 1961.
Tate, Marvin E. *Psalms 51–100*. Dallas, TX: Word, 1990.
Taylor, Vincent. *The Names of Jesus*. London: Macmillan, 1953.
Theiss, Norman. "The Passover Feast of the New Covenant." *Interpretation* 48 (1994).
Thiselton, A. "Influences on Paul." *Review: The Expository Times* 116 (2005).
Trites, A. "The Transfiguration of Jesus: The Gospel in Microcosm." *Evangelical Quarterly* 51 (1979).
Tucker, P. "Speak Lord." *The Gospel Magazine*, November/December 1976.
Vermes, Geza. *The Dead Sea Scrolls in English*. Middlesex: Penguin, 1962.
Vos, Geerhardus. *Redemptive History and Biblical Interpretation: The Shorter Writings of Geerhardus Vos*. Edited by Richard B. Gaffin Jr. Phillipsburg, NJ: Presbyterian & Reformed, 1980.
Wainright, A. W. "The Confession 'Jesus is God' in the New Testament." *Scottish Journal of Theology* 10 (1957).
Wallace-Hadrill, D. S. "A Suggested Exegesis of Matt. 3:9, 10." *ET* 62 (1950).
Walton, J. H. *Ancient Israelite Literature in Its Cultural Context: A Survey of Parallels Between Biblical and Ancient Near Eastern Texts*. Grand Rapids: Regency Reference Library, 1989.
Watts, R. E. *Isaiah's New Exodus in Mark*. Grand Rapids: Baker, 2000.
———. "The Psalms in Mark's Gospel." In *The Psalms in the New Testament*, edited by Steve Moyise and Maarten J. J. Menken. London: T. & T. Clark, 2004.
Weaver, Dorothy J. "Power and Powerlessness: Matthew's Use of Irony in the Portrayal of Political Leaders." In *Treasures New and Old: Recent Contributions to Matthean Studies*, edited by David R. Bauer and Mark Allan Powell. Symposium Series 1. Atlanta: Scholars, 1996.
Wengst, Klaus. "Aspects of the Last Judgment in the Gospel according to Matthew." In *Eschatology in the Bible and in Jewish and Christian Tradition*, edited by Henning Graf Reventlow. JSOT 243. Sheffield: Sheffield Academic Press, 1997.
Weren, W. J. C. "Quotations from Isaiah and Matthew's Christology (Matt. 1:23 and 4:15–16)." In *Studies in the Book of Isaiah: Festschrift Willem A. M. Beuken*, edited by J. Van Ruiten and M. Vervenne. Bibliotheca Ephemeridum theologicarum Lovaniensium 132. Leuven: Leuven University Press, 1997
Westermann, Claus. *Essays on Old Testament Hermeneutics*. Translated by J. L. Mays. London: SCM, 1963.
———. *The Praise of God in the Psalms*. Translated by Keith R. Crim. London: Epworth, 1966.
Whitelam, Keith W. *The Just King: Monarchical Judicial Authority in Ancient Israel*. Sheffield: JSOT, 1979.
Williamson, H. G. M. "The Messianic Texts in Isaiah 1–39." In *King and Messiah in Israel and the Ancient Near East: Proceedings of the Oxford Old Testament Seminar*, edited by John Day. JSOT Supplement Series 270. Sheffield: Sheffield Academic Press, 1998.
Wilson, Gerald H. "The Structure of the Psalter." In *Interpreting the Psalms: Issues and Approaches*, edited by Philip S. Johnston and David. G. Firth. Leicester: Apollos, 2005.

Winn, Adam. *The Purpose of Mark's Gospel: An Early Christian Response to Roman Imperial Propaganda*. Wissenschaftliche Untersuchungen Zum Neuen Testament 2. Reihe 245. Tubingen: Mohr Siebeck, 2008.

Wise, M. O., and J. D. Tabor. "The Messiah at Qumran." *Biblical Archaeology Review* 18:6 (1992).

Wolff, Hans Walter. "The Understanding of History in the Old Testament Prophets." In *Essays on Old Testament Hermeneutics*, edited by Claus Westermann. London: SCM, 1963.

Wood, D. R. W. et al., editors. *New Bible Dictionary*. 3rd ed. Leicester: InterVarsity, 1996.

Wright, N T. *Jesus and the Victory of God*. London: SPCK, 1996.

———. *The New Testament and the People of God*, vol. 1. Minneapolis: Fortress, 1992.

Ziesler, J. A. "The Transfiguration Story and the Markan Soteriology." *EP* 81 (1969).

Zimmerli, Walther. "Promise and Fulfillment." In *Essays on Old Testament Hermeneutics*, edited by Claus Westermann. Translated by J. L. Mays. London: SCM, 1963.

www.ingramcontent.com/pod-product-compliance
Lightning Source LLC
Chambersburg PA
CBHW071941240426
43669CB00048B/2553